Lost Loot

Lost Boot 3

New Jersey ~ New York ~ Pennsylvania

Patricia Hughes

4880 Lower Valley Road • Atglen, PA 19310

Published by Schiffer Publishing, Ltd.
4880 Lower Valley Road
Atglen, PA 19310
Phone: (610) 593-1777; Fax: (610) 593-2002
E-mail: Info@schifferbooks.com

For our complete selection of fine books on this and related subjects,
please visit our website at *www.schifferbooks.com*.
You may also write for a free catalog.

This book may be purchased from the publisher. Please try your bookstore first.

We are always looking for people to write books on new and related subjects.
If you have an idea for a book, please contact us at *proposals@schifferbooks.com*.

Schiffer Publishing's titles are available at special discounts for bulk purchases for
sales promotions or premiums. Special editions, including personalized covers,
corporate imprints, and excerpts can be created in large quantities for special needs.
For more information, contact the publisher.

Other Schiffer Books by the Author:
Lost Loot: Ghostly New England Treasure Tales, 978-0-7643-2816-9, $14.95
More Lost Loot: Ghostly New England Treasure Tales, 978-0-7643-3627-0, $19.99
Maine's Waterfalls: A Comprehensive Guide, 978-0-7643-3113-8, $14.99

Other Schiffer Books on Related Subjects:
Folklore of the New Jersey Shore: History, the Supernatural, and Beyond
978-0-7643-4127-4, $24.99

Empire State Ghosts: New York Legends and Lore
978-0-7643-3418-4, $14.99

Ghostly Connections: Pennsylvania's Lower Susquehanna Valley
978-0-7643-3717-8, $16.99

Copyright © 2013 by Patricia Hughes

Library of Congress Control Number: 2013945559

Designed by Mark David Bowyer
Type set in Burton's Nightmare 2000 / NewBaskerville BT

ISBN: 978-0-7643-4134-2
Printed in the United States of America

Contents

Dedication

To Roxanne Kilpatrick, my good friend, my "research assistant," and a fantastic driver...Thank you just does not seem to be enough to tell you how I appreciate your help and support in making this book a reality. You are an amazing person and I am proud to call you friend!

Roxanne at the Saratoga battlefield in New York.

Special Acknowledgments

To Florence Kissane and Mary Alice O'Brien, for driving me around and sharing the beauty and history of Long Island, New York, from a resident's perspective.

Introduction:

Quest for Haunted Treasure

The supernatural and treasure lore are forever intertwined. The places explored in this book have a mystery attached to them... there are strange rock formations, markings, events, battles, certain dates, and unexplainable feelings that occur when one visits these areas. Each place also has some valuable artifact to be potentially found, whether the treasures were left before people arrived — like the precious metals, minerals, or gems under the Earth — or were buried by the various groups of people who lived here at various times through the centuries. Why do both these circumstances seem to happen in one place?

2001 piece of iron from Tower II.

The question often arises: Why search for haunted treasure sites? The answer is rather simple, despite the fact that complexity itself lies in the search. It is a way to perhaps to find our history and to answer the question of how we got here. So much happens in such small areas, but why? There really is no answer, which is why the exploration of lost treasure is so amazing. The lore and legends always lead to a magical place where many strange events occur over and over again. The supernatural and treasure history are intertwined throughout the history of the region, and the circumstances of why the phenomenon happens in the same place numerous times remains a mystery even today.

Not only are events and places touched by seemingly otherworldly forces, but the same date will also crop up in the same region, triggering large historical significant events to take place. For example, as the reader goes through the book, one date does jump out: September 11. There are many important historical events that occurred on September 11th in the New York region, as well as in the other states. As one searches for treasure with supernatural twists, it is interesting to see that one date occur and reoccur numerous times throughout history.

This book is separated by state and by three different types of haunted treasure to be found in New York, New Jersey, and Pennsylvania, also called the Middle States. The supernatural treasure site divisions are: Native American and Geology; Pirate, Military, and Wrecks; and Precious Gems, Fossils, and Mines. We start our treasure quest with a general need to know information about all three states.

The Native Americans

The Iroquois Nation was considered the most powerful North American tribe. Originally, there were five tribes early on — the Tuscarora tribe joined later. The six Nations League eventually comprised of the Mohawk, Oneida, Onondaga, Cayuga, Seneca, and Tuscarora tribes. The Iroquois were called the Long House People by the settlers and their villages were called castles. The Iroquois' believed that all things were placed on Earth for the use and enjoyment of people, but that people had to be wise enough to know how to use them; for example, saving much of the food harvested for winter, known as the "season of death." The Iroquois have eight clans: Wolf, Bear, Beaver, Turtle, Deer, Snipe, Heron, and Hawk. At birth, one becomes part of the clan of their mother. It does not matter what tribe in the Nation you are part of, but what clan you are part of.

The first people to live in New York came here around 11,000 years ago and are called Paleoindians. This was at the end of the last ice age, and the coast of New York was about one hundred miles inland. The next group was called the Archaic people who lived here from 10,000 to 2700 B.P. (before present). The sea had risen and the coast looked like it does today.

Next, came the Woodland tribes, or Native American tribes, that the Europeans met when they arrived. These were the Algonquians; the sub-tribes were called the Delaware or Lenni-Lenape tribe. The Munsee tribe lived in Lenapehoking, a territory reaching from the lower Hudson River to western Long Island and northern New Jersey to northeastern Pennsylvania. The settlements or villages were in Canarsie and Manhattan. There were other villages, but the exact locations remain unknown. The names of the villages were Rechgawawank, Siwanoy, and Wiechquaeskeet.

The only non-Iroquois tribe to live in the Delaware River Valley was the Lenni-Lenape tribe, meaning "the real people" or "the original people." The English called them the Delaware tribe. According to their oral tradition, they originally came from the Pacific Coast, actually southwestern Canada, and, in alliance with the Iroquois, drove out the Erie and Monongahela tribes. Probably because the Lenni-Lenape tribe's grandfathers were of the race of Great Unami or Turtles that lived on the Delaware River and Manhattan Bay, they were allowed to live here, at least for a time. This tribe claimed to be related to the tortoise whose back looked like an island of the earth. The seers of the tribe said the moodus-jargon noises of thunder and earthquakes were the signs of anger from this turtle, as he jarred the earth on his shoulders. They said he was Hobbamocko (the Devil) and he was worshipped as the God of Thunder.

These Algonquian people were probably who Henry Hudson first met when he landed here. Lenape means "the first come." The Lenape legend of the world origin is that in the beginning there was only water. A turtle rose from the sea. Its domed back drying in the sun became the Earth. A tree grew in the midst. The first man sprang from its roots; then the treetop bent to the ground and the first woman appeared. The Native Americans called the Dutch "swannekens," meaning "people of salt" because they came from the sea.

The Hudson Valley Native American tribes, who were basically Algonkian, were three loose confederacies: The Mahican, who were located on both sides of the Hudson River south of Albany; the Delaware, on the west shore south from the present-day Catskills into New Jersey; and the Wappinger, which were found from the Poughkeepsie region to south of Manhattan. The Montauk tribe ruled Long Island. There were sub-tribes within each confederacy. For example, the Wappinger confederacy had the following sub-tribes: Wappinger, Nochpeem, Kitchawank, Sintsink, Pacam, Wecquaesgeek, Siwanoy, and Manhattan.

The Delaware tribe settled from the Allegheny Mountains to the Atlantic Ocean. They are divided into three groups: the Wolf Tribe, called Minsi, meaning "men of the stony country," lived in the eastern ridges of the Pennsylvania mountains; the Turtle or Tortoise Tribe, called Unamis, meaning "fishermen," lived in the lower Delaware Valley from Philadelphia, Pennsylvania, to Trenton, New Jersey; and the Turkey Tribe, called Unalachtigos, meaning "people living near the ocean," occupied Delaware Bay to the Atlantic Ocean through Salem and Cumberland counties of New Jersey.

The six Iroquois Nation were connected by a 240-mile walk (trail), which is the basis for the New York Thruway between Albany and Buffalo. Tribe villages, or castles, were located all through the region. Knowing what tribe lived in what area can help treasure seekers search for artifacts. Some notable Native American tribes and villages were located:

- The MONTAUK TRIBE was located on Long Island, New York
- The ONEIDA TRIBE was located in Central New York and Pennsylvania; they sided with the Patriots during the Revolutionary War
- The ONONDAGA TRIBE was found in Central New York; they sided with the British during the Revolutionary War
- The SENECA TRIBE lived in the Finger Lakes Region of New York and was called "People of the Great Hill"; they were considered the most formidable of the six Nations, having fought and exterminated the Erie Tribe and sided with the British during the Revolutionary War
- The SHINNECOCK TRIBE lived on the southeastern part of Long Island, New York; basically, their villages were in present-day Hamptons
- The SUSQUEHANNOCK TRIBE was located in the Susquehanna River Valley in Pennsylvania; little is known about them, other than they have an Algonquin name and spoke the Iroquois language. Disease and war caused the tribe to be extinct by 1700. They were called the Andaste by French and the Minqua by the Dutch, which meant "people at falls" or "muddy water people."
- The TUSCARORA TRIBE moved to the Niagara Falls, New York area, and were the sixth member of the six-nation confederacy. The Tuscarora tribe first lived in the Carolinas, but moved north in the early 1700s. There is an ancient legend from this tribe about a white serpent that would come to the shores of their kind and cause great hardship and death. When the Europeans came to Roanoke Island in 1584, it was this tribe that they met. It is thought that may be one reason why the tribe headed north. This tribe also sided with the Patriots during the Revolutionary War.
- The MOHAWK TRIBE lived in the Mohawk Valley. The French called them Agnierrhonons, meaning "people of the flint"; the Algonquins called them the Mahaqua; the Dutch called them the Maquas; and the English called them the Mohawk. In 1649, the tribe destroyed the Huron Nation, which lived on the shores of Lake Huron at that time. This tribe, with the Cayuga Tribe, sided with the British during the Revolutionary War. As an interesting side note: the warriors did shave their hair in a Mohawk style.
- The WAPPINGER TRIBE lived in the Catskill Mountains, which included New York Harbor, between the Catskills and Poughkeepsie, New York
- The WENROHRONON TRIBE was located in northwest New York State, along Lake Ontario and east of Niagara; a common foe of the Iroquois who eventually joined with the Hurons, their tribal stories often have themes revolving around vampires and cannibals
- The MOHICAN TRIBE lived along the Hudson River
- The NANTICOKE and CONOY tribes lived south of the Potomac River
- The SHAWNEE TRIBE lived along the Ohio River

• The ADENA TRIBE was the famous mound builders and lived in western New York and Pennsylvania. They were one of four known tribes who built mounds. These were effigy mounds that contained multiple burial sites, though not all are believed to be graves. Perhaps these were more ceremonial. Many hills, natural or man-made, were used as Native American burial grounds.

Some tribes that also lived in the region were the Pennacook, Mahican, Horicon, and Nawaas; they were dispersed before Samuel de Champlain came with the Mohawk tribe. The Horicons went to the Lake George area, calling the lake "Lake Andratoroct." The Pennacook and Nawaas went to the east bank of the Connecticut River. The Mahican and Hoosac went to Fish Creek, an outlet of Lake Saratoga, which eventually became another war trail between the Hoosac and Mohawk tribes. Lake Champlain became Caniaderaunte, which meant "a dividing line" between the two tribes.

The word "Wampum" is a short version of Wampumpeak, meaning "strings of white shell beads." The more purple in the shell, the more the worth in monetary terms. This type of shell can be found on numerous beaches of the coast today. The Mid-Atlantic sea is rising 1/15" each year, and the beaches of the island are creeping shoreward. The salt marshes left behind will fill up with sand. For this reason, digging for any artifact is a must during the present-day treasure hunt.

Geology

If the treasure seeker must use a map to locate treasure, please remember and know that not all maps were created the same way. Ancient maps are always plotted east to west, following the sun. Also remember that the ancients believed that saltwater was evil and freshwater was good. Also, beware that the same fort region were called different names based on who claimed the area, whether it was the French, British, or American forces.

The site of natural disasters is one place to start your treasure search. For example, an earthquake felt in August 1884 was described in diaries, newspaper reports, and books ruined many homes and businesses in Long Island and Brooklyn, New York, where people ran into the streets in terror and the Brooklyn Bridge rocked like a huge hurricane had blown by. During the same time, in Philadelphia, Pennsylvania, buildings swayed and fell over. In Camden, New Jersey, the quake lasted ten seconds, and every large building shook as huge waves traveled up the rivers.

Another place to search for early settler artifacts is along flooded plains. For example, it was reported that the Espous River in New York often flooded and early settler belongings were constantly being washed down the river.

Ghost Towns

Another place to start a haunted treasure search is to look for old forgotten settlements. One way to find these places is by knowing what type of food of plant was used in bygone eras. Find those plants, and there may be a ghost settler town or lost Native American village to be found nearby.

Garlic was once known as Miner Lettuce because it prevented scurvy in miners. Dandelions found all over the region were used as a coffee substitute, and the flowers were used to make wine. Native Americans would chew the stems like gum.

The plant pissenlit is a French word, meaning "piss in the bed" because it was believed that children who handled the plant would wet the bed. In fact, this plant contains a strong diuretic.

The Corpse Plant, or Indian Pipe, turns black and oozes a goo when picked. It is one of the strangest flowers that grow in this region. Sassafras bark was one of the eastern Native American most valuable commodities. No one is really sure why, but sassafras does not grow further west than Iowa. There is no geological reason why it wouldn't. The eastern tribes sold it to the western tribes.

Beach flowers

Beach plums or cherries

The Mighty Appalachian Mountains

Lower Mine River in Brewster, New York

The Appalachian Mountains were once the tallest mountains that ever existed on Earth, even higher than the Himalayas. This ancient range is 2,000 miles long and was formed during the moment of creation of the supercontinent Pangaea. The crystalline Appalachian Mountains are made of Metamorphic Schists and gneisses of various plutonic (igneous) rocks, created from the heat and pressure of the sandy rock that existed here before the collision. The mysterious kingdom of Appalachia was said to be a real place and supposed to be one of the border lands of North America. This strange mass now lies under the sea and has been the basis of a number "vanished" land and island stories.

What the kingdom of Appalachia really consisted of was a geologist's misunderstanding of what a terrane really was. A terrane is a land mass that naturally occurs, but perhaps because different materials create the mass it led some people to believe that something man-made occurred here. This phenomenon happened due to the destruction of Pangaea. At one time, all the land masses were together, creating the super continent of Pangaea. When the continent split apart, pieces of it stayed together. For example, the state of Maine is part of the Avalon terrane, which is not part of the North American land mass. It is really part of the African terrane, which was once connected to North America as part of Pangaea. More about this splitting event will be explored in the New York section of the book. This paragraph is just a word of caution when searching for lost places — sometimes understanding basic geology can save a person time and effort, if the vanished area is really just a geologic event.

As an interesting side note: The word Appalachia or Appalachian comes from Apalachee, the name of a tribe from northern Florida. When the (Hernando) de Soto expedition returned to Spain, the cartographers of the era began applying the name of the tribe to the mountains. The name was not common to the entire range until the nineteenth century.

Mines

One thing that is common throughout Pennsylvania, New York, and New Jersey is the danger of the mines. There are hundreds of stories about deaths of miners from explosions, flooding, and other disasters. There is no doubt that every mine that is talked about in the book has some sort of supernatural twist attached to the element that is to be found there. People have died while trying to find what lies underneath the ground and many bodies were never recovered. It is important to remember that

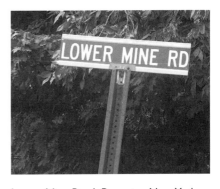
Lower Mine Road, Brewster, New York

mines and their general area are very dangerous. Permission should always be gained before going to these places and great planning and careful consideration should be given when deciding to explore these places.

When exploring any mine location, beware of asbestos. This was the material that the Greeks and Romans used to make dinner napkins. They did not have to wash it — when it became dirty, they threw it into the fire and the napkin would emerge pearly white once again. Asbestos was also used as lamp-wicks in that time. This eternal light was kept in the Temple of Athena and it never burned out. The Greek name for this material was amiantos lithos, meaning "undefiled stone." However, the Romans called the material asbestos, meaning "unquenchable stone."

Precious Gems

Minerals are a naturally occurring solid substance, such as an element, a solid solution, or compound of inorganic origin. Important minerals are found in all three states explored in this book and what type and where they have been discovered is told in each state section. Some general information about the gems to be found in this region starts here.

- In AMETHYST lore, the gem was a cure for drunkenness. Why? When a container is made from this stone, the liquid poured from it looks like water, thus one could drink as much as they wanted without getting drunk. It also is said to keep soldiers from harm.
- AZURITE is a dark blue carbonate of copper. The gem has blue and green patterns all through it.
- The BERYL gem was a cure for laziness and was said to reawaken love.
- The BLOODSTONE gem was very powerful and could change the sun rays into a storm, turn the sun blood-red, or cause thunderstorms.
- The MOONSTONE could bring good fortune. It is a soft material, usually a milky blue gem.
- ROCK CRYSTAL is said to be formed by water flowing together in dark caverns of mountains or "petrified water" by the ancients. It was thought that the water congealed to a hardness created by exposure to intense and long durations of cold. It is really colorless quartz found in mountain caves and caverns throughout the area.
- SPINEL is considered the great imposter of the gemstone world. Many famous rubies in crown jewels around the world are really spinel. It was recognized as a separate gem in 1587. Basically, spinel is a red-color gem, but can also come in blue, called cobalt spinel, but it is very, very rare. Ironically, spinel is becoming rarer than the rubies they used to imitate.
- SUNSTONE is a feldspar, fire-like gem reflection, which are red to orange reflections in stone.

Most gemstones are found by accident. Most discoveries are first made on the surface, in dry riverbeds, rock crevices, or caves. Gems can be organic or made from living creatures, such as pearls, coral, amber, or odontolite, which is Greek meaning "toothstone" and is also known as tooth turquoise. These are fossilized teeth from extinct prehistoric animals, like mammoths, mastodons, and dinosaurs, which have been dyed blue. These are becoming very rare items in today's gem markets. Amber is fossilized, hardened resin of the pine tree, Pinus Stucccinifera, from the Eocene epoch of the Tertiary Period that lived about fifty million years ago. In other words, fossilized tree gum or sap. Yellow and brown are the usual colors found and it was used as jewelry in ancient times. Baltic Amber, also known as "gold of the north" is the earliest used gem in the world. Perhaps this type of discovery was another reason why the Europeans thought that there was a large amount of gold to be found in North America.

One place to look for gem or mineral treasures is in areas that are or were called by the Dutch word "binnewater." It is said to mean "lake, pond, or the old course of a stream after it cuts a new channel." Dry streambeds are perfect places to start a gem or mineral treasure quest. For example, in Cranesville, New York, Lewis Creek is dry most of the time. During its dry period would be a good time to search the area for precious minerals.

The European Quest for Gold

Why did the Europeans really come to the new world? Perhaps it is best explained by those who first traveled here. Christopher Columbus' Journal of the Fourth Voyage 1503 states, "Gold is most excellent. Gold constitutes treasure and he who possesses it may do what he will in the world, and may so attain as to bring souls to paradise."

Gold is the first real metal known to humanity. Columbus, and most Europeans, believed when they came to America they would find the place where "gold grew." Gold was considered the "flesh of the Gods" or "skin of the Gods" by the Egyptians. They believed that gold was not of this world, which may actually be correct. Gold is created and spread through the universe during the stars' dying stages, the Super Nova, though it can be created naturally on Earth and artificially by man today. Gold was called the "sweat of the Sun" by the Incas. This metal, along with Platinum, are called noble metals, which is an alchemistic term, because both are rare. They are also inert minerals or elements, which means that they do not react with any other element. Gold is the perfect reflector in infrared and it is the best known conductors of electricity — it won't corrode and it is a long lasting conductor.

Gold is scarce on Earth, but it occurs in many types of rocks and environments. There are two principal types: lodes or primary deposits and placer or secondary deposits. Fossilized placer deposits can be found in dry river channels and beds under rock debris. There are seven types of places that lode gold is found naturally on Earth:

1. Super-heated waters emerge from "smokers," spring-like vents in the sea floor.
2. Gold-laden water, heated by magma-molten rock in Earth's shallow crust, forms a variety of lode gold deposits.
3. Gold minerals found in hot rocks in and around volcanoes. Low sulfur, gold-bearing hydrothermal fluids form when hot rocks heat ground water.
4. Chemical interactions between hot fluids and sedimentary rocks form deposits of tiny, even invisible, gold particles.
5. Fractures that form in Earth's crust as mountains rise.
6. Ancient gold deposits are found in greenstone belts. They are volcanic belts that are more than 2.3 million years old.
7. Placer deposits form at the Earth's surface when weathering action exposes gold from other, older lode deposits.

Alchemists have been searching for ways to change base minerals and metals, such as lead, into gold since the beginning of time. The Philosopher's Stone was said to be the substance that could turn metals into gold. Though the Stone has never been discovered, other elements have been found while searching for this elusive mineral. In 1669, Hennig Brand filled fifty buckets with human urine and left them until the urine grew putrid. He heated this mix to boiling and when it was reduced to a paste, he heated the residue until it glowed red hot. Strange glowing vapors appeared, which condensed to a liquid and then to a white solid substance that glowed so bright that Brand could read by it at night. He called the substance phosphorus; from the Greek word phosphoros, it means "light-bringing."

In 1924, a Tokyo scientist actually found the Philosopher's Stone, as well as a common element that could be turned into gold. Mercury Isotope 196 can be turned into gold in twenty-three hours. It makes sense actually: Gold is created in the nuclear reactions of a star, so now that people can create nuclear reactions, we can make gold out of other elements. However, it is considered too inefficient and not cost-effective to use and make gold that way today. Throughout the years, there have been no more than 1,000 people engaged in gold beating; these "gold workers" worked in only thirteen states, including having a colony in Red Bank, New Jersey.

Though gold is what was sought when the Europeans first came to the Americas, silver is also a valuable metal and has been found in these states. The book, *The Silver Bonanza*, by Franklin Sanders and James Blanchard, starts with a quote, "The majority monetary metal in history is silver, not gold," which seems to take a different view of this white metal.

There is much more silver to be found in the Earth than gold. Silver has been used as money for over 4,500 years. In early colonial America, the settlers actually preferred silver to gold, though the main reason the Europeans came here was to find gold. Silver was the major monetary metal for the United States until 1873, when it was demonetized. Actually, it was the discovery of the Comstock Lode in 1859 in Nevada that caused the silver demotion in money terms. There was so much silver coming out that it overwhelmed its monetary usefulness.

Organic Gems

Christopher Columbus' list of what items the Spanish Monarch expected him to bring back from his voyages started with "pearls, precious stones, gold, silver, and spice…" Pearls was the first gem on the "to find" list.

Pearls found in this region are from saltwater oysters and freshwater mussels that were here since days of ancient North America. Pearls can be found in any mollusk, but the animal must be of pearl-making variety. A piece of sand lodged in the mollusk becomes covered with lime and nacre, or mother of pearl, also known as conchiolin…thus a pearl is born. Natural pearls take seven years to form and cultured pearls take about three years to create.

Oyster Bay, Long Island, New York

Marine pearl producing mollusks are found from Canada to Florida. In the Atlantic Ocean, the Hard Shell Clam, the Edible Oyster with blister pearls, and the Knobbed Whelk all can yield pearls. In freshwater, the European Pearl Mussel can produce a pearl.

How did the ancient people perceive the pearl's origin? In Rome, they were said to be the frozen tears of the oyster. The Greeks thought that they were the remains of lightning strikes in the sea. In India, it was said that they were dew drops that were solidified in rain.

Fossil pearls have been found from the Cambrian Period about 530 million years ago, and have been found in more than thirty different species of extinct mollusks that were common in the age of the dinosaur. Cave pearls are not pearls created by mollusks — they are ivory white bodies that are inorganically formed in shallow cave pools of rich calcium water.

Pirates!

Pirates roamed the Atlantic coastline during the 1500s. Some famous pirates were well-known to the New York and New Jersey pioneers, and were actually welcomed and liked in many coastal communities. The buried treasure sites will be discussed in each state, but there is general pirate lore that pertains to all pirates.

Pirates used nicknames, also known as aliases, so that law enforcement would not go after the family on land. That is why it is important to know the real name of the pirate as well as the well-known nickname. Perhaps treasure was buried on the land owned by family members.

Pirates actually did wear earrings, which helped with their health, though they probably never really knew why. Acupuncture specialists report that there are pressure points located just above the earlobe that help to improve eyesight, reduce the appetite, and boost energy levels. Though this may be true, the main reason pirates wore earrings was that it was a convenient place to hold wax, which they would use to plug their ears during cannon fire. Earrings were also used as payment for a proper burial because they were made of gold and other precious metals.

Pirates who may have hid treasure in the three states explored in the book are:

- EDWARD TEACH, commonly known as Blackbeard, was also known as "Terror of the Sea." He was a pirate along the North Atlantic coast. He had many wives; the exact number remains unknown, but it has been said that he may have had at least sixteen. One legend of buried treasure relating to him has an abandoned wife left to die to protect his bounty on the Isles of Shoals off the New Hampshire and Maine coasts. Another strange tale about Blackbeard is that he buried one of his wives in his "treasure chest" off Plum Point, North Carolina. Blackbeard was a strange character, but why would he do this? It is believed that perhaps these women overheard something he did not want anyone to know. His legend is so powerful that it is said that after his head was cut off and his body thrown into the ocean, he swam around the British ship three times before his body finally sank to the murky sea bottom.

• HENRY SIMS was an Estonian turned pirate and was actually deported to New England. He became a pirate because he was captured by a pirate crew and roamed the coasts of New York and New Jersey. Many times when people were captured by pirates, they were given a choice — either join or die. It really is no wonder that people would choose to join the crew. He did not have much luck as a pirate, perhaps because his heart was not in it. Unfortunately, he was caught and hanged.

• JOHN AVERY is also known as "Long Ben," Henry Every, Avery or Avary, or Benjamin Bridgeman. He did business in Boston in 1690 and it is said that he buried treasure all along the Atlantic Coast. Very few pirate captains retired alive with his loot, but he did. His ship was called Fancy and he worked with famous Rhode Island pirate Thomas Tew, even taking part in the battle where Tew was killed. During this battle, a lot of pirates and sailors were killed, but Avery is said to have escaped with $600,000 in jewels and loot, making him the richest pirate in the world. In 1696, he disappeared. Though it is probable that he may have changed his name, he disappeared from the records and perhaps lived a quiet life somewhere. His pirate life lasted only a few years.

• BARTHOLOMEW ROBERTS was a pirate captain who did not allow gambling or women on his ship. Roberts arrived in Newfoundland, Canada, in June 1719, the same year that Blackbeard was killed by the British. His first pirate raid was to capture a French ship, which he renamed Royal Fortune, as he started to roam the northeast coast. In 1721, the crew deserted Roberts. A pirate crew would often do that so they could not be convicted of murder. They would maroon or leave a person on an island, away from the shipping lanes, with a keg of grog, which was a real drink of rum and water on-board pirate ships, a loaf of bread, and a gun with one bullet. Roberts was actually rescued by another pirate crew and went on with his pirate career. He captured at least two other ships, renaming them both Royal Fortune. Eventually, he was killed on February 10, 1722 during a battle with the British Royal Navy.

As an interesting side note: It should be noted that most captains of any type of ship during that era did not allow women on their vessels. It was considered bad luck. However, the female pirates of that time were very successful.

Lodestone Lore

People have been trying to find their way across horizon-less water since the beginning of time. No one is really sure who, when, or where the actual compass was invented. It is thought that an item found from the Olmec civilization of Mesoamerica may be an early form of a compass, which predates the Chinese reference to a "direction finder using a magnetized needle" over 2,000 years.

The Chinese dictionary printed in 121 A.D. defines the lodestone as a "stone with which an attraction can be given to the needle." When a needle was rubbed against this stone, the needle became magnetized and could be used to steer a ship. The word in Middle English means "course stone or leading stone." This element is one of only two minerals that are naturally magnetized. The other is pyrrhotite and it is only weakly magnetic. However, only a small amount of Magnetite on Earth is found magnetized or lodestone. One theory suggests that lodestones are magnetized by the strong magnetic fields surrounding lightning bolts. This claim may be substantiated by the observation that most lodestone is found on the surface of the Earth, not buried. It could also have been created from volcanic gases and it has been found in meteorites. It has also been discovered in large quantities of sand.

Magnetite or Lodestone magnetic qualities are caused by electron motion. The moving electrons in the rock create magnetic fields. The stone is also known as "the Herculean Stone." Magnetism was first applied to minerals found in only three places — Lydia, Magnesia, and Herakleia — and was discovered by a shepherd on Mount Ida because the nails of his shoes clung to a piece of the mineral. A combination of magnetite and corundum creates emery, which has been used as an abrasive since ancient times. The word lode originally meant "leader," so the sailors could "follow the stone" to a specific destination and, in mining, miners could "follow" a lode to extract minerals, hence the name.

The year 1190 is the first time that the Europeans mention a compass in books. In 1250, it became a common tool used by sailors. It was the 1300s before it was used in surveying. Columbus used a compass. He proved that it was a verified fact that the needle did not constantly point to the North Star. In 1600, William Gilbert, an English physician, physicist, and natural philosopher, proved that the Earth is a large magnet with lines of force flowing from pole to pole. Previously, it was believed that Angels and Demons and the stars of the Heavens influenced the needle.

Now that we have the general knowledge to start the haunted treasure journey of New York, New Jersey, and Pennsylvania, all you have to do is turn to the next page.....

Looks like New Jersey is still a good bargain in 2011.

Atlantic City is still the gambling spot on the East Coast today. The Taj Mahal Casino is on the boardwalk. There are still places to lose loot in the present era along the Atlantic Coast!

Section One
New Jersey

Overview of the Garden State

Welcome to one of smallest states in the Union, known as the Garden State! Other nicknames are: Clam State, Camden, Amboy State, Jersey Blue State, and the Pathway of the Revolution. There are four states smaller than New Jersey: Rhode Island, Delaware, Connecticut, and Hawaii. New Jersey lies midway between Nova Scotia and Florida. There is no national seashore here, though there is 127 miles of coastline. The state was considered neutral territory during the Civil War and is basically surrounded by water, except for the small strip along the northern border.

Per an agreement between James, Duke of York, and Sir George Carteret, a "pepper corne" was used for rent in exchange for this area to be known as New Jersey. The state was named by Carteret and Sir John Berkeley after Carteret's native island of Jersey in the English Channel. According to legend, New York and New Jersey were separated to pay off a gambling debt and, based on that story, it does seem fitting that casinos came to the East Coast first in Atlantic City.

It can be said that New Jersey started with a bang. A remnant of a massive asteroid impact is found in southern New Jersey, where the ejecta layer of the asteroid has been discovered. There are only one hundred places on Earth where these layers have been seen. Many space minerals only can be found in asteroid impact sites.

In the Triassic era, New Jersey and Mauretania were connected when the giant continent, Pangaea, started to pull apart at the Palisades in New York along the Hudson River. This event ultimately created the Atlantic Ocean about 250 million years ago. The Palisades actually tilted westward, which became known in New Jersey as the Border Fault. This opening happened in the Miocene era and is actually still occurring today. What that means is that part of New Jersey is found in Africa. New York and New Jersey were directly connected to Morocco during this epoch. It is theorized that what once happened here is happening today at the Great Basin in Nevada — the earth is splitting apart and becoming an ocean.

Triassic New Jersey looked very different than what we see there today. It was covered in a red mud layer with lava oozing from it. Where Whippany and Parsippany are located today, a 7,000-foot mountain once stood. Much of the Triassic period rock found in the present is a red color, proving that there may have been an abundance of oxygen in the atmosphere at that time. In the Hackensack Valley, there was several hundred feet of water over the airport, called Glacial Lake Hackensack, filled with many islands. Ancient New Jersey was created seventy million years ago, basically from sand, clay, and marls of shoreline, which is where Camden is now. Northwestern New Jersey was sliced by the ancient Appalachian Mountains.

The Native American tribes here were, starting west to east: the UNILACHTIGO tribe, meaning "people who live near the ocean"; the MINSI tribe, meaning "people of the stony country"; the UNAMI tribe, meaning "people down the river"; and the HACKENSACK tribe. The Hackensack, a sub-tribe of the Lenni-Lenape, lived in a village found in the neck between the river and Overpeck Creek, near the Teaneck Ridge. The Hackensack River is a tidal river that flows to the village of River Edge. The Native American word means "river of many bends," and it starts in New York and ends in New Jersey. Numerous Native American villages were found along its entire length. The region was inhabited by the Lenni-Lenape tribe before the Dutch arrived. New Milford was the site of the last known wampum factory, which existed until the middle of the nineteenth century.

Dinosaur Stomping Ground

Dinosaurs were known to roam this region because of the numerous fossils found. Fossil sites are given throughout the section, but here is a beginning list of what types of dinosaurs once walked through the state:

• DIPLOTOMODON: This dinosaur had a double folded cutting tooth and lived in the Late Cretaceous period. It was a meat eater, and may have been one of the largest carnivorous dinosaurs ever known.

• HADROSAURUS: Meaning "sturdy lizard" and also known as the "Duckbilled Dinosaur," it lived in the Late Cretaceous period and was a plant eater.

• ORNITHOTARUS: Meaning "bird the flat of the foot" from the Late Cretaceous period, it was a plant eater.

• DRYPTOSAURUS: Meaning "to tear lizard" and found all through the eastern part of North America, it was a meat-eater in the Late Cretaceous period and thought to be a natural hunter of the Hadrosaurus.

Whale bone

There have been many dinosaur prints found in the red sandstone and lava flows all across the Hudson Valley, particularly in New Jersey. The dinosaurs that roamed here, or what the most common prints found, are of the Hadrosaur or duckbilled dinosaur. In that age, New Jersey was a sub tropical region and the dinosaurs apparently liked the swamplands that could be found in the region.

In 1858, the first United States Hadrosaur dinosaur skeleton was discovered in Haddonfield, New Jersey. During the building of the George Washington Bridge, skeletons and prints of this dinosaur were found. Dinosaur prints have also been excavated at Fort Lee, Princeton, New Egypt, Marlton, Crosswicks, Mullica Hill, and Lenola.

Fort Lee is the Hudson River fort that was located at the end of the George Washington Bridge. It is almost completely gone today, but on the bluffs near the river, some ruins can be seen. A major battle took place here in 1776. Fossils were found in 1910. A crocodile-like reptile skeleton, called the Rutiodon Manhattanenis, was discovered. This was also the site of the first blockade of an enemy ship during the Revolutionary War.

Near Giants or Meadowland Stadium, thousands of dinosaurs tracks from the late Triassic age were discovered. These prints were made in the late Triassic age by turkey-sized dinosaurs. During this epoch, Africa was east of New York and New Jersey in the middle of Pangaea and this region was an arid valley desert region.

A Mastodon skeleton was found in 1869 in Manninton Township in Salem County.

In North Bergen, the fossil of a gliding reptile came to the surface in 1960. Today, buildings basically cover most of the site. This was the earliest vertebrate to achieve aerial locomotion, named Icarusaurus Seifkeri after the Icarus of Greek myth.

The Duckbill dinosaur and meat-eating mosasaurs were found in the Inversand marl pit in Sewell, Gloucester County. In Poricy Park Brook, Monmouth County, fossils of marine creatures from the Late Cretaceous period lived about seventy million years ago shortly before dinosaurs disappeared from the Earth forever.

At Trenton Falls, which is an eight-foot drop, the Isotelus gigas, a Ptychopariid, came to light in the limestone from the Ordovician era. These fossils were three inches long.

Spooky Sites

Who discovered New Jersey first? It is obvious that the Native American tribes were already living here before the settlers arrived, but possibly a pre-Lenni-Lenape person named the glacial-age or stone-age man called this region home. This is a very controversial theory, but in 1872, it is said that an argillite blade was found along a Delaware River bluff, about one mile south of Trenton. There were also arrowheads, stone blades, and other artifacts that are very different from the Lenni-Lenape people.

Petroglyphs have been found here in caves, crevices, and rock shelters all through state, but is there evidence that Europeans ventured here before Columbus? Some of the inscriptions found on rocks in the area may not be Native American. They are thought to be Libyan, Celtic, and Phoenician.

Officially, in 1524, it was Giovanni de Verrazano who sailed along the coast and is said to have traveled just off Sandy Hook. In 1609, Henry Hudson landed at Sandy Hook on the north coast and explored the Hudson River. In 1614, the Dutch explorer, Cornelius Mey, explored the Delaware River. In 1618, the Dutch built a trading post at Bergen, now Jersey City.

There are strange haunted places found in New Jersey and many of them have a treasure or precious mineral to be found. At the Stone Clock Tower found at the New Jersey Palisades, where Pangaea broke apart, is a place where the treasure seeker could, it is said, to be able to meet Satan himself. It is also called the Devil's Tower and can be found on the road called The Esplanade, about one mile north of the Tenafly-Alpine border in Bergen County. It was built in the 1900s as a centerpiece of an estate called Rio Vista. A Spanish businessman named Manuel Rionda made a fortune from sugarcane in Cuba and he built the estate on present-day Alpine Lookout. All belongings were removed, including the remains of his wife and sister, in 1943 after Manuel's death. It remained woodlands through the 1970s, and there are lots of ghost stories and sightings. To see anything though, a person must complete the ritual of walking or driving three or six times in reverse around the tower. If done correctly, one may see the ghost of Manuel's wife, the devil, or perhaps drive into a tree when leaving.

The wife is said to have killed herself in the tower after seeing husband with another woman; another story is that it was built as a birthday gift, but she died before it was completed. The clock is said to chime at certain times to people walking in the woods. Over the years, as new owners lived in the home, they tried knocking down the tower, but odd deaths kept occurring to the crew charged with its removal, so the tower was left standing. The minerals to be found here, called rare Earth elements, were created during the tearing apart of the supercontinent.

There are abandoned houses off Route 23 on the border of Morris and Passaic counties, near the border of West Milford and Kinnelon, called Demon's Alley. The ghostly town lies in the woods on the road called New City Road. The New City Colony was built in the early twentieth century to house workers constructing the numerous reservoirs of the Newark Watershed. It was abandoned in the mid-1980s. The real question that spooks many people is: Why was this place abandoned? People who had ventured into the homes despite the presence of "No Trespassing" signs, say that many of the residents' personal belongings are still there, including TVs, furniture, and even clothes. Plywood has been nailed over the doors and windows. The actual buildings are now gone, burned by suspicious fires. All remains were demolished in 2002. Claims of the area include the story of a man who moved into area in the 1980s. It was said that he was a cult leader who lured all the residents of this town into a small area, where his cult killed them. One day, the cult vanished and no one talks about what happened.

The Devil's Tree is a cursed tree found in the Martinsville section of Bernards Township in Somerset County. The tree stands alone in a field off Mountain Road. According to legend, a farmer who lived in that area killed his entire family and then hanged himself at this tree. Now if anyone tries to cut down the tree, they will die. The legend goes on to say that even just touching the tree will result in a curse attaching itself to you. As an interesting side note, it is said to be warm around tree — and actually one rock is very warm, called the heat rock. No matter how cold it is, no snow is said to remain here. The tree is also said to be a portal to hell and is guarded by something that drives a black pickup truck called the phantom driver. You will see headlights one minute…and then nothing. Another interesting side note: The area was one of the central headquarters of the KKK in New Jersey.

Many strange rock formations can be found in the state. Though some were created by the glacier, perhaps not all were, and what were they used for or what strange events happened here may be lost to history. What else could still be left here? The Stone Living Room is located in West Milford, New Jersey. These are dolmens, also known as Perched rocks or standing stones. The question here is, who built them? And why? Some of the rocks weigh over four hundred pounds. They can be found on a trail off Glenwild Avenue.

Kinnelon's Stonehenge, or Tripod Rock, is a massive stone laying on three small stones found on Pyramid Mountain in Kinnelon. It is part of the Pyramid Mountain Natural Historical Area and can be found two miles along a hiking trail. More strange rock formations can be found on Bearfont Mountain in West Milford, Passaic County. There is a chunk of pudding stone perched on three smaller stones in a remote location, but can be hiked to on a trail east of Terrace Pond. More erratic standing stones are perched along the parallel ridge near the fire tower on the property of the Newark Watershed. Other standing rock formations are found in Norvin Green State Forest and Ramapo, High Point, and Harriman state parks. High Point State Park, located in the Kittatinny Ridge, is home to a granite-faced obelisk that can be found on the Old Trail or Monument Trail. Interestingly, this trail leads to a swamp area that is the home to fitcher plants and Sundews, which are carnivorous plants and uncommon in the region. Are these glacial erratic rock placements or are they odd formations explained by other geologic events or perhaps something else? What can be said is that there tend to be a lot of them in this area. However, it is known that the glacier stopped at Perth Amboy, so it is probable that these were left by the glacier.

One stone formation, though, cannot be explained by the glacier — the Morris Plains steps. About three hundred stone steps in total exist here, though no one really knows why. Some say they were built by Washington's army during the Revolution as lookouts to warn of British troop movements. Others say Native Americans built the steps, but why?

The steps are flat stones, ranging one to two feet in width, and are located way off in woods, at the foot of Watchung Mountain.

Strange carvings are seen in the rock called Turtle Back Rock, located in the South Mountain Reservation in West Orange, Essex County. The etching looks like a turtle's back, which is probably the bottom of a dry lake bed or ancient molten lava that cooled. After all, First Watchung Mountain is actually a lava hill.

The Garfield rock carvings, which are numerous New Jersey rock pictures, though they have never really been fully documented, can be found on a sandstone boulder located on the Passaic River before Dundee Dam in Garfield. They are believed to date from the Woodland Period or about 1000 BC. There are four symbols carved into it: a bear paw with claw marks, a fish, a phallus, and a set of initials, though probably not Native American. Perhaps it is a warning that bears also fish in these waters? The initials are "AL" or "AI." This was a popular fishing spot for the Native American and Europeans.

Lake Hopatcong

Lake Hopatcong, also known as Brookland Pond, is the largest body of freshwater in New Jersey. It is also the supposed home of the Beast of Lake Hopatcong. First reported two hundred years ago, this creature will drag down swimmers and has been spotted even in the twenty-first century. No one knows what this creature could be. It is said that a carcass was seen at the bottom of the lake in an early era.

Lake Hopatcong

Morris Canal dam

In the eighteenth century, the lake existed in two parts: called Great Pond for the southern part of the water and Little Pond for the northern part of the water. Eventually, one lake was created due to the dam that drowned the land separating the two waterways. Hopatcong is said to mean "honey waters of many coves," but it may actually come from the Lenape word hapakonoesson meaning "pipe stone."

Morris Canal

Near the Lake George region lies the Morris Canal. The Brookland Forge was here in 1750, but was completely covered by the canal. When the canal was drained, a piece of the old forge was found in the dry channel.

In the 1600s, the Nariticong clan of the Delaware Nation lived on the east shore of the lake in a village on Halsey Island, which was connected with the mainland at that time. The Dutch established trading posts, and the first settlers to arrive at the place called the Landing in the Roxbury, in the early eighteenth century was a Christian group known as the Rogerenes.

Ruins from Brookland Forge

The Morris Canal ruins can be seen at the Lake Hopatcong State Park today. It was used for commercial transportation in 1827. The canal raised the lake level by six feet, submerging the shoreline and cutting off Halsey and Raccoon islands from the mainland. The canal was closed in 1924. During the heyday, it was the chief means of transporting coal, iron, and zinc across the state for fifty years starting in 1832. After the canal was abandoned, the ruin of a 1750 Iron Forge was discovered where the lake flowed into the Musconetcong River at the southern end. This forge was used during the Revolutionary War.

The ghost town of Atena was about ten miles from Taunton on Rancocas Creek. The dam was rebuilt after the furnace closed and the mill pond is now called Aetna Lake.

In 1797, in Ocean County, about seven miles south of Barnegat, near the present-day town of Staffordsville, the Stafford Forge once existed. A cranberry bog now covers the site.

Remains of the Morris Canal

Native American populations resided in Pemberton, Burlington County, near Rancocas Creek, over 10,000 years ago. The date has been proven by the artifacts found. In 1859, an amazing sandstone ax inscribed with ten characters was discovered by Dr. J.W.C. Evans. In 1861, archaeologist James Whittall stated that the symbols were actually Iberian and meant: "Stand firm, on guard, parry, close in, and strike." The problem is that today, no one knows what happened to this artifact, but if one was found, perhaps others still exist. Other petroglyphs found in area are said to be Celtic, Viking, or Saxon. The ax is still thought to be Phoenician. Perhaps the tribes traded with others before the Europeans arrived?

Ringwood Manor State Park, found at the northern end of the Wanaque Reservoir, about ten miles southwest of Suffern, New York, was the site of a Native American village.

The Native American Burlington Path and Minnisink Trail were the main routes used by tribes from all over this region that came to the New Jersey coast to feast on the oysters. These paths are found near the infamous New Jersey Pine Barrens.

The Pine Barrens

Also known as the Pinelands, the Pine Belt, or The Pines, the geology of this region started with the depression or sinking of the land below the sea during the Lafayette epoch of the Miocene. The name comes from the Pitch Pine, or Pinus rigida, tree found here, though this type of tree is also found on Cape Cod, Massachusetts and Long Island, New York. The rare plant Schizaea pusilla, or curly grass fern, only grows here.

Pine Barrens

The area is almost as large as Yosemite National Park and covers twenty-five percent of New Jersey. A straight line from Boston to Richmond goes right through the middle of the Barrens. The geographic half-way point is in the northern part of the woods, about twenty miles from Bear Swamp Hill. The exact center of the Barrens is either at or very near a place called Hog Wallow. In the sand under the pine is a natural reservoir of pure water that in volume is equivalent of a lake seventy-five miles deep with a surface of 1,000 square miles. According to the US Geological Survey of 1966, the water was "bacterially sterile, odorless, clear; its chemical purity approaches that of uncontaminated rain-water or melted glacial ice." It is hard to imagine that a seventeen-trillion-gallon lake called the Cohansey Aquifer exists under the region, but it does. The settlers called this region the Barrens due to the sandy soil, over one million acres, that did not support agriculture.

Marshy bog region in the Barrens

Numerous Native American trails were found crossing the Pines, though no tribe lived in here. No tribes lived on the New Jersey coast either; they used the trails for sea-fishing and gathering shellfish. One trail started from Somers Point and extended to the east side of Great Egg Harbor. Another trail started at the mouth of Little Egg Harbor River in the west and joined the first trail near the head of Landing Creek. Another starts by Mullica's Plantation, near Basto, and went in a western direction to south of Winslow. Still another was called the Old Cape Trail, which started in Cape May County. It crossed the head of the Tuckahoe River in a northerly direction and went to the west of the branches of the Great Egg Harbor River to the upper waters of Hospitality Creek. Any Native American path may yield artifacts from thousands of years of use.

Which way to go in the Pinelands?

The first Native American reservation, occupied by the Lenni-Lenape tribe, was here, called Brotherton. It is rather ironic, really, because the Native Americans did not come to this area very often. It was considered cursed by the tribes. They said there were vortexes existing in the area. Headaches, nausea, and feelings of not being welcomed have been reported to occur in this place. Children ghosts have been sighted. On Route 541 in Mount Holly, Revolutionary War Hessian soldier ghosts are also seen. It is indeed a very haunted region. Just off Route 68 is the former and deserted Lakehurst Base, where the Hindenburg disaster occurred — strange lights and sounds have been heard near the site. While traveling Route 30, it is said that every night a young boy is seen playing basketball. It is actually the ghost of a child that was killed here by a car.

Double Trouble State Park is found in the Pine Barrens in Bayville. Why the name? In the eighteenth century, there was a mill and dam constructed here. Legends report that muskrats ate through the dam, which constantly caused major leaks. Every time a leak was spotted, the owner would cry, "Here's trouble!" One day, two leaks were spotted and it is said that he cried, "Here's double trouble!" This moist environment is one place where the insect-eating Sundew plant lives. It is an uncommon plant to be found in New Jersey, but then again, this is a very unique area.

What may live here?

Great Egg Harbor

All rivers in the Barrens drain to the ocean. The rivers in the Barrens are: Basto, Manasquan, Toms, Wading, Mullica, and Great Egg River.

The Wading River is found in the western area of Chatsworth. It is a little lake that is almost dried up due to the washing out of a former dam. In the seventeenth century, it was a ship-building site. It is a cedar swamp area or a place that was once a forest that was drowned by the swamp. Because the place was once a living forest and is now a dead swamp forest, it is an eerie place. As an interesting side note, this river appears to actually disappear! It flows very strongly into the swamp, where it just seems to stop, and then starts at another point down the river. Perhaps it goes underground or just melts into the swamp. No one is really sure. The Wading River forge was located at mouth of River, as it flowed into Atlantic Ocean. The Mullica River was once called Little Egg Harbor River, if looking for treasure sites, always find alternative names for an area.

The Mullica and Basto Rivers flow through the Pine Barrens. Basto is a Dutch word meaning "bath house." Obviously, the Dutch either used the river to bathe or observed that the Native Americans would use the river in this way.

There are two streams that become one just below Pleasant Mills, also known as Sweetwater. The lake was a favorite spot of the tribes that passed through, called Nescochague. Small branches of the river, called Mecheseatauxin and Nescochague, add to its flow.

Jersey Devil and Captain Kidd

This region is home to the Jersey Devil. This monster is described as having a head of a horse, the face of a dog, the legs of a crane, and the cloven hoofs of a deer. There have been lots of eyewitness reports of this creature throughout the centuries. The legend is that the creature was born in the eighteenth century and the horrible appearance of the child destined to become the monster is the result of a curse. Mowas Leeds bore twelve children and the thirteenth, who would become the Jersey Devil, was cursed. Once born, the cursed child escaped through the chimney into the woods and has been there terrorizing the region ever since. It makes ferocious sounds when it hunts. Sightings have been reported in Smithfield for over three hundred years, with most of them occurring in Wharton State Forest.

In the nineteenth century, Commodore Stephen Decatur, an American naval hero, was visiting the Hanover Mill Works to inspect the cannonballs being forged. He saw a flying creature and shot at it, but it flew away. Joseph Bonaparte, brother of Napoleon Bonaparte, was also reported as seeing the creature while hunting here.

Skull found in the Barrens. What could it be?

Captain Kidd is also supposed to have buried a treasure in Barnegat Bay in the Barrens. He beheaded one of his crew to guard the loot and it is said that the headless pirate and Jersey Devil are seen together in the nearby marshes, guarding his buried treasure. The Jersey Devil was even reported being seen with a mermaid in 1870.

I drove through this area in October 2010 at night while a major thunderstorm raged overhead. There was a driving rain, vivid lightning, and a very dark area. It was so different than what we had just passed through getting here on the highway. I knew the stories, but even my friends, who did not know the stories yet, said it was almost too dark. The ride through gave us all a strange feeling.

I went back to the area during the daylight and it was still a strange place. Driving along the road, we suddenly spotted the skeleton of a head sitting on the bridge. It is not a normal sighting and yet it seemed to be perfectly normal here. There are some beautiful homes along the lake here, and we did not see many cars driving through the park. Both times spent in the Pinelands will be remembered! I can see why most people throughout the years say they just cross the region as quickly as possible while getting to their ultimate destination. There is a feeling that one should "keep moving along" here.

Searching Along the Waterways!

Because this region was heavily forested, the only way to reach various destinations was by water. Most Native American villages, European settlements, and military forts were first built along the water. It is also the place where precious minerals and gems are found. Knowing what to expect and where this waterways once flowed is vital to the treasure quest. Please remember that all water channels change. Knowing where they once flowed is the perfect place to start digging. Always remember that today most land is owned by someone. Always seek permission to trespass.

The Passaic River is the second longest river in New Jersey. Passaic is a Lenape word, meaning "valley." Its source is the Great Swamp, which is really an ancient remnant of Lake Passaic. It flows for eighty-five miles and is subject to floods which cause it to leave normal channels. Singac, which is part of Little Falls, is the site of Native American camps. Little Falls is found one mile below this camping place. At Pine Brook the Whippany River enters the river. The Whippany was the river where many Native American villages once existed. Whippany is an Algonquin word meaning "arrow stream." The Native Americans would come here to harvest wood for their arrows. Great Falls are found in Paterson, falling over one hundred feet over traprock. Alexander Hamilton was so impressed with these falls when he traveled through; he thought a mill should be built.

The Ramapo-Pompton River starts its journey near Tuxedo Park. Pompton was settled by the Dutch in 1682. The Oakland area was the site of the largest Native American village in the state. The Ramapo Mountains is a very mysterious place. For some reason there are very few roads or even old trails that exist here. Perhaps it is because there are and were abundant rattlesnakes found. Castle Van Slyke is on top of Ramapo Mountain, where a hidden cache of silver dollars or gold coins is just waiting to be discovered.

In 1942, it was reported that the Metedeconk River was always ice cold, even in the hot summer months. It is fed by deep cold-water streams. The water is also crystal clear, not the usual amber color of most New Jersey water. There is quicksand to be wary of near Georgia, which is also rather unusual for New Jersey rivers!

The Paulins Kill River flows parallel to the Kittatinny Mountain range. The river was called Tockhockonetkong by the Native Americans and mountains were Kittatinny, meaning "chief town." The Chiefs of the Lenni-Lenapes lived and governed their people from this village. The present name of the river, Paulins Kill, comes from the story of Hessian, or German, prisoners taken to the village of Stillwater, where they remained throughout the Revolutionary War. After the war, they were released, but they really liked the area, so they bought land and stayed. One of these former prisoners became an important man in area and the river was named for his daughter, Pauline.

Duck enjoying the water.

The entire Kittatinny valley and mountains were created by major volcanic upheaval. The town Delaware Water Gap is where the Delaware River breaks through the Appalachian Chain. It is the site of famous rock formation of the Native American head at the top. The Kittatinny Mountains straddle the Delaware River in northeast Pennsylvania and northwest New Jersey. The Native American name is said to mean "endless hill," "great mountains," or "endless mountains." The word Pocono, thought to be from the Delaware tribe word pocohanne, meaning "stream between two mountains," probably referred to the Delaware River Gap. As an interesting side note: The old-time loggers would drop red paint over the cliffs, telling new loggers that was the blood of the river-runners who did not make it through the Gap.

Delaware Water Gap

Kittatinny Mountain Gap – Delaware Mountain Gap

Close-up of face in Delaware Mountain Gap.

The Pahaquarry Mine found here is shrouded in mystery. There is historical evidence that the Dutch mined the Delaware Valley for copper in the seventeenth century and transported it, by oxen via the Old Mine Road that led to the Hudson River, to Holland. It was a 104-mile road that followed the east shore of the Delaware River and was said to have been constructed just to move copper. Is it true? Mining was attempted at least five times here for copper and none were successful. What is known is that copper ore litters the trails of the old mine and road. The metal must have come from somewhere. Other mountains near the Delaware Water Gap, the area was called Esopus in that era, may also yield copper. This road does exist and the entire road was used during military operations in the American Revolution. Today, part of the road is under the Tocks Island Reservoir. The question remains: are there treasures still existing here? Today the road is a mountain bike road, but it is considered the oldest public thoroughfare in the United States. At one time, the traveler could use this road from Kingston, New York, to the Native American copper mines at Pahaquarry, just north of Columbia. In 1942, one could still use part of the road from Columbia to Port Jervis.

Old Mine Road

The Millstone River, which Stony Brook is a tributary, is a corruption of its Native American name, Mattawang, meaning "hard to travel." However, no one is really sure why, since it is usually considered placid and easy to canoe. Near Manville and Weston, a 225-year-old grist mill existed on the river. It was actually still in operation until the 1940s. The skirmish of Weston was fought in 1777 between the Minute Men and British. Stone Arch Bridge was built in 1793 across the river at Kingston, New Jersey, which is part of South Brunswick Township.

According to geologists, this river flowed in the opposite direction before the ice age. After the ice age disruption, it is one of the few streams that actually flow north. Anytime a person knows that a dry or changed river bed is around, that is one place where heavy metals and gems may still exist. It may be worth the time to search here. Over the Stone Arch was the route of the Colonial Army following the battle of Princeton in January 1777. This bridge is a replacement because Washington himself destroyed the original bridge to delay the British who were pursuing them. *Author note: Anytime a route is known to be used by fleeing or pursuing armies, it is a good place to search for wartime artifacts.*

The Rancocas River is named for the tribe called the Rancocas, Ankokas, or Ancocas, who lived along the banks. The last chief, Ramcoke, was buried near the bridge at Centerton. It is said that a person who ventures here can still feel the presence of the Native Americans who once lived here. The river passes through cedar swamp and is an amber color. There is an ancient stone altar on the hill in Mount Holly, which is said to still echo with cries of the woman who were convicted of being witches. Union Lake was created by dams on this river. Glassboro is the town where one can still find evidence of the glass-blowing industry that once existed here. German glass-makers created Wistar and Stanger glass on this spot. The dam at Fries Mill on Scotland Run, which is one of the branches of this river, seems to create a lake of perfectly blue water that is unusual for this region. Due to cedar tree influence, most water in New Jersey is naturally an amber color.

The Rockaway River is the gateway to the magnetic iron deposits in Morris County. Most of the mines are abandoned, but at one time, this area provided the United States with most of the iron being used. The name is a corrupted Native American name, Roga Weighwero, meaning, "running out of a deep gorge." There is a lot of fast moving water found. The settlers learned of the iron black stone that existed from the Native Americans, who used the stone for hatchets. Eventually, those pioneers found the source near Succasunna. Bats live in the old mine shafts today, but this ore contained eighty-three percent iron.

One finds the Toms River in South Jersey. This is really a swampy river especially the upper part. The village of Toms River had a block house, another word for fort, built as one of the first buildings. In 1782, Tories attacked and burned this fort and hanged the Captain who defended the fort at Gravelly Point.

Cape May

Cape May is the southernmost point of New Jersey and considered the most haunted city in the country. It was the vacation resort of the Lenape tribe. They stayed here all summer. Hoboken was once a Native American trading post.

Henry Hudson was the first European to see this spot in 1609 from his ship, the *Half Moon*. He claimed the area for the Netherlands. Fourteen years later, in 1623, Captain Cornelius Jacobsen Mey entered Delaware Bay on his ship, *Glad Tidings*, to establish settlements and a fur trading post. The misspelling of his name gave this point its eventual name. Ironically, he never actually set foot on the land that bears his name, but he did name the south cape "Cape Cornelius," now Cape Henlopen, in Delaware and the north cape "Cape Mey."

He dispatched twenty-four men up the Delaware River to establish Fort Nassau, near present-day Gloucester, on the east bank of the Delaware River opposite Philadelphia. It was a log structure, and the first settlement

Cape May Lighthouse

Cape May beach

in the Delaware Valley by the Europeans. However, eight years later, no trace of these men was found. Their fate is unknown and the fort was not established until 1631, eventually becoming a fur trading post, and was abandoned in 1650.

Salem was the first permanent settlement of the English on the Delaware River in 1675. In 1870, the Nordic, Danish, and Swedish fishermen settled at the end of the island and named this area Anglesea, later North Wildwood or Hereford Inlet.

A sunken white cedar forest was discovered here in the 1830s. Great Cedar Swamp lies about seven miles across the neck of Cape May peninsula, following the shores of Dennis Creek and Cedar Creek. As an interesting side note: Lumber cut from this underwater forest is as usable to make furniture as what is made from living trees. It gives off the same scent as those trees cut in green forests. Trees mined from the underwater forest were reported as having been around for five hundred years. There is a legend that one tree cut from this forest was over 1,000 years old. How did the forest become sunken? One reason may be that the land gradually sank. Another thought is that the land was sunk due to a great hurricane. The third reason has been said that South Jersey land sinking prompted the building of Noah's Ark. When the ice age was receding, the ocean was two hundred miles from here. It has been discovered that New Jersey coastline had receded about 160' from 1804 to 1820. The sea is thought to still be advancing. There are records of large ships being built at one time, where only motor boats can go today along the Dennis River. The great salt marsh of the Delaware Bay is said to once have been farmland. The Delaware River, geologists claim, is really an extension of the sea.

Mighty Atlantic Ocean from where the Europeans came!

1.
Pirates, Military, and Shipwrecks!

Lighthouses and Wrecks

All ships must pass New Jersey to get to New York Harbor or the Hudson River. Hundreds of ships were wrecked along the coast and millions of dollars in treasure ended up under the sand at the beaches in New Jersey. The state was also well known for the profession of wrecking and wreckers or moon-cussers. Wreckers were known as land pirates. A mule would pull the wagon of burning hay along the shore to lure ships onto the deadly rocks. The people would salvage whatever cargo the doomed ship was carrying and then would kill the survivors. Any treasure found from a wrecking event is usually cursed and it has been said that at times the victims of the wrecking would come ashore and drag the wreckers into the ocean. During colonial times these shallows were known as a graveyard for ships.

Tucker Island used to be on top of the Atlantic Ocean just off the Jersey shore at the southernmost point of Long Beach Island. It is now under the sea. It was a barrier island in the 1800s and was also known as Sea Haven, Short Beach and Tucker's Beach. In the late 1800s, there were numerous pirate treasures said to be buried here. Spanish gold coins had been found, but no treasure trove.

Severe ocean storms, known as northeasters or improperly called nor'easters, gradually created Beach Haven's Inlet and the once connected land became an island. The island was quickly eaten away by erosion. By the turn of the twentieth century, inhabitants had to leave. In 1955, the whole island disappeared, leaving only a shoal. The buildings remained on the island, but are now underwater. Today, this underwater region is called the Jersey's shore Atlantis.

In the 1500s, the Lenape tribe called Brigantine Beach "watamoonica," meaning "summer playground." The name Brigantine comes from the type of ship, perhaps one of the first of the over three hundred vessels wrecked on the offshore shoals during a two-hundred-year period.

Little and Big Egg Harbor, Brigantine Beach, and Ship Bottom on Long Beach Island are all located north of Atlantic City. Large numbers of gold and silver coins have been found along the beaches over the years. Many wrecks occurred which is why the lighthouses were built. Some of these wrecks can still be seen under the sand or just offshore after a large storm. The seeker can see timbers from off shore from shipwrecks here. That is the best time to search for treasure that may be washed on the beach.

In Ocean Grove, south of Asbury Park, on Route 66 in Monmouth County, a large amount of twentieth century silver coins were found on the beach. It is thought that it probably came from an off-site shipwreck. Also, eighteenth century silver coins have been found on Squam Beach, north of Ship Bottom, on Long Beach Island.

Today, if you are standing at Sandy Hook at the tip and looking east, you would see the open Atlantic Ocean, but millions of years ago, you would have seen Africa from this spot.

Over 4,000 ships have wrecked here since the eighteenth century. In the late 1940s, twenty gold coins were found on the beach, which may have come from a British ship that sank here in the 1740s. Sometimes Sandy Hook is an island and sometimes the ocean throws enough sand at the base, so it becomes once again attached to the mainland.

The pirate Captain Kidd is said to have buried a treasure here on the bay side of Sandy Hook. Think this may be just another pirate treasure story? In 1948, a fisherman found gold coins in the sand off Cedar Street. Could it be part of Kidd's treasure or perhaps it's lost loot from a sunken vessel? No one is really sure.

Sandy Hook Lighthouse is the oldest lighthouse in the United States. This first lighthouse was built for safe entry into New York harbor in 1764. At that time, it was five hundred feet from the northern extremity of the Hook. Now, the tides have piled sand around it, so that it is a quarter-mile from the ocean. In 1776, it was dismantled by the Americans, basically to confuse the British. When the United States Lighthouse Service was established in 1789, there were only twelve lighthouses in operation: Sandy Hook, nine in New England, one at Cape Henlopen, Delaware, and one in Charleston, South Carolina. The most powerful lighthouse in the country is found at Navesink Lighthouse on Beacon Hill Highlands in New Jersey, built in 1862. Its light can be seen twenty-two miles out into the ocean!

Absecon Lighthouse
relocated to Atlantic City.

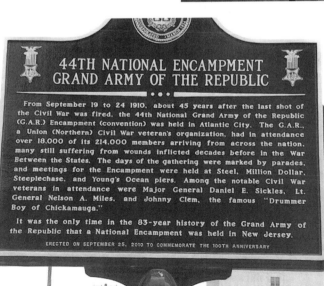

44TH NATIONAL ENCAMPMENT
GRAND ARMY OF THE REPUBLIC

From September 19 to 24 1910, about 45 years after the last shot of the Civil War was fired, the 44th National Grand Army of the Republic (G.A.R.) Encampment (convention) was held in Atlantic City. The G.A.R., a Union (Northern) Civil War veteran's organization, had in attendance over 18,000 of its 214,000 members arriving from across the nation, many still suffering from wounds inflicted decades before in the War Between the States. The days of the gathering were marked by parades, and meetings for the Encampment were held at Steel, Million Dollar, Steeplechase, and Young's Ocean piers. Among the notable Civil War veterans in attendance were Major General Daniel E. Sickles, Lt. General Nelson A. Miles, and Johnny Clem, the famous "Drummer Boy of Chickamauga."

It was the only time in the 83-year history of the Grand Army of the Republic that a National Encampment was held in New Jersey.

ERECTED ON SEPTEMBER 25, 2010 TO COMMEMORATE THE 100TH ANNIVERSARY

Encampment site.

Absecon Light is located in Atlantic City, but was on Absecon Island when it was abandoned in 1933. The lighthouse was built in 1854 at what was thought to be a safe distance from shore, about 1,300 feet away, but the sea kept coming and in 1876 only seventy-five feet remained between the tower and the ocean. It is the third tallest in the United States. There were hundreds of deaths that occurred near the lighthouse, mainly in shipwrecks. It is also known as Graveyard Inlet. There are seven known deaths on the actual property in Atlantic City. This is considered a very haunted lighthouse.

On Absecon Island, there is a stash of pirate loot still to be found and wreckers also enjoyed the shipwrecks that occurred in the region. It is said that the pirates buried their treasure on the northern side of Absecon Island facing Reeds Bay on Route 157, in Atlantic County. Interestingly enough, some treasure was discovered here in the 1930s. The Brigantine shoals are located off the island and old coins are often found in the sand on the beaches. During the 1700s, over 150 known pirates were operating along the Atlantic Coast. It is thought that several may have buried some loot on the island.

The Brandywine Shoal Lighthouse, erected in 1914, is on a shoal that destroyed two previous lighthouses by the waves and grinding ice. The abandoned lighthouse still stands near the new one. Fourteen Foot Bank Lighthouse located in the middle of Delaware Bay. It is considered one of the greatest achievements of lighthouse construction. It stands in fourteen feet of water. In 1887, it was the first lighthouse built on a submarine foundation. Ship John Lighthouse, one of oldest lighthouses on the Delaware River was built in 1877. The lighthouse is named for the ship, John, which grounded here in 1797. The sunken hull increased the area of the shoal. The tower has the wooden figurehead of the John, from the cargo that was salvaged.

The Barnegat Lighthouse, located on the southern tip of Long Beach Island going into Barnegat Bay, is now abandoned, but was one of the most famous beacons along the Atlantic Coast. Built in 1834, the first lighthouse was destroyed by the sea. In 1857 or 1858, the reports differ, another was built by author F. Hopkinson Smith's father. The author worked on this lighthouse while writing his book, *The Tides of Barnegat*. When first built, it was about one mile from shore; today, it is only a few feet from the ocean. The foundation has been weakened by the sea and, in 1930, it was abandoned. Lots of wrecking occurred here too. These particular wreckers were called the Barnegat Pirates. Island Beach State Park, in the Seaside Park area, became an island in 1750, when a storm broke through the sandbar at Seaside Heights. An inlet was opened and lasted until 1812, when another storm closed it. Barnegat Lighthouse is found at the end of the island. It can be seen, but not reached, by the road. A United States cargo ship was attacked by a submerged German submarine in World War I offshore. Barnegat comes from the Dutch word "Barendegat," meaning "inlet of the breakers," for the turbulent water channel that exists.

Ship anchor

At Long Beach, more than 125 ships were wrecked before 1878. It is part of the stretch of coastline named Graveyard of the Atlantic. Here are some of the more famous wrecks of the region:

⚓ *City of Athens* wrecked with $300,000 off Cape May.
⚓ *Live Oak* wrecked in 1769 off Squaw Beach, carrying $20,000 in supplies for the British troops fighting in the Revolutionary War; this beach name no longer exists, so the exact location is unknown.
⚓ A British ship was grounded off the southern end of the Brigantine Shoals with a cargo of tea and silver plate.

⚓ *Cassandra*, a wooden steamer, wrecked in 1867 off Cape May. In 1968, coins were found under her hull that dated from 1804-1850. The coins were coated with tar, as the practice of placing coins in tar barrels for concealment was popular during that era.

⚓ The *Delaware* sank in 1898, just three miles off Point Pleasant; the cargo lost was $250,000 in gold bullion.

⚓ An unnamed Spanish galleon is said to have sank off Fort Mercer.

⚓ *Betsy*, a British ship, wrecked during a storm in 1778 off Cape May; the cargo was $1.5 million in silver coins.

⚓ The Spanish treasure ship *Juno* sank with $3 million still aboard in 180 feet of water near Cape May.

Captain Kidd and Other Pirates

Anywhere along the New Jersey coast or Long Island, New York, many residents tell the story of a pirate ship that was Captain Kidd's and the treasure spot where he buried his treasure and murdered a member of his crew to watch over the loot forever. The treasure seeker must always take the Captain Kidd buried treasure legends with a grain of salt. Kidd was a pirate, did kill a member of his crew, and did bury treasure in New York. Those are the known true facts. He just was not a pirate long enough to have buried all the treasure that are attributed to his name. The entire Captain Kidd story is very sad. He was not a real pirate, but a privateer; his letter of marque has been found.

Below are some of the lore of Kidd pirate treasure. Though Kidd may not have buried the treasure, it should be noted that perhaps some pirate did bury treasure on this spot. It just may not have been Kidd. These stories have preserved over time, so perhaps there is more to the story than meets the eye.

⚓ There is said to be Kidd's treasure buried on Cape May in Del Haven under the present-day offices on Cape May Point. It should be noted that it is a fact that pirates would stop here for fresh water. More on this treasure can be found in the Cape May section of this book.

⚓ Kidd buried treasure in Ocean City and the Highlands. In 1948, a lobsterman found gold coins on the beach of the Highlands — actually a lot of gold coins were found that year. The coins were thought to be part of Kidd's treasure, but they were dated 1730, years after Kidd's hanging in London. They are most likely from a wreck somewhere off shore in the ocean.

⚓ Kidd buried treasure on Sandy Hook. This loot is buried in a grove of pine trees near Raritan Bay, but the trees were destroyed long ago. Or perhaps it may be found north of Sandy Hook, near Whales, or Wales, Creek on Cliffwood Beach, on the border of Monmouth and Middlesex counties near Aberdeen. During Kidd's era, there was an island called Money Island. Earlier, Spanish gold coins were found there, hence the name. The island has eroded into the Raritan Bay. Nearby, there is a Treasure Lake, where more gold coins were found, which is why the name was changed from Duck Lake to Treasure Lake. Two Elm trees are called Kidd's Rangers. One was near the mouth of the Matawan Creek in Keyport. The other was located in Rose Hill, which is a cemetery today. Is it any wonder that it is considered one of the state's most haunted cemeteries? Legend says that these trees were used to guide Kidd to his treasure. The treasure is said to be in the middle of these trees, which ironically is exactly where Cliffwood Beach is located.

⚓ Another Kidd treasure is to be discovered on an island at the mouth of Tom's River or in a cave in a notch in an iron pot on the Passaic River

⚓ Close to Atlantic City on Brigantine Beach, there is a Kidd treasure still to be found. It is also said that a fisherman once found $100,000 on this beach. The story is that in 1698, a young man named Abner, who was walking the beach with his wife Mary, saw the Kidd pirate ship. What is in question is how did he know it was Kidd's ship? The truth was that perhaps a pirate ship was roaming this region, but it was always said to have been Kidd's ship. So, Abner and Mary witnessed Kidd and his crew burying a large treasure in a large sand dune and then the Captain killed the pirate crew member to guard the loot. The reported that they could never retrieve this prize though, because the pirate ghost would always scare them away. The name Brigantine was named for a brig that was wrecked here in the eighteenth century.

⚓ There is a story that Kidd became romantically interested in an Ocean County resident named Amanda. Because of this romantic interest, he anchored his ship in the mouth of the Mullica River or in the vicinity of Oyster Creek, just south of Long Beach — the stories about where differ — and decided to bury his treasure on Brigantine Beach. However, he was betrayed by a crew member and had to leave the area before being caught.

Other Pirate Tales

The pirate JOHN BACON had a base of operations during the Revolutionary War era on the northern end of Island Beach, about ten miles north of Ship Bottom in Ocean County. He is said to have buried several caches in the area. One that is on Long Beach was buried during the early 1780s. He was considered the scourge of the Jersey Coast, and was shot by a band of patriots in 1783, ending his pirate life.

Another pirate, JOE BRADISH, used Turtle Gut Inlet near Wildwood as a base and buried treasure here. Pirate treasure is also buried on the Cedar River about one mile southwest of Cedarville, on County 553 in Cumberland County.

The famous pirate BLACKBEARD also visited the New Jersey coast. It is said that he sailed into Little Egg Harbor, making one of the small islands to the back of Brigantine Beach his headquarters. Eventually, the British did come to the unnamed island looking for him, but he had already buried his treasure and was underwater, breathing through a reed, while they searched the small island for him; however, he successfully hid until the British left. Blackbeard is also said to have been seen near and around Philadelphia. Another place that he left buried loot is thought to be on Long Beach.

A pirate named BLUEBEARD is said to have buried his treasure in Salem County in a field, close to a cave where he lived. Perth Amboy is another town that claims a pirate treasure, but the details are vague.

Seven Mile Beach or Five Mile Beach — the story differs — tells of pirate loot buried in 1710. That year, on the Stone Harbor sandy barrier island, the only person on island was the life-saving station person. There were no other buildings on the island then, and the station was on the south end. He reported that he saw a ship and crew come ashore, and bury something. He tried to find the treasure, but never did find anything. In 1944, visitors were having a picnic with children. The children were digging and playing in the sand dunes. The next day, the mother found five strange coins in her child's pockets. The child said he found them in a box buried in the sand. The coins were Spanish in origin and pure gold minted in 1706. This discovery started a mini treasure hunt and though the box was never found, over two dozen coins were found. That is all that has been found since. Is there still more?

Pine Barrens

Pirates or privateers would move their stolen goods across the Pine Barrens. It is isolated and difficult to get through. It is thought that during the Revolutionary War American privateers captured more than 1,000 British ships and moved $20 million through the Pinelands. The New Jersey pirates are said to have moved so many ships into the Barrens' rivers that hulls and timbers are still to be found in the riverbeds.

This place was a smugglers great hiding place. This was the region where Pine Barren robber and Tory, Joe Mulliner and his one hundred-member gang called the Refugee gang, lived during the Revolutionary War era. Their hideout was an island in the middle of the Mullica River just south of Pleasant Mills and only half-a-mile from his wife and home, called "the forks." This gang held-up stages and burned and pillaged farms. He also held-up wagon trains carrying supplies to the Basto Furnace.

His justification for this type of behavior was because he was loyal to the British Crown during the Revolutionary War. It is said that he accumulated a lot of gold and he is thought to have buried some here. He was called the Robin Hood of the Barrens, though he really did not give to the poor, he was well-liked by the people living here. He was caught and hanged at a nearby birch tree near the Read Manor House. He was buried near the road and monument does mark the spot. The question remains: did he spend all his stolen loot or is it still hidden somewhere in the area?

There was said to be over twenty-five gangs that once used the Pine Barrens as they base of operations at one time. There could be stolen loot from criminals in Monmouth County still hidden at Colt's Neck.

Pine Barrens

Farmingdale was the haven for the criminals Jacob Fagan and Lewis Fenton in the late 1700s. They were called the monsters of wickedness. The numerous caves found here were used as hideouts. The caves were man-made, braced with timber. There was a small trap door for access.

Military Plunder

Throughout various wars, the military marched through the state. Anytime there is a battlefield or fort, there may also be major pain and sacrifice there, and looking for artifacts from these places often leads to seeing the battle still raging. Such places include:

⚓ Moody Rock is a place where Tory's once hid plunder obtained during the Revolutionary War.

⚓ Great Egg Harbor is a massacre site. In 1778, the British killed the Patriot troops in a field located three miles from Tuckerton, Ocean County.

⚓ Bound Brook, Somerset County, just off the Raritan River, is the site of a fight between the Patriots and British in 1777. Many military supplies were reported abandoned.

The Native American tribe who lived on the Raritan River was called the Naraticong. This river's name means "river beyond the island," which is speaking of Staten Island. Some believe the name comes from Roaton or Raritanghe, a tribe that had come from across the Hudson River and displaced the existing tribe, or perhaps Raritan is the Dutch word wawitan or rarachons, meaning "forked river or stream overflows."

The Raritan River, with both north and south branches included, is the largest river in New Jersey. It is one hundred miles from its headwaters to Raritan Bay at Perth Amboy. It is also said that it is a Native American word, meaning "forked river" or "smooth running" or "gentle." The Native American villages of the Naraticong tribe were located all along here, the River was their highway. There are lots of deposits of iron found in the mountain area along the river. Two mills were found at Clinton, both over two hundred years old, in 1942.

High Bridge was once the site of a large waterfall; today it is a seventy-five-foot dam. The South branch of the Raritan once hosted a covered bridge. The South and North branch join at a place, named by the tribes in the region, called TuccaRamma-Hacking, meaning "the meeting place of the waters." Below the TuccaRamma-Hacking was one of the earliest-known Native American villages found in New Jersey. Many artifacts have been discovered here.

Raritan River

New Brunswick, along the river, was settled in 1681. It was called Inian's Ferry, for the obvious reason that it was here that the ferry crossed the river. The oldest road in New Jersey crosses the river at Albany Bridge and is the route General Washington passed on the way to his inauguration as the first President of the United States.

During the Revolutionary War era, Haddonfield was the camp for the British. This site is located ten miles east of Camden on State 70. In 1778, the British killed a large number of American dragoons at the Baylor Massacre Site located in Bergen County on Highway 53 between Routes 116 and 90. A mass grave was found in the area. Also, many farms were destroyed by the British in the region. When armies march through territory, the settlers flee and usually leave quickly without their belongings. What is not taken by the invading army may be left for the future to find. Sometimes the settlers returned, but sometimes they decided to find a safer place to live.

British troops buried two chests of gold coins during the Revolutionary War on Apple Pie Hill, three miles southwest of Chadsworth, County 563 in Burlington County.

Princeton was settled in 1682, and is the oldest settlement in the state. It is located at the head of the Raritan and Delaware Rivers. Both Washington and his army and the British army stayed here during the Revolutionary War. Major battles were fought in the region and the town was held by both the British and Americans during the war.

General Clinton camped for weeks in 1778 in Monmouth before going to the Monmouth Battlefield. Ruins of colonial times have been discovered. The Monmouth Battlefield is located west of Freehold in Monmouth County. After the British sacked Philadelphia and were bringing 1,500 wagons of supplies and plunder to New York City, they were attacked here by the Patriots. It is said that the British buried much of the plunder, and though some was found by the Patriots, it is said that a lot is still missing, just waiting to be found.

Tories raided some Philadelphia Whigs or they robbed the treasury of the United States of American during the Revolutionary War, the stories differ about what was robbed. Anyway, they retreated into the Delaware Valley and got to the town of Vernon in Sussex County and buried the $120,000 on a knoll somewhere in the Great Swamp.

Shabbakonk Creek was the site of battle during the Revolutionary War in 1777. The battlefield is found south of Lawrenceville on US 206. Often, military gear can be found at these sites.

Trenton, the headwaters of the Delaware River, was settled in 1680. Originally, it was called the Falls. A number of battles from Revolutionary War took place here. On December 26, 1776, the Continental Army won the first major victory against the British forces during the Revolutionary War.

The *Hussar*, a British Frigate, sank near here on November 25, 1780; $580,000 in treasure was lost. The ship struck Port Rock, nearly opposite upper Randalls Island, and sank, with everyone on-board, including American prisoners. About 150 people died in this wreck.

In 1903, the barge *Harold* sank close to the shore off Sewaren in the Delaware River, west of Bridgetown on County 49 in Cumberland County. A diver found some of the treasure off Sewaren from this wreck. Exactly 7,678 silver ingots, each weighing about one hundred pounds, were recovered, but the cargo shifted and 1,800 silver bars still remain in Storys Flat on the muddy bottom of Staten Sound. In 1950, silver bars were also found on the beach at Ben Davis Point.

Springfield is the site of a Revolutionary War battle fought along Vauxhall and Galloping Hill roads. This was a very bloody battle and basically destroyed much of the town. It was also one of the last major battles in the north. The British moved further south to fight at this time. It has become known as the Forgotten Victory. Perhaps there are also forgotten artifacts lying beneath the bloodstained ground too.

Delaware River

Hopewell is located on County Road 518 in Mercer County and may be the site of 100,000 pounds of lost gold and silver coins. A British pay wagon was attacked here in 1778, and it is said that the Patriots buried the treasure around the area, but were killed by the British reinforcements.

Unionville is another town where many Revolutionary War artifacts have been found. Many are plowed up by farmers, but one farmer found an earthen jar containing $1,000 in gold and silver coins here.

The Wildwood region is where Turtle Gut can be found. It was also the site of a major water battle on June 29, 1776 between the ship called *Nancy* and a British warship. The *Nancy* ran herself aground, unloaded her cargo, and set the ship up as a booby trap to explode when the British boarded.

There was a trolley that once traveled from Wildwood to Poverty Beach. Those trolley tracks are now underwater. Why are the trolley tracks under water? Not really sure, either erosion or the ocean has risen.

Forts

The fort built at Sandy Hook was called FORT HANCOCK. The Americans and British fought over one hundred skirmishes in New Jersey alone during the Revolutionary War. Artifacts from this era can be found in the battlefields of Trenton, Princeton, and Paulus Hook.

FORT NONSENSE was built in Morristown by Washington in 1777. It was probably used as a beacon site, not actually a military fort. The soldiers who built the fort thought that it was unnecessary and was designed to keep them busy, hence the name. This fort was an earthen fort; the natural hill was cut into terraces. It was rebuilt after it gradually crumbled. However, nothing remains of the site today.

JOCKEY HOLLOW, located about three miles from town, was another place where the fledging United States army suffered horribly during the harsh winter of 1779-80. Proper huts were not built before winter, and the smallpox epidemic killed many of the men. Portions of the actual barracks remained until the 1930s. The story is that in January 1781 troops of the Pennsylvania Line mutinied against the authority of the Continental Army. Being poorly fed and unpaid for twelve months finally convinced the men that their officers had deceived them. They snapped and killed Captain Adam Bettin, who attempted to restrain them. Meanwhile, the British offered them a considerable sum to fight for Britain. The soldiers became furious at that request and turned over these spies to Army officers who executed them on the spot. The mutiny was subdued with many of the men being discharged from service. Another story of this area is that when two mutinous soldiers attempted to commandeer Temperance's, the daughter of one of the officers, horse, she pretended to submit and then whipped the soldiers to let her horse loose. She led the horse into the farmhouse and closed the windows and doors. The soldiers searched the woods and barn, but never thought to search the house for the girl and horse.

FORT TINICUM was in Chester. Tenaconq was the Native American name for the fort, and it is found at the mouth of Salem Creek on the shore of New Jersey.

FORT MERCER is in the Red Bank Battlefield Park on the Delaware River. It was an earthen fort during the Revolution. Many British soldiers were killed here in 1777.

FORT NASSAU is also on the Delaware River. It was the first Dutch fort built in Gloucester County in 1623. In November 1777, the British landed. Their ships, the HMS *Augusta* and HMS *Merlin*, were run aground on Gloucester Beach and blown up. Fragments could still be seen at low tide during the 1990s.

FORT MOTT was erected in Pennsville on the Delaware River in 1838 on Finns Point. This fort never saw action, though men were stationed here. It became a state park in 1951, so the area was left abandoned for many years. From this location, one can view Pea Patch Island in the middle of the Delaware River, where FORT DELAWARE is located. This is a haunted fort where prisoners from the Civil War are said to still roam. This fort will be discussed in the Pennsylvania part of this book.

Treasure to be Discovered

During the 1930s, a farmer named Arthur Barry is said to have buried $100,000 in gold coins somewhere on his farm near Andover, County 517, Sussex County. On another farm near Hanover Neck, about six miles east of Morristown, on County 10, Sussex County, the owner in the 1800s hid $50,000 in gold coins under a large tree. Somewhere near Caldwell on County 506, in Sussex County, a cache of $12,000 in gold coins lie buried on the estate of William Besthorn. The farmer Hendrick Dempster buried $50,000 in gold coins on his farm near North Bergen, US 95 in Hudson County.

A farmer named James Gilam hid a large treasure on his property at Finns Point on the Alloway River, near Quinton, County 581, in Salem County. In 1921, a farmer named Vincent Conklin buried a large treasure near his barn about one mile east of Tabernacle, on County 532 in Burlington County.

Bootleggers buried one and a half million dollars near Lake Manetta, south of Lakewood, State 9, Ocean County. The bandit Bunker Kid is said to have buried his plunder near Newton, on State 206, in Sussex County.

Several gold coins were buried in the late eighteenth century near the Seven Star Tavern on the north banks of the Salem River near Sharptown. The White Horse Tavern located in Bordentown, is said to have been the place where Joseph Bonaparte buried most of his treasure. In Salem County, Peter Louderback, the owner of the Seven Star Tavern, found between Sharptown and Swedesboro, is thought to have buried his treasure close to the tavern in 1780.

Ghost towns in New Jersey include Ongs Hat, which has a tavern ruin, and Old Half Way, located in Burlington County. The abandoned town of Topanemus was in Monmouth County and the town Quaker Bridge also has tavern ruins. However, nothing of either of the above towns exists today.

A strange find in Unionville, Sussex County, was excavated by workmen. They were digging and found a flat stone, one feet wide and two feet long, in a four-foot deep hole. On the bottom, Spanish dollars laid, with the date 1781. What the story is and why they were there remains a mystery.

Mountains are dangerous places. There are parts of the Kittantinny Mountain Range that are airplane crash sites:

- In 1932, a Millbrook Monoplane crashed here. Both passengers died.
- In 1942, a C-47 Transport crashed around Walnut Valley.
- In 1944, a B-17F crashed at Millbrook.
- In 1948, a Swartswood Army C-47 crashed on the mountain.

On Hackettstown Mountain, or Schooleys Mountain, the story is that a fortune was buried by a guest at the health resort. It was buried along the grade up the slope near the old stone huts of German settlers. Schooleys Mountains Springs was known to the Native Americans as a remedy for rheumatism and skin problems and has been used as a spa place by the settlers since 1770.

Towns Where Treasure May Exist

• CORNWALL: It is said that a sealed jar found in 1871 was filled with ancient coins, about $1,500 worth.

• ASHBURY PARK and STONE HARBOR: Numerous British and Spanish coins have been found along the coast.

• FOLSOM: A farmer is said to have buried his fortune on his farm in 1915.

• BURLINGTON: Legend has it that over $200,000 is buried in town.

• MORRISTOWN, NEAR HANOVER NECK: $50,000 was buried under a big tree in early 1800s.

• VERNON: Robbers buried large amounts of gold and silver coins taken from settlers in caverns and caves around the region.

• BELVEDERE: Home to a hermit who is said to have distrusted banks. Apparently it is thought that he buried his life-savings, said to be silver and gold coins, somewhere near Harkers Hollow. In the same town, a cache of ill-gotten gains was buried by a man named Parson Hardin, thought to be a member of the Pine Robbers gang in the late 1700s who escaped justice. It is also said that his ghost haunts the location where the money is located.

• HOMESTEAD: Another hermit resided here, but it is also reported that he owned a farm. What is consistent is that he also distrusted banks. He buried $35,000 in gold coins in town, and it was never recovered.

Cape May Park

Cape May Lighthouse

2.
Cape May

Being on the ocean, it is no surprise that Cape May has numerous stories about pirate and military treasure. In 1698, a French pirate only known as Canoot captured ships below Cape May and came ashore to bury treasure somewhere on the beach.

The Cape May Lighthouse was built in 1823 to guard the Delaware Bay, and was the second lighthouse in New Jersey, though that actual first site was taken by the sea. The second tower, built in 1847, was also taken by the sea. The present site, built in 1859, is 1,000 feet inland.

The Lenni-Lenape tribe are said to have had a village; whether it was permanent or temporary is still being debated in this region. In the seventeenth century, a subdivision of the Lenni-Lenape tribe, called the Tuckahoes, lived near the Tuckahoe River, and the Kechemeches lived between Cape May Courthouse and Cape May Point. Dutch whalers settled here in the 1600s.

In 1685, the first permanent village was established by *Mayflower*

World War II bunker

descendants. The village was on the banks of the Delaware River in Portsmouth, called New England Village, or what is today called Townbank. Nothing remains of this site today because the land has eroded into the ocean. During World War II, the bunker seen on the beach was part of the Harbor Defense Project and served as a military base. During the Korean War, the bunker was used as a radio transmitter station for the Navy's Atlantic Fleet. World War II bunker still exists on beach on Cape May. Visitors could once visit this place, but it is no longer permitted.

The pirates of the era, including Kidd and Blackbeard, stopped here to fill water casks from Lilly Pond or Lilly Lake, sometimes spelled Lily Lake or Pond, because spelling was not very important and not every person who recorded information could spell well. The pirates were never bothered by residents when they visited. In some respects, they were welcomed. Kidd's captors claimed that he received help from the people of Cape May because the Quakers there disliked gaols or jails, and refused to help send anyone to jail. Many of the residents suffered imprisonments in England due to this belief. There was a lot of contention between the British and residents for many years. For example, during the Revolution, British war ships would land here and raid Cape May often. The residents became so angry that they dug a ditch around Lilly Pond and let the ocean in to make their own drinking water brackish. It also made it undrinkable to the British. It did discourage them from coming.

A report by Colonel Quary to the British Lords of Trade in 1699 actually mentions that Kidd used Cape May as a hideout. The report states: "I have, by the assistance of Col. Basse, apprehended four more the pyrates (sic) at Cape May. Hee (sic, Kidd) hath been here (Cape May) about ten days and the people frequently goes on board with him. Hee (sic) is in a sloop with about fourty (sic) men and a vast treasure." So, based on this report, it was believed that Kidd must have left a treasure here, but though thousands have dug up the sand, only Cape May "diamonds" have been found.

Cape May "diamonds" are colorless quartz crystals. The Native Americans of the region thought that these crystals had mystical powers. The largest crystal ever found was the size of a hen egg and weighed eight ounces. When I visited this area, in direct sunlight the white sand does sparkle with little lights all though it. Though I did not find a crystal large enough to photograph during my visit, I can see why the settlers thought and hoped that there were diamonds to be found here.

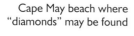

Cape May beach where "diamonds" may be found

Higbee Beach, also known as Diamond Beach, is where the treasure seeker can find arrowheads and fossils, as well as those diamond-like quartz stones. The ghosts of Thomas Digby and his dog are said to roam this beach. Digby has been dead for well over one hundred years.

The *S.S. Atlantus* was one of the twelve experimental concrete ships built during World War 1. The weight caused it to be deemed impractical. In 1926, it was used as a ferry dock, but a major storm hit and the ship broke loose, grounding on Sunset Beach. Though many tried to free the ship, it just would not budge and so it remains where it landed today. When I visited the region, it was really an amazing sight to see the ship just rotting in the ocean. *An interesting side note: Cape May diamonds are found especially just south of the sunken concrete ship, in the water at the waterline.*

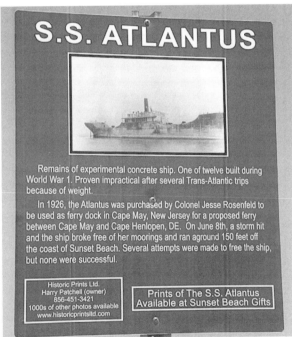

SS *Atlantus* wreck site

Remains of experimental concrete ship. One of twelve built during World War 1. Proven impractical after several Trans-Atlantic trips because of weight.

In 1926, the Atlantus was purchased by Colonel Jesse Rosenfeld to be used as ferry dock in Cape May, New Jersey for a proposed ferry between Cape May and Cape Henlopen, DE. On June 8th, a storm hit and the ship broke free of her moorings and ran aground 150 feet off the coast of Sunset Beach. Several attempts were made to free the ship, but none were successful.

Historic Prints Ltd.
Harry Patchell (owner)
856-451-3421
1000s of other photos available
www.historicprintsltd.com

Prints of The S.S. Atlantus
Available at Sunset Beach Gifts

SS *Atlantus* wreck

Wildwoods
beach sign

Wildwoods Beach

Wildwoods
beach sign
backward

3

Precious Gems, Mines, and Ghost Towns!

New Jersey is known as one of the world's richest sources of minerals and fossils. In Notch Brook, near Paterson, the first pearls were found in the United States in 1857. It was a 93-grain pink pearl and sold to Tiffany & Company. They called it the Tiffany Queen and resold it to Empress Eugenie of France.

Iron Ore Towns

Iron is found in the bogs, Pompton Mountains, and the Ringwood River, which is a branch of the Pequannock River. Iron is rarely found in the earth in a pure state. It is usually found in veins and fragments throughout rocks. The iron in the rock must be smelted, or melted, out. The iron is heavier and will sink to the bottom of the liquid, which is why the furnace iron ghost towns were created.

The roads through the Pine Barrens are old colonial stagecoach routes and trails leading to charcoal pits or are lumber roads and connecting roads between bog iron ore communities that may no longer exist. For example, five of these roads end in a place called Washington, but nothing is there now except stone foundations. Some vanished towns include: Hanover Furnace, Speedwell, Martha, Calico, and Munion Field. The people who settled in the last town were actually Tories, or those loyal to the British Crown during the American Revolution, and Quakers who could not live up to the Quaker code in the eighteenth century. Another group who came to the Pinelands was Hessian soldiers who deserted the British Army. They settled on or near Mount Misery. The German name for the mountain was Misericorde, where the name misery comes from. They lived in the northern part of area.

Iron was also found in the bogs. Most of the vanished towns were iron towns or bog iron towns. Graves in the Barren are sometimes adorned with iron tombstones. The iron industry lasted about a century after the American Revolution and reached its highest development right before it vanished in the 1830s. Why did they vanish? Because iron ore was found in western Pennsylvania and was superior to the bog ore.

Indian Spring flows into Great Egg River and an old iron forge and dam are found near Weymouth. Penny Pot was settled in 1686 by the English and the name comes from that time when the area reminded them of their home in England. The Teakwood Dam here was created by salvaged teak timber found from old warships and battleships. It is a rare dam building material, actually the only one known in United States built with teak wood. The dam is said to have $75,000-worth of teak wood in it. There are also iron forge remains from the eighteenth century forge here. Some of the first cannon balls for the Continental Army were cast in this forge. *An interesting side note: Indian Springs has flowed continuously through wet and dry seasons for centuries. The reason is not known.*

Atison is another iron town, and iron walkways and windowsills are still found here. The town was said to be the site of Atsayunk, a Native American village. However, remember that the Native Americans did not live in the Barrens. They camped and traveled through the area on the way to the ocean. For this reason, it's possible to find Native American artifacts throughout the region. Charles Read, owner of the Read Manor, where the Robin Hood of the Revolutionary War was hanged, was considered the greatest iron master of the Province in 1750. The Colonial Manor house found in town is haunted. Under the highway bridge, the ruins of early forges can be found. There was an old mill across the river that was used in Colonial times.

The ghost town, called Quaker Bridge, was named for the bridge there spanning the Basto River. To reach Quaker Bridge, one must follow a single track sand road through Pine Barrens. It was an important stage route in the eighteenth century. It is located four miles from Atison Furnace on Old Tuckerton Road. It was a village from 1809 to 1849, but no sign of this village exists today. Mulliner was said to visit all these ghost towns in his day, but he was killed in 1781 before Quaker Bridge existed. Beware of myths and lore about people — he was a real person, but, like Kidd, his legacy far outweighs what he may have actually done.

Basto Iron Works is found here too. Iron forges here supplied Washington's army with iron during the Revolutionary War. In October 1778, the British attacked Chestnut Neck, destroying the storehouse and the entire town. The Chestnut Neck site is covered today by a boat yard, but it was the American privateer base during the Revolution. The British marched toward Basto Furnace, which was creating munitions for Washington's Army. They pitched a camp a few miles from the furnace in the woods, but messengers sent word to the furnace and the men ambushed the British. The British retreated and Basto was saved. Basto is a ghost town today. Landing Creek, across from Lower Banks State Park, is the site of Gloucester Furnace, which is also a ghost town today.

Ringwood Manor and Iron Works is located on Country Road 17, close to the New York border, in Passaic County. Iron was discovered here in 1740, and Ringwood was an important furnace during the Revolutionary War.

In Oxford, a cannon ball from the French & Indian War, fought 1754-1763, was found in the furnace cinders. This area is haunted by Jerry Mack, an employee who was found dead at the furnace in the late 1800s. The workers who saw his ghost never would tell what happened or return to the furnace again.

Minerals and Gems

There are many minerals and gems to be found in New Jersey, including copper, granophyres, fowlerite, willemite, prehnite, smoky quartz, agate, zinc, titanium, gold, silver, and pearl.

New Jersey amber is one of the richest deposits of amber ever found on the coastline, with fossils of one hundred unknown species of insects and plant trapped in the resin. For example, a flower that was embedded in an oak tree was ninety million years old. The oldest moth, oldest feather of terrestrial bird in North America, oldest black fly, oldest mushroom, and oldest mosquito were all discovered in this amber find. The fly and mosquito were from the Cretaceous period and may have fed on dinosaurs.

Some places to find amber are: in Sewell, Gloucester County, on a tributary of the Mantua Creek; in Neptune City, Monmouth County, along the Shark River; and in Trenton, Mercer County, in Lignite at Crosswicks Creek. Also in Trenton, zircon and Black Jasper have been found in the Delaware River at Washington Crossing State Park.

On the upper continental slope off the coast, the grey color mineral Reidite was discovered. It is only found in one other place in the world: Barbados. It is created by high-impact, shock-metamorphosed zircons. Remember that New Jersey is the site of an asteroid impact.

Places Where Gems & Precious Metals May Exist

The question arises as to why so many precious minerals are here? It's due to the geology of the area, but perhaps it's also the reason for the strange creature that is said to roam here. Sussex County is known as the New Jersey Bigfoot region. There have been numerous reported sightings of Bigfoot here, as well as in Lake Owassa, Newton, Wantage, and the regions of Somerset County, near the Great Swamp area and Hillside. The following is a listing of possible locations for gems and precious metals.

- STERLING MINE, OGDENSBURG, SUSSEX COUNTY: 345 minerals have been mined here, including: green Willemite; red Calcite; black Franklinite, a rare Earth mineral; Tephroite; marble; zincite; large crystal spinel; andradite; chodrodite; titanite; silver zinc deposits; heminorphite; and uvite tourmaline. Why are there so many minerals here? The answer is because of the zinc, manganese, and iron-rich sediments found in the pre-Cambrian seafloor. All this material was swept up in the event that created the Appalachian Mountains. This event occurred over one billion years ago, and Franklinite, willemite, zincite, and hemimorphite are some of the minerals here that are not found in other places. Zincite is one of first new minerals found in North America. One unique aspect of the minerals found here is fluorescence — they light up under fluorescent light. The entire region is surrounded by marble. Today, the mine is filled with water and covered over. The minerals found are over a tenth of the world's known varieties, thirty-five of which have never been found anywhere else.
- FRANKLIN FURNACE, FRANKLIN, SUSSEX COUNTY: 345 types of minerals are found here, including green Willemite; red Calcite; black Franklinite, which is a rare Earth mineral; Tephroite; Rhodonite in marble; Chondroite; Nickeline; zincite; allanite; ferroaxinite; Johannsenite; Fowlerite; and Vesuvianite or Cyprine. These were found in the dumps of the New Jersey Zinc Company mines, in the Blue Apatite (Atlas Quarry) and Palmer Zinc mines. It is said that all the minerals were gone by 1954. The entrances have been capped with cement.
- WALPACK COPPER MINE, near BUTTERMILK FALLS, SUSSEX COUNTY: This mine opened in 1980. However, there is a deed from 1755, which states that there was a copper mine located here. There is also said to be a gold mine in this county. In 1880, gold was discovered in the mountains near Allamuchy.
- KITTATINNY VALLEY, near LAFAYETTE: A lead mine was used here in the Revolutionary War. In 1864, on the western edge of Sparta, zinc and lead were mined about one mile apart in the swampy areas of the Kittatinny Valley.
- SUSSEX COUNTY (in general): Silver mines also existed here. Today, they are all on government property: the Perry Mine in Montague, the Snook Mine in Stokes State Forest, and the Silver Mine in Walpack near Haney's Mill. In Byram, there's the Cascade Mine, named after the cascading waterfalls just a few feet away. The mine is over 150 years old, just off the Sussex Branch railroad trail, only a few feet from the Silver Mine. Today it is reclaimed by the forest.

More minerals found in Sussex County include black zircon and, in the Andover Mine, Actinolite, Serpentine, hematite and magnetite, and zinc and copper. The mine opened before the Revolutionary War and closed in 1863. In the Limecrest Quarry, blue and brown Zircon can be found in marble, corundum, and tourmaline; in Edison, graphite, marble, and molybodenite; in Sparta, Unakite; and in Rudetown, Diopside and Serpentine have been found. The treasure seeker will need permission to hunt.

Sites of Minerals

For a small state, the amount and variety of minerals to find is amazing. Below is a list of places to dig for these rare precious minerals, gems, and elements.

- SUMMIT, ESSEX COUNTY: Agate, Prehnite, and Amethyst at the Houdaille Construction Materials Quarry. On Mount Arlington, black Zircon is found. Paterson has a lot of minerals beneath its streets, including Natrolite, Prehnite, greenockite, calcite, Babingtonite, apophyllite, analcime, thomsonite, scolecite, laumontite, heulandite, stilbite, and chabazite.
- MONTAGUE AND VERNON, SUSSEX COUNTY: Silver mines.
- MONTVILLE, MORRIS COUNTY: Yellow and green Serpentine; in Dover, Sunstone can be discovered from the Alan Wood Iron Mine and from the dumps on Mine Hill.
- PHILLIPSBURG, WARREN COUNTY: Green Serpentine was mined from the Royal Green Marble Quarry.
- SECAUCUS AND HUDSON COUNTIES (in general): The very helpful mineral Magnetite was discovered here.
- Vernon, Sussex County: Magnetite has been found at the old Bird Mine. It is an unknown magnetite mine. The Bureau of Mines tried to find this mine in the 1970s, but was unsuccessful.
- WANAQUE, PASSAIC COUNTY: In the New Jersey Highlands, a Magnetite mine was worked in late seventeenth century through the twentieth century.
- CASTLE POINT, HUDSON COUNTY: Serpentine.
- OXFORD TOWNSHIP, WARREN COUNTY AND PARAMUS, BERGEN COUNTY: Garnet is found at the Hoit Mine in Oxford Township and on the Green Farm in Paramus, Bergen County.
- BERNARDSVILLE, SOMERSET COUNTY: Amethyst has been seen. In Bound Brook, agate, amethyst, and jasper have been mined in the New England Quarry.
- WATCHUNG, SOMERSET COUNTY: Carnelian and Quartz can be found, and the seeker will be able to dig in green sand to find them. Quartz is the most common mineral on Earth. What is not common is the green sand found.
- CLIFTON AND HAWTHORNE, PASSAIC COUNTY: Agate has been found in the Houdaille Industries Quarry and Braen's Quarry. Amethyst has also been reported in Clifton.

Delaware River Gap

So ends the journey for treasure in one of the smallest states in America. However, it is easy to say that there are large numbers of supernatural lost loot to find here! Now, on to the next part of the quest...

Section Two:

New York

Overview of the Empire State

Welcome to the Empire State and the Excelsior State! This is the only state that has boundaries on a Great Lake and the Atlantic Ocean. At the turn of the twentieth century, New York City was considered the most haunted city in America, and one ghost story flows through all of New York. After the Civil War, President Lincoln's funeral train passed through New York State. Thousands of mourners came to see this slow-moving train. The procession went from New York City, passing through the Hudson River Valley, through Buffalo and Albany. To this day, residents claim to sometimes hear the horn blowing of that long-ago train as it passed through the region. Phantom sounds are sometimes heard where tragic events occurred or when a lot of suffering is felt in one area — as was the case was when Lincoln was assassinated and his funeral train traveled to his last resting place.

Strange occurrences happening in New York may be due to the fact that there are lay lines here, as well as all over the world. The theory is that along these lines, remarkable events occur. One place said to have lay lines is East Bethany, where the haunted site of Rolling Hills is. A lot of death occurred at Rolling Hill while it was a poorhouse. People were just buried in the backyard. Over 1,700 people died here and it was considered one of the worst poorhouses in the state after the Civil War. Many children, women with no husbands, and the insane were buried in unmarked graves and in the fields throughout the region.

It seems that all types of creatures have been drawn to the East Bethany area for millions of years. Near the Lackawanna Railroad, Devonian shale was excavated, filled with well-preserved fossils, including Lampshells or brachiopods, snails, molds of clams, and massive horn-shaped coral fossils.

New York Harbor is the best natural harbor ever found on Earth. Sailors commented that there was a sweet smell when they entered the harbor. Was it the numerous tulip trees that once existed? The answer is yes. Also contributing to the smell was the abundance of wildflowers. It was said that this wonderful smell could be scented off the coast of Maine when the wind blew the right way. An interesting side note: An ancient Tulip Tree once grew, thought to be around two hundred years old, through a Native American shell heap at the site of an old Native American village, called Shora-kap-kok. It was located west of Broadway and 208th Street, along the Spuyten Duyvil Creek; it was destroyed in 1928.

Ironically, as sweet-smelling as this region was when the Europeans first came here, since prehistoric times people have thrown their garbage into the East River. There are also numerous sunken ships in the rivers and bay, adding to the ultimate pollution of the region. Both the East and Hudson Rivers are tidal rivers, meaning that they flow both north and south, depending on the tides. As an interesting side note: The answer to the question of how and why did the Native Americans first come here is that, according to oral tradition, they came from the west seeking a river that flowed two ways and discovered the tidal Hudson River.

Dirty Hudson River in 2011

Native American Settlements and Geology

The East River did not exist 12,000 years ago. Over the millenniums, New York has been landlocked, a bog, a swamp, a grass land, a desert, under ice, and underwater. New York Island is just the top of a land range. The last ice sheet rose to the wrist of the Statue of Liberty and moved about a foot a day. It was the fastest ice age and glacier movement ever known. New York State was under water during the last age of the dinosaur. The region was sub-tropical, much like Louisiana is today.

The Palisades of the Hudson River was the exact place where the supercontinent Pangaea finally broke apart 180 million years ago. It must have been a terrifying sight for anyone around. Here, the volcanoes grew and erupted. The infant Atlantic Ocean pushed Africa and North America apart. Giant tectonic plates lie deep below New York and the Tappan Zee Bridge lies in the Palisades. This entire region is called the Triassic Lowlands and lies in hardened magma rock, which was once 1,000 feet deep. The Palisades was known as Weehawken by the tribes living here because they resembled "rows of trees." This is a very unusual geological formation — the only other one in the world is in Ireland, near Finsal's Cave, and it's called the Giant's Causeway.

Hudson River,
Piermont, New York

Tappan Zee Bridge

Over 450,000,000 years ago, Coney Island was a beach. There was a fossil found here called a sea scorpion, and this creature had the ability to leave the water environment and roam on land. A living descendant today is the horseshoe crab. Forty miles northwest of New York City is the Hudson Highlands, where a treasure seeker can find the oldest rocks in the Appalachian Mountains. About one billion years ago was the time before Pangaea, when the continents were together again on a supercontinent called Rhodina. It was at this time that North and South America collided, thus creating the largest mountain range ever known.

The Wisconsin Glacier caused a deep fjord that is still retreating, creating the Hudson River. The New York bedrock is called Manhattan Schist, a metamorphic rock similar to gneiss and marble, which is often revealed in embedded minerals. Manhattan schist has a lot of mica. It shines, which is one of the reasons that early explorers felt the rock here was mineral rich.

Glacial erratic stones are large rocks dropped by glaciers as they retreated through New York and can be found in park areas. Fossil remains of woolly mammoths, white bears, and ground sloths as large as elephants have been found in New York.

In 1609, Henry Hudson was searching for the northwest passage to China when he sailed his Dutch ship, *De Halve Maen,* or the *Half Moon*, into New York Bay and along the Hudson River. The river was not called the Hudson at that time though; it was called the Mauritius River, which meant, in Dutch, "Prince Maurice's River," the "Nassau River," or the "Manhattan River." Hudson also called it the Noort or North River because the Zuydt or South River was the Delaware River and the Connecticut River was called the Fresh River.

The Hudson River is 315 miles long from its source in the Adirondack Mountains to the Battery on the southern tip of Manhattan Island. Whatever the name for this river, it is considered haunted. For many years after Hudson's death, it was claimed that people could still see his ship sailing up the Hudson searching for that non-existent northwest passage to China. The Hudson River was called Muhheakantuck or Mahikanituk by the Native Americans, meaning "river that flows two ways." It is a tidal river that changes directions four times everyday. The East River, like the Hudson and Delaware Rivers, is a tidal river. It is not really a river, though; it is a continuation of the Long Island Sound. New York is the same latitude as Athens, Greece. However, no warm current enters the bay, so it is colder here in the winter than in the Mediterranean Sea.

Could it be a T-Rex fossil? No, but fossils can be found throughout the region.

The Dutch West India Company had two goals when it first organized in 1621 and claimed Manhattan Island: the first was to capture gold-filled Spanish treasure ships and the second was to establish a trade relationship with the tribes in the region. The fur trade gathered over 60,000 guilders and the pirate and privateer plunder gathered more than sixty million guilders. Is it really any wonder then that many considered being a pirate a lucrative career?

Throughout this section, the stories of the New York Native Americans will be told. Numerous artifacts can be found in a variety of areas. For example, in 1892, George W. Chapin, a logger, found Native American pottery in a hole on the shore of Cayudutta Creek, between Fonda and Johnstown. It was the site of a Mohawk fort around 1600. The brass and copper beads were of Iroquois decent. The village here was called Gandawague in the sand flats west of Fonda. It is also said that the Native Americans buried a great deal of plunder in a cave not far from Conesville. A Native American village with many relics was also discovered between Amsterdam and Patterson. Wallkill was known as Twischsawkin, meaning "the land where plums abound." Three prehistoric rock shelters have been found here, and the area is abundant in flint and chert, from which the Natives would make spear points and arrowheads.

There is no doubt that the Native American culture created many of the names that are used today. Here are just a few examples: Manhattan, meaning "the island"; Cohoes, meaning "canoe falling"; Copake, meaning "snake pond"; Taconic, meaning "full of timber"; Mattewan, meaning "good furs"; Poughkeepsie, meaning "safe harbor"; wassaic, meaning "rocky place"; wicopee, meaning "end of land"; coxsackie, meaning "owl hoot" or "place of wild geese"; canarsie, meaning "at the boundary or fence"; tuxedo, meaning "lake of clear, flowing water"; hoosac, meaning "place of stones"; schodack, meaning "place of fire," because this island was the traditional Mahican capitol and site of the council fire; Hackensack, meaning "lowland"; tappan, meaning "cold springs"; kayaderosseras, meaning "lake country"; sacandaga, meaning "marsh or much water"; esopus, meaning "river"; mohonk, meaning "raccoon skin coat"; ashokan, meaning "to cross the creek"; Armonk, meaning "beaver"; cahppaqua, meaning "well-watered place"; Mount Kisco, meaning "land on the edge of a creek," probably meaning Croton River; Kitchawan, meaning "large and swift current"; Croton, meaning "wind or tempest"; muscoot, meaning "place of rushes." Finding out why someplace was named or what the name means may help the seeker to know what treasure might be buried there or what events could have happened there. More names will be given throughout the book to help in the quest. As an interesting side note: We also still use words given to us by the Dutch, including boss, cookie, dumb, and snoop.

1

Manhattan

Believe it or not, New York City, when first seen by the Europeans, was hilly and heavily forested. The only tree that might still exist from that era may be located in Central Park. The Honey Locust Trees has large thorns that evolved spines to guard against the American Mastodon that roamed the region. The Central Park trees still have major thorns that may show what the area looked like many years ago.

Manhattan Island is part of the New England Upland physiographic province. What that means is that it is the eroded root of a mountain over four million years old. More than 170 mineral varieties were once found here. South of the Narrows, at the entrance to the New York Harbor, lies the old channel of the Hudson River. In glacial times, the Hudson flowed 120 miles further out to the Atlantic Ocean. This would make the present-day river actually a drowned river, as the glacier melted and overfilled the older Hudson River channel, which is one of the main reasons why the Hudson River is so deep and ships could easily navigate the lower end of the river. The Mahican tribe called this river, Muhheakunnuk, meaning "great waters constantly in motion" or "river that flows two ways." It is a tidal river. When unhindered, this river has significant tidal activity. It reaches all the way to Troy, which is 150 miles away from the mouth. The river is brackish for sixty miles, up to Newburgh.

Who first arrived in New York after the Native Americans? Well, there are stories that it may have been the Viking, Leif Erickson, who landed in Manhattan, but officially, the Italian explorer Giovanni da Verranzzano is said to have arrived here in 1524. Traveling on the ship *La Dauphine*, Verranzzano and his crew are said to have visited the Native American village on Governor Island, called Nut Island by the Dutch later, just off Battery Point, and named it Mahicansac. He called the upper bay, the Gulf of Santa Margherita, and New York, Angouleme. He called the Hudson River, Vendome, after a French Duke. It is also said that he described the river as the "River of the Steep Hills" and "Grand River." According to a letter he wrote to the French King, "A violent contrary wind blew in from the sea and forced us to return to our ship, greatly regretting to leave this region which seemed so commodious and delightful, and which we suppose must also contain great riches, as the hills showed many indications of minerals." This letter may have sparked the mineral interest of what New York had to offer by the Europeans.

New York City was first a graveyard. Hudson's crew fought the Native Americans on the land that the city now stands. The dead were buried here in September 1609. As an interesting side note: Hudson founded Manhattan on September 11, 1609.

The Manahata Project found a 1782 British map that showed how the island looked before it became a city. Times Square was surrounded by hills and three streams. The Tulip trees that were there were said to have lived more than three hundred years. Four hundred years ago, this area was a swamp with Red Maple trees. The south end of the island, at Inwood Park, still retains the foliage of what New York had, including the rocks. There were low hills about one hundred feet high and sandy beaches along the Hudson River. The Harlem River was a pristine waterway with marine animals.

Manhattan Island was the Native American name of a small, ten-mile-long island located at the foot of Grand Street on the East River. At low tide, it was a small peninsula; at high tide, the water covered the narrow roadway extending from the shore, thus making an island of what remained. The Native American word is said to mean "place of the whirlpool" or "dangerous stream of rushing water." In the East River once existed the whirlpool called Hellgate. It was reported that over 1,000 shipwrecks occurred here annually. It has since been destroyed and most of the dangerous rocks were removed by 1851. The actual whirlpool was located where 90th and 100th Streets are today. This whirlpool was named Hellgat by Adriaen Block; it meant "Hell Channel" and perhaps was so named because his ships were wrecked here. However, going through the whirlpool was a fifty-mile shortcut from the Atlantic Ocean through the Long Island Sound. The biggest reefs were called Hallet's Point off Astoria and were destroyed in 1876. Flood Rock was located near Roosevelt Island and was destroyed in 1885. Still, one wonders what may remain under the water from the numerous shipwrecks that occurred so long ago?

The tribe that lived here were called Monatuns, meaning "people of the whirlpool." They were also called Manhattoes. However, Manhattan Island has a variety of meanings, it seems. It was called Manahata by the Munsee tribe, meaning "island of many hills" or "heavenly island;" Menatay, meaning "island"; Mahatuouh, meaning "place for wood gathering"; Mahahachtanieuk, meaning "place of general inebriation"; or Manhattan, meaning "rock island."

Whatever the tribe was called, they were part of the larger tribe, the Wappinger, that belonged to the Confederacy of the Algonquian. Native American artifacts have been discovered on the east bank of the Hudson River, in Poughkeepsie, near Wappingers Falls, on Avenue A and 120th Street. In 1900, Native American skeletons were found at Seaman Avenue, Tottenville, and Staten Island. There were arrowheads found in the bodies. It is obvious that they died in battle. There is a small rise of land on the southwest corner of Dyckman Street and Sherman Avenue, which ran into Sherman Creek at one time, called the Knoll. Shards and pottery have been found here. There have also been skeletons found, but ones that have lead buttons. It is thought that the Knoll is probably the graves of early settlers. At a place called Isham's Garden, between Isham Street and Seaman Avenue, the soil was white from shell fragments found. Other Native American artifacts found were arrowpoints, flint chips, hammerstones, sinkers, and pottery.

Indian Cave is located in Inwood Hill Park at the foot of West 210th Street. Pottery, bones, weapons, cups, dishes, spear and arrow points, fishing tools, net sinkers, a bone harpoon point, pipes, pendants, ornaments — one was carved with a human face — and implements were discovered. To see these artifacts now, they are in the American Museum of National History. Also, glacial potholes can be found in the park. Archeologists excavated Cold Spring, the extreme end of the Island in a shell heap and found more arrowheads. There are also three rock shelters found at the foot of the hill, called Cock Hill, in the northern part of Manhattan.

The area was called Shorakpok by the Native Americans. Legends tell that at Shorakapok Rock once stood a tulip tree where Peter Minuit, the Dutch settler, purchased the island for $24 in 1626 from the Munsee tribe. This lore should be taken with a grain of salt. The Munsee tribe, like all Native American tribes, did not believe they owned the land, so how could they really sell it? They believed the land was created by Kishelemulong to be used by all. The settlement was along Seaman Avenue. On the west side of the street was a Native American gravesite. The intersection of Broadway and Isham Street was a Native American village about 2,700 to four hundred years ago. Pottery has been found here.

The Dutch reported finding a large shell heap on the west shore of Fresh Water Pool, which was bounded by the present Bowery, Elm, Canal, and Pearl Streets. They called it Kalch-Hook or shell-point. There were reports of a village called Catiemuts overlooking a small pond near Canal Street. It was also said to be a lookout spot. Canal Street was originally a forty-foot canal with trees along the side. A stone bridge crossed at

Broadway, which is now under the pavement. In 1886, on Kingsbridge Road, known as Broadway today, and 220th Street, arrowheads, wampum, pendants, bowls, harpoons, cups, and pottery were found.

In 1661, there was a Native American village called Sapokanican near Gansevoort Market; it is Greenwich today. The current Main Street was on the shore at that time and the Hackensack tribe would land here to trade. The village was between Bethune and Horatio Streets. Native American artifacts were once found, including a toboggan, Lacrosse stick, snow shoes, and skis. A grooved stone axe was found at 77th Street and Avenue B. Also, an arrowhead was discovered at 81st Street and the Hudson River. There have also been Native American items found on the campus of Columbia College.

In the seventeenth century, the Bronx was part of the large territory of the Munsee tribe. They called the area Siwanoy. The boundary was from Hell Gate in the East River to Norwalk, Connecticut. It is thought that Clasons Point was the site of their village, called sankapins. There was a wampum factory at Castle Hill Park, and at Ferry Point Park was the Native American graveyard. This area was considered sacred to the tribe.

The settlers called Brooklyn, from the Dutch word Breuchenlen, after the ancient city on the river Vecht in the Province of Utrecht. It was also known as Bracola, Broccke, Brocckede, Broicklede, and Brocklandia. These words describe a moist meadow plain area. The Native Americans cultivated maize here. The tribe that lived here was called the Marechkawiecks; they were a sub-tribe of the Canarsie tribe of Long Island.

At the Harlem Ship Canal, which is today 220th Street and Kingsbridge Road, a large deposit of shells were found with pottery shards. The strange thing about this find is that the shells were so wedged and packed together that a pick could hardly penetrate them. The Harlem River Deposit existed at 209th and 211th Streets, along the west bank of the Harlem River. A shell heap was here too, but these shells were different because they were all red. In 1903, archeologists thought they had uncovered a Native American gravesite on 211th Street, but it was found to actually be a Slave graveyard. Shell heaps and stone sinkers were found, as well as hammerstones, all from the Native American era. These sites were obviously used over many years for a variety of reasons: in Harlem, on Avenue A between 120th and 121st Streets, arrowheads were found in 1855 and in 1938, there was the "tree of hope" near 131st Street and 7th Avenue. It was believed that if a person rubbed his back against the tree it would bring them good luck. The tree is no longer there.

A Native American village called Reckgawawanos was located at Yonkers. The main village of the Lenni-Lenape tribe at Yonkers was called Nappeckamack. Many relics were found here. On Spuyten Duyvil Hill, near

Berrien's Neck, there was once a Native American fort and village called Shorckappock. A lot of shell deposits were found. Spuyten Duyvil was a one-mile channel connecting the Hudson and Harlem rivers, meaning "Devil's Spout" — no doubt a reference to the strong and wild current found here.

Richmondtown is the exact geographic center of the island. Daniel Wandell dug up $10,000 in gold on Richmond Road at Concord while digging a trolley pole. A Paleo-Indian site was found. During that time, 11,000 years ago, Staten Island was a hilltop. Staten Island comes from the Dutch word Staaten Eylandt. The area was called Aquehonga, Manacknong, or Eghquaons by the Lenape tribe.

In Tottenville, a Lenni-Lenape Native American burial site was found called Indian Burial Ridge. About 120 artifacts were found here, including a fluted spear point, arrowheads, and bone tools. Many beads made of copper were discovered in the 1950s on the southwestern tip of Staten Island, on the shore of Arthur Kill. Major archaeological artifacts of the tribe and burial grounds were found on Ward's Point. By 1670, the tribe had traded this town to the Europeans.

The Dutch settlement on the island was called New Amsterdam and was located from Wall Street to South Street, which today would be from the seaport to City Hall Park and Foley Square. Fort Amsterdam was located at the foot of Manhattan from the base of Broadway, facing the East and Hudson Rivers. In 1612, Adrian Block's crew of the Dutch ships the *Tiger* and *Fortune* traded with the Hudson River tribe and built huts on Manhattan Island. In 1624, Dutch and French Protestant refugees, led by Cornelius Mey, established the first permanent settlement, Fort Orange, in Albany. By 1625, the Dutch settler Willem Verhulst founded the colony of New Netherland, now renamed Manhattan, to New Amsterdam. Wall Street was actually where a wall was built by the Dutch to keep the Native Americans out. The wall was nine feet tall.

All streams that once flowed in New York are now buried. Three streams flowed to the Hudson River from Times Square, including the Maiden Stream, where women would wash clothes. It was known as Virgins Path, but was also at one time a lover's lane before being changed to Maiden Lane. The Dutch name was "T'Maagde Paatje." It was also known as Green Lane. The stream still runs beneath the pavement of the road. The street is curved because it follows the old stream path. It became the street of jewelers, goldsmiths, silversmiths, and gem dealers. Minetta Street is a Dutch word meaning "little one." The name was to distinguish this second creek from the larger creek not far away. This little creek originated in the marsh in Washington Square and still flows under New York City. The third stream that flowed from this river was called Spuyten Duyvil Creek by the Dutch, or perhaps the larger creek than the one called Little One or Minetta? There are also stories of a creek that runs under Second Avenue and 52nd Street. It was called DeVoor's or Old Mill Creek. Could this be the location of the third creek or Spuytun Duyvill Creek? There was yet another stream that flowed along 21st Street, called "krom mesje," meaning "little crooked knife," where the corruption of Gramercy comes from. The freshwater pond that gave the Dutch their drinking water lies under the Criminal Courts' Building on Centre Street. Collect Pond was where the Tomb's Prison was covered with Canal Street. By 1798, it was reported that it would be best to cover the streams located in New York City, as they were not fit to drink any more. Even animals did not come to drink from them.

There have been reports from the Dutch that there was a village lying between the North River and the stream called Manetta or Bestavaar's Kill. The name of the village was Lapinican. Chinatown's Canal Street was originally part of the waterway that may have allowed the Native Americans to sail straight through the island at high tide.

Pearl Street was on the East River waterfront in 1660. Many Dutch artifacts were discovered here, from coins, called jetons, to goblets, bowls, pipes, beads, wampum, wine bottles, and plates. There was also a Dutch Silversmith Shop, located on Wall and Water Streets, where beer bottles, pots, medicine bottles, crucibles, and glassware were discovered. Artifacts from the sites above were destroyed in the September 11, 2001 terrorist attacks.

The Manhattan Island hoax occurred in 1824. A charismatic speaker named Lozier stood in Manhattan's Centre Market and announced that, because of all the buildings recently constructed, the southern tip of Manhattan was too heavy and was in danger of sinking. The solution, Lozier said, was to saw the island off at the northern end, tow it out to sea, turn it 180 degrees, and re-attach it. He said that the mayor of the city had put him in charge of the project. He hired hundreds of people to work on the project, ordered saws, oars, and other construction items, set the delivery day of cattle, chickens, and hogs, so the workers would have enough to eat. The big day arrived, and workers, spectators and a marching band met at Spring and Bowery Streets to see the project start. Only Lozier did not come. He was found in the Bronx, but apparently the people did not want others to know they had been duped, so no charges were brought against him.

Most streets in New York City are perfectly straight, except Broadway, which followed the original diagonal trail created by the Native Americans who lived here. Broadway was called Heerewegh by the Dutch, meaning "highway." In 1805, an iron bolt was found in Central Park, which was part of the grid that created New York's streets' system. It was decided that the island's hills would be leveled and the valleys filled, in a plan called the grid, and that this farmland would become a city. All streets would be straight. Iron bolts were set in lead and then stone. The story is that while the plan was being made the sun caused a gravel screen, casting a shadow across the plan, and that is the way the streets were created.

The Hudson River had a major logging industry at one time. During high flow times, the logs could travel seventy to ninety miles in mere weeks. However, during dry times, it may take two years to go the same distance. The log drives and jams caused many river drivers to die in the Hudson River. Perhaps that is another reason that the entire Hudson River Valley is considered haunted. In 1872, the Hudson River reached its logging peak: 213,800,000 board feet were milled by the logs that moved along this river.

There are over forty islands located in New York City Harbor. Many of them have a dark history, and are sometimes called the sad New York Islands. Below is a partial list of what has happened at some of these islands:

- Vissher's Island, also known as Winthrops Island, is where Adrian Block's ships were wrecked in 1614, after sailing through the Hellgate whirlpool. The Hudson River once flowed down Greenwich Street. In 1916, workmen excavating a subway station on the corner of Greenwich and Day Streets found the keel and rib timbers of Captain Adrian Block's ship, *Tijer* or *Tiger*, which had been burned by the riverside in November 1613. The remains can be found in the Museum of the City of New York.
- Rikers Island is found at the head of the East River, where it comes into Long Island Sound. It was once the city prison.
- North Brothers Island, also called Roosevelt Island or Welfare Island, was once an infectious hospital center, a poorhouse, and a prison. It is a very strange place and the ruins are falling down today. Ironically, it is also the site of the fasting-growing area in New York today. Once a place most would avoid, it will likely one day become a tourist site.
- Hart Island is out in Long Island Sound and was a reform center. There is also an unknown burial site, a memorial to unknown people buried here. It is a white obelisk on the north end of the island. Unknown and unidentified people found in the city are buried here twice a week.
- Governors Island is off the southern tip of Manhattan. The original pioneers from Holland camped here before going to Manhattan. The Dutch called it Nut or Nutten Island because it was covered with Hickory Trees. Today, it is a Coast Guard base. It is the largest Island in the harbor and there was a Native American presence here. Native American artifacts found here date to the Late Woodland period, 1,000 to four hundred years ago. These items include pottery and stone flakes, left over from

making tools. It is thought that perhaps this was a campsite for the tribe. Spear points from an even earlier time have been found. It was a Dutch trading post in 1620; archaeologists found a Dutch Windmill, built in 1625, that was part of the trading post. Fort Jay was built in 1755, in the center of the island, during the French & Indian War. There is a gravesite here, though it is thought to be British soldiers stationed here during the Revolutionary War or perhaps American Prisoners of War. Before the War of 1812, the fort called Castle Williams was built. This is just one of the eighteen forts guarding New York City. Castle Fort Williams was abandoned in 1996 to cut costs. It is a very haunted island with numerous ghosts sighted from various eras.

• BEDLOE'S ISLAND, or Liberty Island, is next to Oyster Island. Pirate treasure belonging to Captain Kidd is said to be buried here with a horrible evil creature guarding it. A soldier's ghost is also said to be guarding guns at Fort Wood. A Native American trash heap, or midden, was discovered, as were pottery and spear points.

• ELLIS ISLAND, is also known as Gibbet Island or Oyster Island, as it was called by the Dutch, who found a profitable oyster bed here. It was also where the British hanged pirates. It is a very somber and unsettling place. Human remains were found under the main building. Could the building have been built over a Native American gravesite? The Delaware Tribe blessed the bones in 2003. Fort Gibson was built in 1790 and was on the southeastern part of the island. In 1891, the first emigrant was processed here. Her name was Annie Moore from Cobh, Ireland. Ellis Island is the smallest island in the harbor, but today, due to the landfill, it is nine times larger than its original size.

An enduring legend has been here since the beginning of the settlement. According to Peter Stuyvesant, the first Dutch Governor of New York in the 1600s, the famous ghost ship, *The Flying Dutchman*, sailed through the narrows of New York harbor. When the ship failed to stop, the gunners of Manhattan fired their cannon at her, but the balls "went whistling through her cloudy and imponderable mass."

Three Native American and Dutch wars were fought on the grounds of Manhattan: Kiefts War — Kiefts was the first governor of New York before Stuyvesant — in the 1640s; the Esopus War in the 1660s; and the Peach War, which was fought in September 1655. They were started basically because of the bad attitude of the Dutch with the tribes. Take the Peach War, for example: this war was started because a Dutch settler saw a tribe woman taking a peach from what he said was his orchard and shot her.

On Isham Street, British glass, coins, and hardware were buried here from the Revolutionary War. In the Academy Street Garden, located between Academy and Hawthorne Streets, running to Seaman Avenue to Cooper Street,was a British campsite during the Revolutionary War. Many artifacts have been found, including buttons, gun-flints, and bullets. Native American artifacts have also been found, including a red jasper-like stone and shells. During the Civil War, this area was a training ground for Union military units. Many camps were located on the east and north shores of the island and one was located in New Dorp.

Despite having such a pleasant name, Golden Hill, New York, is the site of the first battle of the Revolutionary War in January 1770, called the Battle of Golden Hill. This was the original name of John Street, on the east side of Williams Street. The name of the hill came about because during the Colonial period there was a legend that a great amount of gold was hidden here. It is known as Williams Street today and is located between Wall Street and Hanover Street. However, it has also been known as the Glassmakers Street, Smith Street, Smeedes Straat, Smit Straat, Suice Street, Smee Straat, the Suice, De Smee Straat, Burghers Path, Burger Jorisens Path, King Street, and Burger Jovis Path. Golden Hill Street was really an old wheat field filled with golden wheat, not hidden gold.

Chinatown's lost loot legend starts on Doyers Street. The origin of the name is not known, but it may have been for Anthony H. Doyer, who lived here in 1809. The lore is that the Doyer family buried $35 million in gold in the walls of their home, but it has never been found.

The British Revolutionary War American Prison Ships site is in Wallabout Cove; however, no monument marks the spot. The 11,500 victims were buried on the western side of Fort Greene. The prison ships were the *Whitby, Good Hope, Old Jersey, John,* and *Falmouth.*

2.

Long Island

This barrier island was built in the last ice age. The glacier left sand, gravel, and rocks to form Long Island and it is one out of only three islands in the world that was created this way. The ice also left a depression that later filled in, creating Long Island Sound. This water is almost entirely encased by land and has a lot in common with the Mediterranean Sea. Long Island Sound has been called a really deep valley that is submerged today. Still others say that Long Island split from Connecticut because of an earthquake and the fault is Long Island Sound.

The island is 119 miles long, larger than the state of Rhode Island, and is about twenty miles wide. There are numerous types of islands found throughout the world. There are linear islands lying parallel to the coast and peninsulas, or "almost islands," connecting to the mainland. There are arcuate islands, like Martha's Vineyard, and elliptical islands, like those found in the Boston Harbor. There are rectangular and straight-sided islands, like Sardinia and Puerto Rico; zigzag islands, like the Belcher Islands in Hudson Bay; and isolated islands, like Sable Island off Nova Scotia.

Violent storms can and do change the shape of the island. Jones Inlet was created during one such violent storm. When first created, residents tell that the spot where the inlet had broken through there was low water. Where the sand washed away, they could see a meadow many feet below of what would have been the high-water mark. The meadow had been covered for many years, and there were curious footprints in the sand of that meadow. They were the prints of cloven hoofs — it was later determined that the prints were buffalo put there many years before.

There is a ghost ship of a British War ship that is seen in Long Island Sound; it was seized and destroyed by farmers off Throgg's Neck in 1777. Conscience Point is the 1640 landing place of the first colonists who settled in Southampton. It was the first English colony in New York State. The next was Setauket, settled by Puritans from Boston in 1650. The Native Americans called Hampton Bays, Long Island "good ground," and planted fields and crops here. The people living here in the early 1900s called the Hamptons "The Gold Coast" because all the very rich families built mansions here.

Long Island Sound

Conscience Point

New London Lighthouse during a severe
thunderstorm

The Conscience Point Landing Site

Native American Sites

The Native American name for Long Island was Gawanasegeh, meaning "Long Island." On early maps this place was called "The territories of the people of the Long House called Hodenosauneega." This island has a four hundred-mile coastline, where thirteen different tribes once resided. Montauk was where the ruling tribe of Long Island, called the Montaukett or Montaukets, lived. The Cariarsie tribe resided in Jamaica and Coney Island, which was where Hudson landed, located in Kings County. Coney Island is a Dutch word Konynen Eylant, meaning "rabbit island."

Sag Harbor

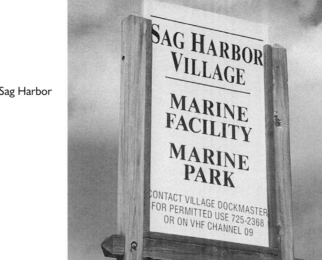

The Sag Harbor waterway

The Rockaway, Meracock, and Massapeague tribes lived on the southwest side of Long island. The Masssapequas, which lived between the Hempstead Plains and Islip Township, were exterminated in 1653. In the north, the Matinecock tribe lived, and in the East, the Nissaquogue, Setauket, Corchaug, Secatogue, Shinecoc, Patchogue, and Montauk tribes. On Shelter, Ram, and Hog islands lived the Manhanset tribe. The Corchauge tribe lived on the North Shore and Catchogue, meaning "the greatest or principal place," was the Sachem's home. Morton National Wildlife Refuge is found on Nayack Road in Sag Harbor and was the village of the Montauk and Shinnecook tribes. Glen Cove is also a Native American village site, and quartz arrowheads were found in a cornfield near Mount Sinai Harbor. They are thought to be from the Nonowantuc tribe, a sub-tribe of the Setauket. Numerous Native American artifacts are found all along Long Island, including arrowheads and stone axes. As an interesting side note: All the tribes here paid tribute to the Pequot tribe of Connecticut.

The tribes made canoes out of tulip wood by digging and burning out the tree trunks. There are stories that the tribes could sail across Long Island to Rhode Island in these canoes. Apparently, they were sea-worthy. Flint quarries abound here. There are sites where arrowheads, spears, and tomahawks were made and can be found today.

A Massapeague tribe fort was excavated in Fort Neck, Queen's County, in 1653. Evidence of Native American life has also been found at Stony Brook and Wading River. Acombamack was the name of the Native village where Bellport now exists. The name means "over against the fishing place." Powells Cove is another place where arrowheads, knives, and axes have been discovered. In 1958, a boy found a 5,400-year-old, Frontenac Island-type missile head. It is also said that the mysterious Ohio Mound Builders were here in 100 B.C. The French Fort, Frontenac, was located on Lake Ontario.

There was also a Native American fort located at Fort Pond Bay. This place is also a very old Native American burial ground. Ancient footprints have been located in the granite here, and, according to legend, the granite has several red spots on it because they are the marks of blood from a Native American chief killed here by an enemy's arrow. It is said that the great evil spirit Mutcheschesumetook arose here and, when chased away by the tribe, left his footprint in the granite.

Spooky Spots

Huntington was a place that the Native tribes considered too taboo to visit. It was purchased by settlers in 1653 from the Manticock tribe. Nothing would grow here and was considered cursed land. The region was nearly impassible for horses and wagons to go through. Numerous ghosts abound here, with sightings reported as recent as 2006. There is the vision of an old hospital that appears, though it burned down years ago, and it is said that the ghosts of the hospital's patients still haunt the area. There are even reports of phantom police who roam the road. Assawanama, in Huntington, means "the midway fishing place" or "the fishing place between the forks of the creek."

Mount Misery of Long Island is an 854-acre, dense, thick area of woods — and it is considered the most haunted woods in America. Long Island also claims the most haunted lake in America, Lake Ronkonkoma. A one-mile landlocked lake, it was created by glaciers about 17,000 years ago. As the blocks of glacial ice plowed deeply in the land and melted, they created great kettle holes, which is how the lake was made. It is fifty-five feet above sea level, 4,300 feet long in diameter, and ninety-seven feet deep at maximum. The lake beach is known for its white sand, and it is said that at times the lake seems to have no bottom, but it really averages seventy feet deep. It is fed by hidden springs that no one can locate. Geologists have said that it would be impossible to drain the lake. The lake was created by an iceberg and punched a hole through to the underground water table, which continues to feed the lake and which is why the water is always fresh. The name comes from the Native Americans and means "boundary fishing place." It was called Sachem's Pond by the tribes in the region and was the boundary line between the Secatogue, Unkechaug, Cetalcot, and Nissequogue tribes. Today, it is the dividing line between the towns of Islip, Smithtown, and Brookhaven.

The lake is also cursed and males should not swim in it. They can and have drowned here. The Native American legend is that a maiden fell in love with a settler. It was a forbidden love, and the princess killed herself by drowning in the lake. The curse was that she would take a male life every year; there were 160 drownings in 135 years and only one of the victims was female. There have also been sightings of the Native American princess by visitors and employees of the various hotels and inns that surround the lake. There is also the legend of a young Native American warrior who jumped into the lake and killed himself for love and his body appeared in the Connecticut River. This is a variation of the story that the lake is thought to be bottomless.

In Boonville, there is a place called Lovers Lane located on the Old French Road. It is said to be haunted by French settlers desperately trying to get to Canada. Fort Le Boeuf, built in 1753, also known as Le Beauf, was located near a swamp on the French Road. Moodna is a Dutch word from Moordenaars, meaning "murderers' creek" because lore says that a colonial family was murdered here. Seventeenth-century Dutch maps show that the Native American village in Ossining was part of the Mohegan tribe, called Sint Sinck, meaning "stone upon stone." This may refer to the extensive beds of limestone found in the southern part of the village. The word Sicomac means "resting place for the departed" or "happy hunting ground." This is the name of an area of Wyckoff that, according to legend, was the burial place of many Native Americans and possibly Chief Oratam of the Hackensack tribe.

Fire Island

Fire Island, a sunken maritime forest, can be found off Long Island. It is forty miles long and only half-mile wide. It is the northernmost Ilex-dominated forest on the Atlantic Ocean. It is a *Ilex Opaca* (American Holly), *Sassafras Albidum* (White Sassafras), and *Amelanchier canadensis* (Shadbush) forest almost three hundred years old. The island is considered a barrier island and, like all barrier islands, it is slowly retreating landward, rolling over on itself. The sunken forest floor is lower than the dunes between it and the sea. The water is slowly building, as well as narrowing, the east end. Storms also help this process along.

Huracan was what the Carib tribes of the Caribbean named their storm God. In 1690, the settlers say that the Great Gut increased to nine miles in width. The 1690 hurricane probably cut an inlet nine miles wide through the peninsula near the western part of Fire Island. This channel, which separates Fire Island from Jones Island, is now called the Fire Island Inlet. Still, though, it was kind of connected to the mainland. The great storm of 1782 changed the course of the victory of the Battle of Long Island since the resulting hurricane destroyed much of the French fleet coming to the aid of the Patriots. In 1931, a storm smashed the channel known as Moriches Inlet through the Peninsula, detaching more of Fire Island.

The Great Hurricane of 1938, also known as GH38, cut right through Long Island over Fire Island. This hurricane finished disconnecting the island from the mainland and created Shinnecock Inlet. It was one of the most severe weather systems to ever hit New England. Sebastian Junger, an author from that era, reported that the GH38's waves actually shook the Earth so hard they were registered by a seismograph in Alaska. The average hurricane that hits Long Island, when they do come, often has the input energy of ten thousand atomic bombs. Anytime a natural disaster occurs in an area, artifacts of that time may still be hidden underground. It is as though time stood still for that moment. Consider Pompeii or other areas that were destroyed by a natural event.

Fire Island is a very eerie place even today. No cars are allowed on the island without permission. Though pirates passed this island a number of times, no one is really thought to have landed here. Why? Perhaps because it was used as the place to send people afflicted with the Plague.

3

New York's Valleys

Hoosac Valley

The entire Hoosac Valley was a battlefield during the Mohawk and Mahican tribal war fought between 1540 and 1669. This location is chiefly between the Taconic and Green Mountain range. The passes here were bloody war paths between Montreal, Canada, and Cohoes Falls, New York. Warriors would go through the forbidding Hoosac Mountain, which went between the Hudson-Champlain and Connecticut River valleys to get to Manhattan and New England. The Hoosac Pass of the Taconacs was called the Pass of Thermopylae. This major war path held over forty forts guarding the borders of New York, Massachusetts, and Vermont, all within seventy-five miles. For example, Fort Massachusetts was an English fort found in the upper Hoosac Valley.

The bear clan, of the Maquara and Mohawk tribes of the Iroquois Confederacy, began the war with the Hoosacs and Mahicians in 1542. In 1545, they forced the Sachem, Uncus, and his Passaconaway tribe to leave the area. They eventually settled in Connecticut and adopted the crest of the Great Unalachti, part of turkey clan. The wild call of the turkey sounded like Pequat, so this clan chose a new name for their tribe, Pequot. In 1609, some members of the old clan still lived here. The nephew of Uncus lived in Castleton on the east bank of the Hudson River and considered himself the Sachem.

Many Native American artifacts have been found in the Hoosac Valley region, especially at the junction between the Hoosac and Hudson Rivers, including Mahican quartz, Mohawk flint arrows, scalping knives, tomahawks, clay pipes, and hominy-pounders. At the site of a Native village, called Mingling Waters, that once existed at the meeting of the Tomhannac with the Hoosac River, a ceremonial Calumet or peace pipe was found.

The Hoosac golden legend of St. Croix, which means "the holy cross," was formed by the junction of the Walloomasc with the Hoosac Rivers. In 1542, this place was blessed by a French missionary. It was also the meeting place of the tribe living here. The tribe considered this a spirit cross of the rivers and was located just above their village. It is considered a haunted, as well as sacred, place. The "gold" part of the story is part of the legend of Modoc and what he brought to this region. The myth goes back to the Delaware and Mahican traditions to the time of Modoc's voyage to America in 1170. The story of Modoc has been told in connection to the possible existence of Welsh colonies in America:

> The Mandan tribe was known as the "white Indians." They are said to have access to the metal gold that a Wales crew may have brought with them when they traveled here. It is conjectured that the tribe mixed with an ancestor of the Madogs of Llanfydnach Wales. Prince Madog was a younger son of the King of North Wales in the twelfth century. In Richard Deacon's book, *Madoc and the Discovery of America*, he states that in 1170, the Prince sailed from Wales and arrived in Mobile, Alabama, and sailed up the Alabama River and disappeared. Travelers in the 1800s reported seeing fair-skinned, blue-eyed, blonde-hair Native Americans in the area that spoke Welsh words. The tribe was destroyed by Smallpox before 1796.

Weeping Rocks are located in Pownal, New York. The Mahican tribe held a tradition that they would not be conquered until these rocks wept, and this belief led to a century of battle between the Mahicans and Mohawks. Eventually, the Mahican warriors retreated to a shelter under the Pudding Stone Cliffs and saw the waterfalls, or teardrops, fall over the mountain. The Mohawk warriors were close by and killed all the Mahican members. Though the Mahican Chief tried to get help from the tribes in Massachusetts, in 1669, the last battle took place on a hill known as Kinaquarione, just east of Hoffman Station, New York. Until 1669, the Hoosac Tawasentha, or burial field, and shrine of sacrifice was found in a fifteen-acre meadow on the south bank of the Hoosac River, opposite the Fallen-hill in Old Schaghticoke. There was a natural obelisk of limestone that rose about one hundred feet from the riverbed beneath Fallen-hill. It was called Hobbamocko's Altar or the Devil's Chimney. The Mahicans hung offerings to appease the fiend of calamity. The pudding stone cliffs that form the Weeping Rocks are sand hills of glacial drift found on all the headwaters of all the rivers of the Hoosac Valley. There is a myth that these mounds were used as burial places by pre-historic Ohio Native Americans. Sea erosion during the pre-Cambrian era created them before the mountains rose. Rare plants, including the walking fern, cliff-brakes, and spleen worts, can be found here. Below Hell's Gate, a perfect oxbow forms where a Mahican camping ground once existed. The falls form about and below Devil's Chimney.

The Hoosac Kitsmac, or powwow priest, used the stone to carve symbols of the wakon-bird, or spirit dove, to appease the moodus upheavals/noise of Hobbamocko, meaning "God of Thunder." To the Mahican tribe, the Moodus upheaval/noise came from these distorted pudding rocks being thrown against other rocks, which is why they were used as sacrificial stones to appease the angry God. There are more of these types of Moodus Upheaval, or Pudding Cliff Rocks, in the thermal sand springs about two miles south of Williamstown.

The largest falls on the Hoosac River are Quequick, or Quiquek, in the Schaghticoke Village. The falls flow 160 feet in less than two miles between Devils Chimney, opposite Fallen Hill through a ravine, and Hells Gate, which is a narrow pass not more than twelve feet wide.

Many cohohas, or cradle hollows or potholes, are found here and were used by the Native Americans as mortars to pound corn with stone pestles. These types of relics can be found all through the area.

The Taconic Mountains, which start in the northeast at the Fishkill-on-the-Hudson and go two hundred miles along the New England/New York border, are built with lots of marble inside. The Native Americans called the summits of the range Manitou Aseniah, meaning "spirit stones." The mountain is named from the corruption of the Native American words Tohkone, Tachan, and Taghkan, followed by the affix "izen," "ic," or "ac," meaning "wooded, rocky mountain place." Tohkonac was a bubbling sand spring west of the Taconic Range, near Copake Lake, purchased from the Mahicans in 1683. A lot of caves were also found in this region. An interesting side note: The name "Taconic" has over fifty different spellings in the Albany Archives.

Glacial pothole

Mohawk Valley

The mighty Mohawk River — its Native American name of Tenonanatche means "the river flowing through the mountains" — is the only entrance through the Appalachian Plateau between Georgia and the Saint Lawrence Valley. In the Mohawk Valley, there is a story that links this spot with the mythical city of gold in Maine called Norumbega. It has been speculated that the Norumbega River was not the Penobscot River, but actually the Hudson River and Manhattan Island was the lost golden city, not Bangor, Maine. However, there are no legends in Native American lore to substantiate that claim. There was also no hidden, secret golden city found by Henry Hudson when he traveled by Manhattan. It would make sense that he may have noted that fact in his logs. John Fiske, author of the book *Dutch & Quaker Colonies of America*, claims that the Hudson River, not the Penobscot River, was the Norumbega River and that the golden city was located at a pond near a gloomy prison called the Tombs. He suggests that perhaps the name was a corruption of Anormee Berge, which means "Grand Scarp" in French. Another place for this golden city is said to be Albany. This is a myth of golden fortune to be found that endures in the entire northeast corridor.

The Native Americans of this area claim to have come from the Asiatic-Mongoloid people who crossed the Bering Strait. It seems that they may have come here by way of the Niagara Peninsula and were originally of Algonquian linguistic stock. The New York tribes — Seneca, Cayuga, Onondaga, Oneida, and Mohawk — were called the Five Nations Confederacy and were part of the Iroquois Confederacy. They are also known as the League of Five Nations. The tribal council place was on Pompey Hills. Later, there were six nations when the Tuscarora tribe joined the confederacy.

The Mohawk tribe, or "people of the flint," lived in the valley. The Mohawk tribe is said to have been driven out of Canada by the Algonquians in the late sixteenth century, which was likely a reason for the constant warfare between the two tribes in later years. To further prove this may have happened, the Great Iroquois and Mohawk settlement, called Hochelaga, was near Montreal in 1535. However, in 1603, Champlain found Algonquin tribes living here. The word Iroquois is probably a French nickname from the translation of two Native American words, Hiro, meaning "I have spoken," and Cooer, meaning "approval or disapproval, depending on the inflection." The word is also said to have been an Algonquian epithet meaning "real snakes." The Mohawk were the sworn enemies of the Abenaki tribes in New England. They called them "eaters of living creatures."

The Mohawk Valley is not a Native American term, actually. Mohawk is said to mean "people of the flint" and referred to the Iroquois tribe the Mohawk, which was what the English called them. The Native American name for this valley was Cahaniaga or Agnierrnonons or "the land of Konoshioni." The Mohawk tribe were the keepers of the Easter door of the Long House. They called themselves "Ganegaono," which meant "flint owners." The Iroquois called themselves Onkweonweke, meaning "only real men." Their chiefs, or nobles, were called royaneh. The Mohawk tribe was considered the most war-like of the Iroquois Nation. They were also known as the "red-knife people" because they used copper knives.

The Mohawk tribe were very superstitious about dreams and nightmares. It seemed that nightmares plagued the Mohawk, at least it is recorded that they talked about them. It was their belief that if they turned their moccasin soles up on the ground before sleeping, the nightmares would not come true. If an enemy warrior or a dangerous animal entered their dream-world for three nights in a row, they were convinced that the dream would become reality and that the enemy or animal would kill them in the near future. If any Mohawk heard an owl the night before a battle, that event was postponed, for the owl was a warning of impending disaster. The howl of a black dog at night meant the death of a chief or Shaman of the tribe.

Native American Sites

Native American villages would usually change places within ten years, which is why it's very difficult to locate them. However, many Native American artifacts tend to be, and are, found in numerous locations. Perhaps the same tribe would have many village sites in one generation. For example, one village has been called numerous names by various explorers: the Mariaville Hill site was called Gandowogue by the Mohawk tribe; Onekagoncka in 1634 and Onekagoncke in 1642, both names were given by explorer Van Curler; Osservenon in 1642 and Oneougoure in 1646, by explorer Jogues; Carenay by explorer Vanderdonk in 1656; Adriuche by explorer Hendric Cuyler in 1686; and Kline by author W. Max Reid in 1898. It is very easy to get confused about where to hunt. To make things more complex, the names are not usually the name that was given to the village by the tribe who lived there.

In the town of Kline, arrowheads, pipes, and hatchets have been found. The Mohawk village was called Adriochten, Adriuche, or Adriutha, and was located a short distance below Amsterdam. The village was thought to be near Lewis Creek, near Adriutha Falls, also known as Buttermilk Falls. These falls were fifty feet tall in 1898 and were located in Cranesville. There are no waterfalls today, except during heavy rain. Somewhere in the area between Lewis Creek and Eva's Kill, opposite Kline, is the Mohawk village site known as Adirutha. Numerous relics have been found in the hills in the north part of the river. About one mile west is Cowilligan Creek; from the Native American word Canowaroda, it means "place of canoes" on the south side of the Mohawk River on a hill near Kline. Another village can be found on Mariaville Hill, near Mariaville Pond, called Kinaquarone. It is a rich find with many Native American relics.

Early Mohawk villages are really hard to find. Since they were called by different names and moved numerous times, there really aren't many records of them. Here are examples of where some villages may have been: In 1790, the Onondaga Castle found on Onieda Lake, or also known as the Onieda Castle, was a Native American village and where the six Nations held Council. It was a very important Native American site. The Canajoharie Castle was located somewhere on the Mohawk River and the Lower Mohawk Castle on the lower Mohawk River. There were three other Mohawk villages on the Mohawk River called Andagaron, Teonontogen, and Osseruenon. Unfortunately, that is all the information known, and this is where the luck in treasure hunting comes into play.

A Native American village was in Danube in Herkimer County. On the north side of the Mohawk River, on a hill between Fort Johnson Creek and Dove Creek, Native American artifacts were found. A Mohawk fort and village, found between Johnstown and Fonda near the Cayudutta Creek, were lived in during the 1600s and discovered in 1892. The scientists have discovered pottery, bone tools, brass and copper beads, and flint implements in a ravine near the western bank of the river.

To sum up the relationship of the Mohawk tribe to all the others who arrived in their valley, the message found at the beginning point to this region seems to say it best. On the rock at the entrance to the Mohawk Valley, there is a life-size statue that says: "Hail to the Sunrise — Mohawk Indian — the Mohawks of the Five Nations...For 90 Great Suns They Fought the New England Tribes. The New York Mohawks That Traveled This Trail Were Friendly To The White Settlers."

Schenectady

The town of Schenectady is located in the Mohawk Valley on the Mohawk River. It is a corruption of the Native American word "Schonowe," meaning "the gate" or "place beyond the pine plains," and the Dutch name for the area, Schoonachtendel. "Schoon" means beautiful, "Achten" means esteemed, and "Del" means valley. Eventually, the area was called Schenectedy. The tribal village, called Nsarcane, or Niskayuna, from 1661 to 1669, was located halfway between Schenectady and the bend on the Mohawk and Hudson Rivers. It was a capitol of the Five Nations. The early Mohawk Valley village site, Garoga, was about ten miles north of the outlet of Garoga Creek into the Mohawk River. On the south shore of the Mohawk River, past Schenectady, there was a village called Little Nose.

Hiawatha, who is said to be the founder of the Confederacy of the Five Nations, once lived in Schenectady. On the west end of Union Street, on the bank of the BinneKill, a Mohawk castle once stood. This is where Hiawatha dwelled. In the lore, the mystery of Hiawatha is that he was a great and wise man who did amazing things in life and then just seems to have disappeared. He didn't die, but was just gone.

Wonderful Waterfalls

Little Falls, located on the upper Mohawk River, were one-mile rapids and two hundred to four hundred feet high in 1755. It was the spot in 1840 where Professor Louis Agassiz found proof that the glacier covered all of New York State to the Atlantic Ocean. At that time, the Mohawk Valley was the only outlet from Lake Iroquois, now called Lake Ontario and Lake Spencer, which are called Lake Superior, Michigan, Huron, and Erie together. Eventually, the individual lakes formed and found a natural outlet to the sea, so the Mohawk Valley dried up. As an interesting side note: Lake Champlain was called Iroquois Lake by the Native Americans when Samuel de Champlain first met the tribe living there in 1609. Perhaps Champlain misunderstood what lake was being talked about.

There is also a one hundred-foot Lovers Leap located at Little Falls. The lore is that a Native American maiden and her lover, who were being chased by an enemy tribe, jumped off here to their deaths together. The darker truth may be that it was not really an enemy tribe, but just a different clan of the same tribe who chased the lovers over the cliff. Three different clans of the Mohawk Tribe lived here: the wolf, the bear, and the tortoise. Two warriors of the wolf and tortoise clan were in love with the same maiden from the bear clan. The maiden decided to be with the warrior from the wolf clan and the tortoise became jealous. He took the girl to a cave where he kept her captive. The wolf warrior rescued her, but they could only escape by going over the falls and dying together. A cave was discovered directly across from Lover's Leap.

New York's two great rivers, the Mohawk and Hudson, join at Cohoes Falls, meaning "canoe falls" or "place of falling canoe." The Dutch called the Mohawk River "Macques Kill," which is closer to what the Mohawk dialect called Gahaoose, which means "shipwrecked canoe." It was once a great fall site, now it is usually dry. The sound of Cohoes falls was recorded as early as 1642, though no one knew what those loud sounds were. In 1656, Adrian Van Der Donck visited the region and reported in his notes that the falls were 100-150 feet high and said to be falling over firm blue rocks. In 1898, they were reported as being seventy feet high, almost perpendicular, and one hundred feet wide.

Three islands are found here — Peebles, Van Schaicks, and Green Island — and they break the Mohawk River into four branches. Green Island, or San Gowson Island, is West Troy today. It lies on the west bank of the Hudson River. While the workers were building the dam here, early human remains were discovered. Prior to 1850, it was used as a camping area for the St. Francis tribe. It was also the site of the ancient Dutch settlement called Watervliet. In 1540, a Jesuit Father went to Green Island with fur traders and called the island St. Ange, place of the Holy Angel, and it is still known as Nastagione. It is not known what the Native American word means. It was also the site of a massacre in 1690.

Hudson River in Troy, New York

The Native Americans also have a legend about Cohoes Falls. Before the time of the Europeans, a young maiden was working at the riverbank when she fell asleep in a canoe. The canoe slipped off its moorings and headed down the river toward these falls. There was nothing that this girl could do and the canoe dropped over these mighty falls. It is said that no remains were ever found. In 1655, the Dutch also tell this story, except it is a Native American wife and child who is killed here by going over the falls. In 1642, another visitor said that they "could barely hear each other at this site. As you come near the falls, you can hear the roaring, which makes everything tremble, but on reaching them and looking at them, you see something wonderful, a great manifestation of God's power and sovereignty of his wisdom and glory." It must have been quite a sight to behold.

Finger Lakes Region

The Finger Lakes lie in the north-south valleys in western New York. It is believed that the lake valleys once contained southward flowing rivers, which were backed up by the dams of glacial debris formed during the ice age. The new or post-glacial drainage was forced to seek the northward course it now has. In 1779, the six Nations were occupying this area.

This region is the place to find spectacular waterfalls. In Letchworth State Park, about thirty-five miles south of Rochester, three waterfalls and the gorges can be explored. The Seneca nation lived here and are part of the Iroquois heritage. In the Naples Valley, on the southern tip of Canandaigua Lake, the Seneca called it "the chosen spot" or Kanandarque. Montour Falls are found here and are almost as high as the Niagara Falls. The Seneca called this phenomena Chequaga, meaning "tumbling waters."

Hudson Valley

Albany

The Native American tribe had many names for Albany, including Pempotuwuthut or Chescodonta, meaning "place of council fire" or "fireplace of the Mohican Nation" by the Mohicans; Scheneghtada or "through the pine woods" by the Iroquois; Gaishtinic by the Minci; and Moheconneuw, meaning "the place where the waters are never still," by the Mahican. The town was used as a council fire site until 1545, at which time the fire moved to Castleton, called Schodac, on the east bank of the Hudson River in the neutral forests around Ticonderoga.

In 1524, Verrazzano sailed up here on his ship, *La Duphine*. He called this river the LaCorande. The Mohawk Tribe, called Maquaas by the Dutch, lived on the west bank of the Hudson here and the Mahican tribe, called the Mohegans by the Dutch, lived on the east bank of the river. The Dutch called Albany, Rensselaerwyck or Fort Orange or Aurania, which is another word for Orange.

Old Schaghticoke is a Native American burial site. "Weapons of rest" have been discovered in burial sites, including a Wakon-bird stone, a rare find that is a quartz bird of paradise or dove. Fort Schaghticoke was built in 1703. On Haver Island was a Mohawk settlement, called Moenemines Castle.

Albany has five streams or kills — kills are creeks in Dutch — and the largest are Norman's Kill; Beaver Kill, also known as Buttermilk Creek; Ruttenkill; Foxenkill; and Patroon's or Mill Creek. Guilderland is a very hilly town with lots of falls. The main stream here is Norman's Kill; the branches are Bozen Kill, named derived from Boos, meaning "angry," due to the falls and rapids; Black Creek; Wildehause Kill; and Hunger Kill. The Native Americans called Beaver Kill "Tawawsantha."

In the present-day Albany area, opposite the present-day town, there was a French fort or French fur trading post called Castle Island, which was destroyed by flood in 1540 before it was completed. The island was also known as Van Renssalaer Island, Kasteel Island, Martin Gerritse's Island, and Patroon's Island. Since the late nineteenth century, it has been referred to as Westerlo Island, which was once five separate islands: Castle Island or Westerlo Island, Cabbage Island, Bogart Island, Marsh Island, and Beacon Island. This island has been constantly destroyed by flooding and rebuilt. Filling in the shallow creek and the coastal areas of the Hudson River ultimately destroyed the three smallest islands: Bogart, Marsh, and Beacon. They merged with Cabbage Island in 1929. Island Creek was still separated from Westerlo Island, the mainland, and Cabbage Island. Normans Kill, or Normans Creek, separated Cabbage Island from the mainland. In the 1930s, Island Creek was filled in, connecting Westerlo Island to the mainland. The Canadian Pacific Railway's Kenwood Yard and railroad tracks sit on the site of the original creek. A park just north of the Port of Albany is at the site of the former northern terminus of Island Creek with the Hudson River and retains the name Island Creek Park. By the 1950s, Cabbage Island had merged with Westerlo Island, but with the Normans Kill still flowing along its southern and western banks.

The Iroquois applied the word Schenectady to Albany, which makes finding any treasure very difficult if one is looking for Native American artifacts said to be in the Schenectady region but was really in the

Albany area. What the Iroquois were probably speaking of was that this Schenectady was beyond the opening or beyond the pine trees, probably in reference to the Karner sand plains. The Karner Sand Plains is where rare plants and animals are found. It is one of the only places to find a rare subspecies of a butterfly species called *Lycaeides Melissa Samuelis* or the Karner Blue Butterfly.

UFO Sightings

There have been many sightings of Unidentified Flying Objects, or UFOs, here and in Syracuse. Airplanes are reported to be taken over by unknown lights in the sky here. However, the area is also the site of great hoaxes. In 1820, Philo Cleveland, a farmer, was clearing his land when he found a stone with strange lettering on it. The lettering was as follows:

Leo X De____L.S.
VI 1520- + ^

The stone was taken to the museum of the Albany Institute and archaeologists thought it could mean: Leo X by the grace of God, sixth year of his Pontificate, 1520. L.S. was the initials of the deceased, a cross meant that he was a Roman Catholic, and an inverted U meant he was a member of the Masonic Order. They thought he was a native of Spain.

OR

Perhaps this was an adventurer from Spain who knew about the story of the lake to the north whose bottom was lined with silver, which were the salt at Salina Springs, and died. This was his grave.

OR

H.R. Schoolcraft, a scholar of the day, thought that perhaps it was a sign from a group of men that came over with Ponce de Leon in 1512 and wandered here utterly lost.

OR

Henry A. Holmes, the librarian at the New York State Library, felt that perhaps it was a memorial to a Spanish person who was captured by Native Americans and that he left this stone here after becoming a chief of the tribe.

In 1897, the stone was proven a hoax. The point here is not to believe the first item read about a region or treasure, like the silver-lined lake for instance. Researching for lost treasure means that the seeker must always be willing to read one more story about the treasure. It may be the one that proves or disproves the ultimate story.

The Catskills

The Catskill Mountains are not really mountains, but peaks that are really just lofty ground between the valleys of a deeply dissected plateau...so the Catskill Mountains are really an illusion. It is a small part of the Allegheny Plateau, which runs from Tennessee to Canada. Eventually, erosion will destroy this illusion of mountainous range and the Catskills will be no more. No wonder it is a magical place where mysterious events occur.

The region was named in 1609. The name comes from the Dutch word "Kaatskills." The word kaats, means "wildcat," and kil or kill, means "creek or small stream," so the word means "wildcat creek or stream." The Native American word for the region is Ontiora or Onteora, meaning "mountains of the sky." In 1655, the Visscher map of New Netherland showed the Catskill Region was named "Hooge Lankt van Esopus," meaning "the Highlands of Esopus." The word Esopus is an Europeanized form of an Algonkian word for "brook or small stream."

Spooky Train Trestle near Sleepy Hollow, New York

The Catskills are also known as the "Blew Mountains" or "Blue Mountains" by the British. When Henry Hudson sailed up the Hudson River to the region, he called the Hudson, "The Great River of the Mountaynes." Living in the northwest was the Iroquois tribe, known as the copper tribe, to the north was the Machian tribe, and in the west and southwest was an Algonkian-speaking tribe, located toward present-day Margaretville and Arkville. There is no gold or silver in the Catskills, but the Shawangunk Mountains showed minute traces of lead, gold, and silver, but not in paying quantities.

To the Dutch, this was a scary place filled with ghosts, wild animals, and the Native Americans. Wildcats, or Bobcats, existed here and killed not only livestock, but also people! They felt that the area was a place of darkness and doom. Even the Native Americans did not venture into the mountains very much and they usually did not have settlements there. Their oral lore says that Manitou, their great spirit, guarded the Catskills. However, there were two lesser spirits, Gitchie, the good spirit, and Mitchie, the evil spirit, that also roamed here. The Iroquois legend of this place is that the mountains were created when Ontiora, an evil spirit, was transformed into this form because of his misdeeds. Is it really no wonder that this would be a perfect place to hide lost treasures? In the places that are haunted? In the places that are haunted, there are so many spots to choose from. For example, in Glen Falls lies the famous haunted "Coopers Cave." North Creek, also known as "The Crik," is a mining town. There is also a cavern here that is haunted. Who knows what could still be hidden in these not-so-real mountains? There is a Dutch legend about a crew that could not locate the area where they buried a treasure because of a shift in the shore line and channel of Annsville Creek. They swore they would remain there forever...or until they found the gold. At low tide, people claim that the ghosts of this crew are still searching while a white hound howls.

The Native American tribes found here were the Oneida, Esopus, and Brothertown tribes. Native American rock shelters have been found in New York, New Jersey, and Pennsylvania. In Woodstock, New York, in the Catskill Mountain area, one of these shelters was discovered by Professor Max Schrabisch. Inside, many items were found, including arrowheads, bones, potsherds, and implements. The Esopus tribe lived in this shelter. A rock shelter was also found in the Shawangunk Mountains.

In the Catskills, the mountain passes are called "The Cloves," which comes from the Dutch word, Kloove, meaning "a cleft or gash in the earth." In the earlier days, the cloves were an easier access through the mountains, but it was very scary. It was common, and almost expected, for landslides and large crevices in the earth to be found. People crossing the mountains through this the cloves often disappeared. The Dutch stated that the Devil created the Catskills...that *his* footprints were all over the hills. They were perhaps dinosaur prints, but the real question is why did the Dutch say this? Perhaps it was because they believed that the Native American tribes that often went through the clove were following the Devil, but why would they think that? Perhaps it was easier not to like the tribes if this fact were true. To make it easier to believe, the loggers, farmers, and pioneers all claimed to see the Devil here and even had encounters with him.

The Native American legend of the creation of Kaaterskill Clove is that the evil spirit, Ontiora, was transformed into the Catskills for his misdeeds. His bones became the rocks; his flesh, the rising ground; and his blood, the sap of trees. He lay prone with one knee raised, his face to the sky. His forehead is vast and rough, his nose long, his eyes are North and South Lakes, from which tears flow down in streams that wrinkle his cheeks. The Clove is a deep gorge or valley lying west of Palenville. It is thought to be about one million years old. Tannery was the first use of the Clove due to the large amount of hemlock trees available. Once the deforestation occurred within a fifty-year period, Palenville became a tourist site, proclaiming to be the home of the fictional character Rip Van Winkle. There are many tannery foundations and ruins that can be found. Claryville Tannery was in Sullivan County and the Hunter, also known as Edwardsville. The New York Tannery was located at Red Falls.

Kaaterskill Falls was a prospecting place for the Dutch. This is a two-drop waterfall site in the eastern Catskill Mountains on the north side of Kaaterskill Clove. The falls drop 260 feet or 231 feet in height, making it one of the higher waterfall sites in New York. There are other waterfalls in the area, including Fawn's Leap, Buttermilk Falls, and Haines Falls, though the trails that once led to these sites are long gone.

It was in Stony Clove that most of the sightings of the Devil encounters were made. This is present-day Route 214 and it is not as scary today as it was in bygone days. Most cloves were considered places where one could see Hell. Devil's Kitchen, in Plattekill Clove, was a place where boulders were considered the pans of the Devil. In the nineteenth century, actual guided tours were given there to meet the Devil. The Devils Pulpit, a six-foot-wide and seven-foot-high rounded top, was found in Stony Clove, as was the Devils Tombstone. It is a campsite today, but campers will tell of a strange feeling that comes over them when they stare at the stone at a certain time of day. Perhaps the Dutch really did feel something and it was magnified because of the strangeness and unknown quality of the land that they came to.

Catskill's Haunted Corner

Many Catskill legends are a combination of true events and embellishments. Another example is the lore of Big Indian Creek. It is said that a Native American fell in love with an European settler who happened to be married to someone else. One day, they decided to run away together and go to Big Indian Creek Valley. They were found by the husband and he shot the Native, who crawled into a great hollow pine tree to die. The true story is that a Native American lived in the region during the Revolutionary War era. He would travel to the settlement periodically to raid and burn it and did kill a child during one of these raids. It is said that a settler hunted him down and shot him, burying the man in a "pine bower."

Quassaick Creek is also known as the Vale of Avoca. It is said that Native American ghosts can be seen paddling canoes here. Sleepy Hollow lies to the north and east of the area and is within walking distance of Tarrytown-on-the-Hudson. This is the area of an old roadway. The East India Company made a good profit in this region with the fur trade, but also with the looting and hiding of the riches found on Spanish treasure fleet ships. This is the Tapanzee Waterway, and the Pocantico River flows through here en route to the Hudson River. Called the Highland of the Hudson, it was the route taken during the Revolutionary War, so many military artifacts can be found throughout the region. The Sleepy Hollow lore is powerful and was enhanced by the stories of Washington Irving. This town is said to also be enchanted by a German doctor and Native Americans held powwows here. The Tappen Zee in the Hudson River, between Westchester and Rockland Counties, has numerous ghost legends. There is a story of a man who did not respect the Sabbath and is doomed to row this river until Judgment Day.

In Newburgh, there is a tale from earlier times. Henry Hudson told a story of the red devils dancing in the stone chambers in Newburgh. He called the area the Danskammer, meaning "dance chamber or ballroom." On his voyage in 1609, the crew supposedly saw Native Americans dancing around a fire at the site and they thought they were looking at the "Devil's Dance Chamber," so the Dutch called it Teufel's Danskammer or the "devil's dance chamber." It was a low, rocky point in thirty-six feet of water. The point was broken off in 1890 when the steamer *Cornell* rammed into it. The lighthouse was built on the fragment that fell into the water. The site was the usual meeting place for ceremonial dances. On this rock, the Native Americans would perform powwows. They would be painted in ceremonial paint, build a huge fire on the rock, dance, jump, and sing, as they saw signs of the Evil Spirit or Devil. If it came in the shape of a predator, it was a bad omen; if it was a harmless animal, it was a good omen. Peter Stuyvesant's crew also went by and were reported to be "horribly frightened by roystering devils." They thought the tribe members were reveling noisily and without restraint.

There was once a lighthouse here called Danskammer Point Light. It was demolished, and there are stories of settlers being killed at this place by Native Americans and other settlers. The point is located two miles north of Newburgh on the west side of the Hudson. The structure was forty-four feet high. In 1914, the lighthouse and lighthouse keeper were struck by lightning. Though paralyzed by this event, the keeper stayed at his post until daybreak. He was able to resume his duties after visiting the doctor.

Thunder Mountain, also known as Dunderberg, is the southern gate to the Hudson Highlands. It was said to be populated in the Colonial era by a crew of goblins. They would torment the ships that passed by there; however, if the sailors paid homage to Mein Heer, or the keeper of the Mountain, then the ship would be spared any pranks.

Hudson River

Pound Ridge was the site of a sheep shelter and Native American village. Today, Ward Pound Ridge Reservoir is the largest county park in Westchester County with over 4,000 acres. This is the place where the Delaware Tribe would pound saplings into the ground and herd animals into the area for food. There have been numerous Native American artifacts found here, as well as petroglyphs. There are places to visit called Indian Rock Shelter and Bear Rock Petroglyph. I visited this park during a very hot New York afternoon in July 2011. I was able to see an actual Delaware tribe totem and strange stone carvings. This entire region does have a feeling of eeriness surrounding it. There is no reason why this should be, but one can feel the history that abounds here. The trees seem close together and dark, with strange carvings. I can see why Washington Irving chose this place to be the setting for his scary stories. I can also understand why the Dutch felt so alone and afraid of everything here.

Kieft's War was fought in 1640-45. It was the Dutch versus the Munsee tribe. In 1643, the Dutch killed more than one hundred members of the Munsee tribe living in southern Manhattan and New Jersey, which caused an uprising. In February 1644, the Dutch army killed five hundred to seven hundred members of the tribe, including children. They encircled Siwanoy, the village here, and set it on fire. The tribe was burned alive. The settlement is thought to be near Pound Ridge in Westchester County. After learning the history of this place, it does not seem so farfetched that there really are places that give people a very uncomfortable feeling.

Delaware Native American totem — one side light, meaning creativity; the other side dark, meaning destruction.

Native American petroglyphs

4.

The Adirondacks

These mountains are found in northeastern New York, and are really the Laurentian Highlands of Canada. They are crystalline rocks. Marble was created here from the limestone base. This whole region was created in an old Silurian sea, called the Grenville. *Cryptozoon proliferum*, a spectacular form of ancient cauliflower called Eozoon, fossilized in these hills. During that time, the sea was surrounding the mountains and a barrier reef was created. When the glaciers scraped by, they exposed on the mountainsides "petrified sea gardens," which can be seen near Saratoga Springs. This species generally grew in crumbling layers that formed biscuits, or domes, and spread out over layers. The mountains do not form a connected range like the Rocky Mountains do. They are an eroded dome consisting of many peaks, either isolated or in groups.

Adirondack State Park

The Adirondacks and Catskills are probably the tops of islands with Late Devonian forests; remember that the pre-Atlantic Ocean surrounded the region during the Late Devonian era. These mountains were a moist environment, with lots of streams flowing toward the sea. Where the streams and saltwater met, deltas were formed. These deltas spread until they formed a lowland area covered by the early first forests. The first trees grew in swampy woods. Existence of these forests was discovered in 1869, when a flood raged down the Schoharie Creek and exposed fossil trees near Gilboa called Eospermatopteris. They were about twenty to forty feet high with swollen, onion-shaped bases. The roots ran out in all directions, like the present-day palm trees.

Adirondack is a Native American word that may mean, "winter-hunting season," "dismal wilderness," or "beaver hunting grounds." It may also mean an insult used by the Iroquois toward the Algonquin who traveled through here. That word would mean "tree-eater." The story behind the insult is that the Iroquois thought the Algonquin were incompetent farmers who had to eat tree bark to survive. The actual story may be that the Iroquois jumbled a word from an unknown tribe in the Saint Lawrence Valley in the 1500s. The word originally meant "they of the great rocks," but when the Iroquois used it, it became "they who eat trees or bark eaters."

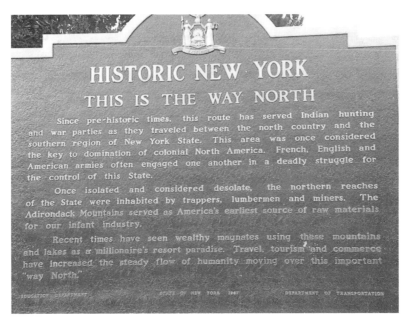

"The Way North"

In 1570, a geographer from Spain reported these mountains, calling them "the Avacal." On later maps, it is called Irocoisa. The Iroquois name for the mountain region is Cauchsachrage, meaning "Beaver Hunting Country." The Native American name for the mountains is Aganuschion, meaning "Black Mountain Range," or Hodenosauneega, meaning "hilly place." They have also been called the "Mountains of St. Marthe" and "Corlear's Mountains." Another name for the mountains by early settlers was the Peruvian Mountains; French explorers are said to have called the mountain this, supposedly named because of the mineral treasure, magnetite, found here.

There were many battles with the Algonquin from Canada fought in the region. It was considered a dark and bloody ground and a dismal wilderness. When the Europeans first started to go to this region, it was so dark with the shade of Evergreens that they would whisper "it was the dark country." There is still a feeling about this place, sometimes called a spirit of place, and as D.H. Lawrence once said of the area, "the doom here that must be atoned for seems to whisper in the very dark trees." Even the Native Americans felt these dark woods should be avoided, so there was no permanent Native American village here. The region was used as hunting ground or a battlefield only. Many war and hunting implements have been found here. It is probably best described as a buffer zone between the Iroquois and Algonquin tribes.

Adirondack Park is the largest in the United States. Covering 5.7 million acres, the park is larger than the state of New Hampshire. The bedrock of this range is thought to be 1.2 billion years old.

Officially, the range was discovered by Samuel de Champlain in 1609. It has a dark history. It was thought that it was through here that the Mohawk tribe traveled after leaving Canada and was called the "way north," passing through Clifton Park. It was thought to be the prehistoric path for Native Americans and lots of battles were fought here with bloody and horrifying results.

There are over one hundred peaks ranging from 1,200 to 1,500 feet in height and the mountains are still growing. Some of the highest peaks here are: Algonquin Peak at 5,114, Haystock at 4,960, Skylight at 4,926, Whiteface at 4,867, Dix at 4,857, and Giant at 4,627. This entire region is also known as "The Wilderness" or "The Wilderness of New York" and "Great North Woods." Ouluska Pass, on Mount Seymour, is a Native American name, meaning "place of shadows." The Adirondack Pass, also known as Indian Pass, is a huge gorge between two mountains, Wallface and McIntyre. The pass is northeast of Lake Henderson, and is one mile long and, in some places, over 1,000 feet high. The Native American name is Henodoawda, meaning "path of the Thunderer." It was so named because of the sounds created when a thunderstorm enters the gorge.

Adirondack Mountains

The highest peak, Mount Marcy, was called Tahawus by the Native Americans; it is said to mean "he splits the sky," stands 5,344 feet, and is over a mile wide. This place was not climbed until 1837. It is considered the oldest mountain on Earth and is the source of the Hudson River. Summit water from a lake called Lake Tear of the Clouds, or Lake Tear for short, is the beginning of the mighty river. This tiny lake sits between Mount Marcy and Skylight. The lakes are very cold, which is one of the reasons there are no fish here. It annually overflows and re-fills with melted snow. This process is called "scouring." The original name, Tahawus, is not really a place, but, to the Seneca-Iroquois tribe, an expression that literally means "it cleaves the sky." It refers to an expression of truth so powerful that when uttered by a human being it ascends to the heavens and is an effort to penetrate the realm of the abode of eternal truth. The mountain points upward to the heavens as an ever-present physical reminder of the supremacy of truth.

Important waterways in the area are the Hudson, Black, Oswegatchie, Grasse, Raquette, Saranac, Schroon, and Ausable rivers. The glacier created over 1,300 ponds in the region, as well as causing many waterfalls and rapids in the rivers. Among the lakes that were created include Lake

George, The Fulton Chain, the Upper and Lower Saranac, Big and Little Tupper, Schroon, Lake Placid, Long, Raquette, and Blue. Sacandaga Lake is a Native American word, meaning "drowned land," though, ironically, it is a man-made lake.

Lake Avalanche was once part of Lake Colden, but was cut-off due to avalanches. Opalescent River glitters with labradorite or opalescent feldspar. It is usually a rich blue color, but sometimes it is green or even gold. There is a legend here of a place called Lost Pond. This body of water has never been seen by any living person. It is said that two men did visit this place, but died after telling of it. It is said to exist in Long Lake Township, somewhere on Seward Mountain, near the Cold River — and it is said to have the best fishing in the world.

The Clintonville Pine Barrens is a nine hundred-acre region that is home to two rare plants and two rare moth species. The Clintonville is a pitch pin-heath barrens that sit on a sand delta deposited 12,000 years ago by glacial melt water. The sandy, well-drained soil gives life to the unique pine barrens natural community.

The Saranac tribe had a temporary summer village here. It was at the end of an Indian carry that ran from upper Saranac Lake to Stony Creek, near Spectacle Ponds, that connected with the Raquette River. There was an old path here called the Eaglenest Trail of the Saranacs, with a clearing at the end, which was a council place. Arrowheads made of red flint have been found throughout the area and there is a Native American lead mine here, but the exact location is unknown. It is said that the mine is located between two lakes, north of Rainbow Lake and south of Mountain View. North Elba was the site of another summer village in Essex County. The story here is that Rogers Rangers destroyed this village on their way to Canada. However, there is no real proof of that to be found. As an interesting side note: There is evidence found of a battle between the European and Native Americans on the Boquet River, but exactly who fought is in question. There really aren't many Native American legends of this region, though there is the story about an old Indian face that appears in lower Ausable Pond. Saranac Lake was called the "dark cup" by the tribes that traveled through. Lake Placid, Tupper Lake and Saranac Lake are known as the "Tri-lakes Area."

Whiteface Mountain, in the Lake Placid region, is where one of the finest views of the Adirondacks can be found. The Lake Placid outflow is a major contributor to the Ausable River. Rainbow Falls, found on the river falls, is seventy feet high. Whiteface can be found in Wilmington in Essex County. The Mohawk name was Theianoguen, who was a famous Mohawk chief killed near Bloody Pond in Lake George during the French & Indian War. The Algonquin name for Whiteface is Wahopartenie, meaning "it's white." There is an apparition effect known as Viloa's Rings or "The Spectre of the Brocken" found here.

Lake Placid itself could actually be two lakes because an island splits it in two. In the extreme southern end of the eastern part of the lake, there is a small body of water called Paradox Bay. It is connected to Lake Placid by an inlet that was famed for a strange event that occurred here. The flow of the water through the inlet used to reverse its direction at short and regular intervals, first forward and then backward. Early books tell of this phenomenon. How and why this happened is not known. It ended in 1890, when the inlet was deepened.

Some of the Native American names probably have very interesting stories and may hold the locations of treasures still not found today. Stony Creek Ponds were called Wampum waters; wampum was the money used by Native Americans.

It was difficult to get through these woods. Roads through these forests were once paved with logs called corduroy roads and definitely not easy to travel. However, perhaps there was one reason to try to maneuver through these woods. Sunday Rock is located on the Raquette River at South Woods. Since 1925, there has been a plaque here that stands at South Colton, also known as Three Falls. This was considered by the pioneers as the gateway to the woods and a way to freedom and happiness. Who called it Sunday Rock? Was it the river loggers, a person who held religious services there, or a merchant who went fishing there on Sundays? No one knows. Over time, it became a place for wishes to come true and for ghosts to appear.

Along the Hudson River, in the Lake Sanford area, a skeleton was discovered at Cranberry Lake. A hunter found a body buried here, which, it is said, was taken out by a doctor to examine, and no one has seen it or heard about it since.

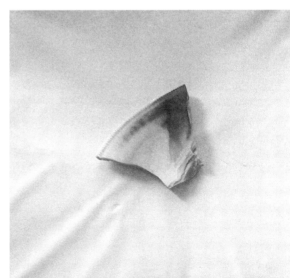

Wampum

Woods in New York

Lake George

Lake George was created during the Ordovician Period by the thrust of a rock lying down in the sea against the edge of the Canadian Shield. This immense collision created the White, Green, and Berkshire Mountains. It also caused the crack in the shield called Logan's Fault, creating Lake Champlain and Lake George. Streams once flowed in and out of Lake George. Though dry today, one flowed south from Northwest Bay through a vanished gap; glaciers dammed the gaps with debris, between Pilot Knob and French Mountain. Another now-dry stream flowed north of Tongue Mountain and may have run past Rogers Rock and into a no-longer existing gap to join the rivers flowing out of Lake Champlain. The four Ice Ages scoured all the material from the Lake George region, which, at five hundred million years old, is the oldest coral reef in the world. Fossils have been found on the Isle La Motte, located northwest of Plattsburgh.

A two-mile great carrying place by Native Americans was from the head of Lake George to Lake Champlain. It is reported that the Earthquake of

1663 caused the forests to be overthrown and streams cast out of their old channels and into new ones. The earthquake came from Logan's Fault. It is thought that more earthquakes could occur on that fault as it continues to this day to stabilize.

Lake George is, ironically, called "Queen of American Lakes," though it is named George. The entire region was called Lake Horicon, or Les Horicans, by the tribe living here, meaning "silvery waters." Another Iroquois word for the lake is andiatarocte, meaning "where the lake is shut in." The French name for Lake George is Lac du St Sacrement. Lake George was first seen by Father Isaac Jorgues, a French Jesuit Missionary, in 1646.

Lake George

The Champlain Valley Corridor was a borderland between two Native American enemies; in other words, this entire region was a battlefield. Artifacts over 8,000 years old have been found. The battles were between the Iroquois and Algonquin Nations, specifically the Mohawk and Abenaki tribes. After the Native American tribes stopped fighting here, the English and French continued the tradition between Lake Champlain and Lake George. The fighting did not stop there, though, as the area became known as the bloody frontier during the American Revolution.

Lake George Battlefield today

Saratoga

Saratoga is the European interpretation of the Iroquois word Serachtague, Kayaderoga, or Saraghoga, meaning, "place of swift or rapid waters" or "hillside country of the quiet river." In the Iroquois language, Saragh means "swift water" and aga or oga means "the place of or the people of," so Ticonderoga means "the place where the lake (Lake George) shuts itself." Sacandaga means "place of the people of the roaring water" and Niagara means "place of the falling waters." It is said that Saratoga Springs was considered "smelly water" by the tribes here. It is also thought that "soragh" is a Native American name for salt, and thus the name means "the place of salt or salt springs." There is also a spring near here called Chalybeate, which was another name for the Saratoga area in earlier times.

Centuries before the Europeans came the Hoosac and Mahicansac tribes claim they had fishing villages and had built fishing weirs at Ochserantogue, the place of swift waters of Fish Creek, which is the outlet of Lake Saratoga. It became the national fishing and hunting grounds for the Abenaki tribe. The Horicons and Algonquins of the Adirondack and Ticonderoga fishing grounds knew Fish Creek as Saratakee, the place where the muddy moccasin heel of the Mohawk and Huron showed on the rocks. Fish Creek became the place of herring and a war trail between the Mohawks and Hoosac tribes well before the settlers arrived. Arrowheads are often found on the banks of Fish Creek. On the south side of Fish Creek, ancient Native American pottery was found in 1874. One Mohawk chief, Tha-yen-da-ne-gen or Joseph Brant, his English name, stated to settlers on Fish Creek that a treasure had been buried here during the Revolutionary War era. Exactly what was buried or by whom is not documented.

An abandoned home in Saratoga, New York.

Saratoga is a region known for strange happenings and rich treasures. To start things off, Lake Saratoga can be seen from every compass point: it can be seen in the south from the Catskill Mountains, in the west from the Kayaderosseras Mountains, in the north from Palmertown Range and French Mountain near Lake George, and in the east from Potash Kettle, near Luzerne. This makes the area very unique. Lake Saratoga is five miles long and was considered the best Mohawk hunting grounds. Bear Swamp, located on the east side of Saratoga Springs, was the "place where game abounds." It was a very scary place to the settlers, much like the Black Forest was to the German people. It is thought that strange mirages can be seen here. For example, water appears on the road and illuminated buildings can be seen in the middle of the swamp. These are all what is called cloud refraction properties, but, in an earlier era, these sightings would have been terrifying.

Lake Saratoga

There are three bodies of water that surround and drain the swamp. Lake Lonely, also known as Little Lake or Owls Pond, is where echoes occur. Round Pond is a clear, small, and black water pond. Black water ponds occur throughout the region and are places where anything can happen, good or bad. The third body of water is Barhydt's Lake. At one time, rare swamp flowers were found here, including the Water bean; ladies slipper or Chid; Indian Moccasin; a fern called the Adder's Tongue, and Lobelia Cardinalis. Also known as "Indian Bright Eye," the Lobelia Cardinalis can also be found on Bloody Pond near Lake George.

The Native American legend of Lovers Leap of Lake Saratoga starts like this. During the war of the Six Nations and the Algonquians of the North, a chief of the Algonquians was captured by the Mohawks. He was condemned to die on the following day by the slow torture of impalement. While he was a prisoner in a cabin, the daughter of the Sachem brought him food, fell in love with him, and decided to save him. They descended the hill near Ramsdell's Cove, but before they reached the water, the cry went up that he was missing. They reached a canoe, but the war party followed. They tried to flee on the opposite shore, but the tribe continued to follow. They reached the rest of the hill overlooking the lake. Not wanting any of her tribe or her lover to die, she decided that they should die together. Clasped in an embrace, they jumped over the cliff and perished. Another Native American legend is a superstition attached to the lake: the Mohawks believed that its stillness was sacred to the Great Spirit and that if someone spoke unflatteringly about the water, the canoe of the offender would instantly sink.

A Native American village was located on the Kayaderosseras Flats and had been there for thousands of years. Lots of Native American artifacts are found here, including stone hatchets, scalping knives, fish spears, pestles, and pottery. In the mid-1800s, one extremely strange relic found was a Native American skull with a tomahawk in the back of his head. There have been many battles and wars fought here, and the entire area is considered dark and bloody. The grounds are called Kayadrossera, ironically meaning "land of the beautiful lake or the winding river." It was the hunting and fishing grounds for the five Nations. Needless to say, the tribes did not like the settlers being here and did everything they could to discourage settlements. Between the years 1642 and 1645, the Iroquois retaliated against settlers near Mount McGregor. This was a war trail and it was used by the tribe in 1690 for the Schenectady Massacre. A year before, it had been used when the Iroquois headed to Montreal. In 1693, it was used when the French went to destroy the Mohawk tribe.

Mount McGregor, north of Saratoga, is called the King's Station area. It is a Native American battlefield, long known as an Indian burial ground.

Jacques Cartier heard of Saratoga Springs in 1535. The incredible curing water was located thirty miles north of Albany, in the foothills of the Adirondack Mountains. Jacques had just discovered the St. Lawrence River and heard of the magical curative powers of a spring that came from a rock near present-day Saratoga.

In 1767, a Mohawk medicine man, called War-ra-ghi-ya-ghy, told the settlers of the medicinal properties of "High Rock Spring or Round Round," thus began the story of the Saratoga mineral springs. This magical water was found on the Ballston Lake Road to Saratoga, to the springs of a tributary of Lake Saratoga called the Kayaderosseras. These medicinal springs are said to contain various proportions of muriate of soda and carbonates of soda, lime, magnesia, iron, and acid gas. The recommended uses for this water are bilious, dyspeptic, or calculous complaints. It can be used for diseases of the skin or chronic rheumatism. Once discovered, the queen of spas was created, Saratoga Springs. In 1767, Sir William Johnson, who was wounded during the Revolutionary War, came to this spring on a stretcher. The Native Americans led him here, and he drank the water, which the Native Americans said was a cure for almost everything. He was able to walk away from the springs after drinking the water. Today, this particular spring flows beneath the ground.

Suddenly, one day, the High Rock Spring waters receded. The St. Regis tribe who dwelled on the banks of the Mohawk River had an oral legend about why this happened: A sorcerer held orgies at the spring and animals were often killed when the sorcerers came to drink. One day, a beautiful girl came to bathe, but there was something very wrong or the girl was sick and the water recoiled and retreated forever, and so the poem continues:

> ...far in the forest's deep recess,
> Dark and hidden, and alone,
> Mid-marshy ferns and tangled wood,
> There rose a rocky cone.
> Deep printed in that beating heart,
> Forever to remain,
> In spite of tears, there was a guilty stain.
> The guilty one in frantic fear,
> Filled with desponding shame,
> Nor was she ever hear of more,
> And no one recalled her name.

Author's Note: There was a peculiar smell in Saratoga when I visited in 2011 — was it due to the polluted Hudson River or the sulfur in the water here?

Hoyt and Little Falls are built on foundations of lime-secreting algae known as Cryptozoon, also known as fossil cabbages. This algae seems to contain a high degree of radioactive potassium, which may be one reason for the therapeutic value of the Saratoga mineral waters.

Even the buildings in Saratoga today are haunted, perhaps due to the unique water found here? The Canfield Casino was built in 1870 by John Canfield. In 1907, gambling was outlawed in town, so now the building is the Saratoga Historical Society and it is considered very haunted. Other ghost stories abound in Saratoga County. For example, a Dutch family filled up their well because it was haunted by a headless woman killed there by Canadians and Native Americans in 1748. There is also a haunted site in Little Falls called Beards Castle. It is a restaurant today, and footsteps, as well as screams, are heard. Ghosts have been seen and suicides have occurred.

The year 1832 was a strange time in New York. Meteors were seen throughout the year all over the state. The moon was a deep gold color. No birds were seen in Saratoga at all and the woods were reported to be silent that year. Could it be that the horror of the battles fought on this ground gave it an eerie feeling that even nature stayed away? What was going on?

Saratoga Battlefield

Cannon from Battlefield

Thousand Island Region

The Native Americans called this area, Man-i-to-anna, meaning "garden place of the great spirit." The Iroquois legend about this place is that when God was summoned to Heaven, one thousand flowers fell and created the thousand islands in this narrow channel of the Saint Lawrence River between Canada and the United States. However, there are actually between 1,800 and 2,000 islands documented, according to the National Geographic Society. All these islands were settled by Native American tribes and numerous artifacts are reported discovered here.

Buffalo, Niagara, and Lake Erie Region

The Niagara River is not really a river — it is a gorge, channel, or strait that joins the upper lakes with Ontario. It is also the place of the most treacherous white water found in the world. It was created during the last era of glacial melting, called the Wisconsin Thaw, about 50,000 years ago. This thaw actually carved out most of the major waterways of North America east of the Rockies. This is a serpentine, winding river course. Niagara Limestone was created in the sea that existed 425 million years ago. This vast ocean stretched from Chicago to New York. There are lots of sea fossils discovered here. As an interesting side note: the St. Lawrence River is not really a river. It takes the water of all five Great Lakes to the Atlantic Ocean. It is really the last link to the single-most important, longest, navigable inland water system on Earth. The Great Lakes are really freshwater oceans that cover 87,000 square miles. The five lakes are: Lake Superior; the twin lakes, Huron and Michigan; Lake Erie, and Lake Ontario. All the lakes eventually drain to Lake Ontario.

An amazing and strange discovery was found of Celtic origin: ungrooved axes and hatchets. Where did they come from? Perhaps through trading with the Native Americans of the region? Originally, the Niagara area was the territory of the Attiwandaronk and Kahkawh, also known as the "neutral nation." However, even though they were an Iroquoian tribe, they were annihilated by the Five Nations. Many artifacts have been found in this region, including pottery, spear points, knives, Hammerstones, net sinkers, hoes, axes, polishing stones, beads, vessels, and pipes.

Buffalo is known as "Queen of the Lakes" or "City of good neighbors" and is the home of Niagara Falls. Niagara was a Native American stomping ground and were occupied, until 1698, by the Mohawk, Erie, Huron, Tuscarora, Neuters — called this because they were a peaceful tribe — and Seneca tribes.

Niagara Falls

Niagara is an Iroquois word meaning "a neck" between two bodies of water or "thunder of waters." Niagara Falls are two falls; on the American side, they are called Rainbow Falls and on the Canadian side, Horseshoe Falls. These twin cascades were probably one waterfall about 10,000 years ago. The thunder sound — the pure power of the falls — must have been a place of wonder, awe, terror, and worship for anyone who lived near there.

The mysterious mound builders are said to have lived here about 2,000 years ago. We do not know much about these people. The Mound Builders came from the Ohio Valley and vanished before the settlers arrived. The settlers found seventh-century pyramidal burial mounds in the vicinity of Niagara. What happened? No one knows. The Iroquois tribe took over the region and even they have no lore explaining what happened.

The Niagara tribes created two principal deities: Holder of the Sky and Great Voice. The Holder of the Sky represented wisdom and the Great Voice represented fear, war, and natural disasters. According to legend, Native American maidens were sent over the falls on the first full moon each spring to satisfy the Great Voice. Always be wary of legends and explore the lore deeply. They are fun to listen to, they can make stories exciting, and sometimes hold an element of truth, but this one is not true — the Iroquois did not make human sacrifices! However, people did die at these falls. Numerous daredevils have tried to defy this magnificent falls site and most died while trying. The holy grail for the tight-rope walking community was crossing Niagara Falls. In earlier times, walkers would try to cross the 1,100-foot gorge directly below the falls, usually only holding a pole for balance. Stephen Peer had actually accomplished this feat a number of times, but, in 1887, it is said that after drinking with friends he attempted the walk one more time. He fell to his death. Niagara Falls was completely frozen in 1911. It must have been a very cold year. There are very rare photos of this amazing event.

There are five islands on the Niagara River before one reaches the falls: Squaw Island is found at the mouth of the Scajaquada Creek; Strawberry Island is found in the center of the river; Grand Island, the largest island in the river, is seven miles long and was forested; Goat Island is where the lower falls starts; and Navy Island is the second largest island, located directly opposite the mouth of Usher's Creek. After Navy Island, the divided channel becomes one channel again.

There have been Native American artifacts found along the banks of the Niagara River, including copper tools from as far away as Wyoming, war clubs with fangs of bears, and wampum belts. The portage of the falls was nine miles. It started at the east bank, just above the upper rapids, and terminated at present-day Lewiston, New York. It was considered the most difficult portage in North America — a person actually had to creep on all fours in some sections, just above Lewiston.

Taughannock Falls, near the head of Cayuga Lake, plunges 215 feet. They are the highest waterfall east of the Rockies and thirty-three feet higher than the Niagara, though the Niagara Falls, over limestone and the gorge, is lengthened about one mile each year. At Taughannock Falls State Park on Route 89, about eight miles north of Ithaca, the Continental Army came through here in 1779. This same army came through the Finger Lakes region. The Cayuga tribe lived here when the Army came through. This place is named based on a legend: Chief Taughannock of the Lenape Tribe was thrown over the falls to his death after a battle with the Cayuga tribe.

As an interesting side note: Predicting into the future, it is thought that as glaciers occur Buffalo will be under ten million tons of ice in the year 10,662.

Pirates, Military, and Shipwrecks!

Supernatural Loot!

Sewanhacky, on Long Island, means a "place of shells" that was used for wampum by the tribes.

Isle Royal is an island in the St. Lawrence River, off the port of Waddington in Lawrence County. The lore is that treasure was buried here by the French Commander of the fort in 1760. The worth is somewhere between $10,000 to $100,000. Treasure Island is another island on the St. Lawrence River, between Louisville and Roosevelttown on County 37, in Lawrence County. It is so named because during the Revolution Lord Amherst buried $100,000 here.

Also during the Revolution, Tories hid a large amount of plunder in a cave in the Shawangunk Mountains, outside of Summitville, in Sullivan County. Another Tory legend takes place at Butlersbury Mansion. Built in 1742, this mansion was located on Switzer Hill, near Fonda, in the Mohawk Valley. This was the home-base of the Tory Raiders, John and Walter Butler. During the Revolution, they raided the Patriots homesteads all over the Valley and buried this plunder somewhere near the mansion.

In 1776, Tory Robert Gordon is said to have buried $75,000 in the marshes, called The Haven, on the Poultney River, on State Highway 4, about a mile northeast of Whitehall in Washington County. He was killed by Patriots, though, and his treasure was never recovered.

The town of Berne is where mineral springs are found; these springs are sulphurous in nature. It is also the battlefield between the Tory's and Patriots, with the Native Americans, during the Revolutionary War. Two stockades existed near Middleburgh, and plunder is said to have been abandoned in the region during the battle. With terrible torture having occurred on both sides, this is considered a massacre site.

The Sulphur Springs Treasure, buried by a traveling salesman between North Pitcher and Pitcher in 1900 near the ruins of the Sulphur Springs Health Resort, contains two chests of treasure. Gold coins have also been found in the area.

Marshy area in New York.

Farmer Tracy Maxwell is said to have buried $135,000 in paper currency and jewelry near his barn. His farm was located two miles west of Surprise in Greene County. In Peekskill, a Dutch farmer claimed that he constantly saw the ghost of a British Spy who was hanged here by General Putnam.

The Loomis outlaw gang is said to have buried $40,000 in Montezuma Swamp, located near Seneca Falls, on County 96 in Seneca County. They were considered horse thieves, counterfeiters, and arsonists. Another band of outlaws buried gold coins near or in Wynd or Wind Cave near the town of Knox, on County 157A, in Albany County. During the 1930s, gangster Dutch Schultz is said to have hidden an iron box containing over $7 million in paper currency, gold coins, jewelry, and uncut diamonds in a stand of pine trees on the banks of Ecopus Creek, about five miles south of Phoenicia, in the Catskill Mountains. In the same area, a bootlegger in 1935 is said to have hidden $2.5 million dollars of gold coins and paper currency, but closer to Phoenicia or perhaps he buried the same amount in paper currency in an iron box on the northern side of the Ashokan Reservoir.

A Revolutionary War treasure is said to be buried near Yankeetown in Woodstock. Local farmers said that a pyramid of rocks was the marker for the treasure. During the 1930s, a silver spoon with a Masonic emblem was found on a Woodstock farm where it was said that a "box of silver and a pitcher of gold" was once hidden by the family.

A Revolutionary War British paymaster hid $150,000 in gold coins near the northern tip of Lake Colton, near the town of Colden. The Bennington Battlefield is located on Route 67 near Walloomsac in Washington County. A major battle was fought here in 1777. Another Revolutionary War battlefield is located off US 20, between Sharon and Sharon Springs, in Schoharie County. This battle took place in 1781. Treasure hunters have found artifacts in this area. A payroll chest that was for the American military of the Revolutionary War was buried on-shore in Chaumont Bay under a large oak tree. It has never been found. In Kingsbridge, legend tells of loot being buried around the home of W.O. Giles, who was a Tory anticipating defeat in the Revolutionary War. A gold coin was found with the date 1772 nearby.

In Manchester, on Cumorah Hill, also known as Morman Hill, Gold Bible Hill, and Inspiration Point, is the place where Joseph Smith said he found the set of gold plates that he translated into English and published as *The Book of Mormon*. According to Smith, this name was revealed to him in a vision as a hiding place of gold plates and it has since been applied to the hill.

At the peaks of the Blenheim Mountains, it is believed that Native Americans raided settlements and hid all the valuables they stole from the settlers in the region. It is interesting to note, though, that Native Americans did not usually climb the mountains. In the Ramapo Mountains, gold and silver plate and jewels were found.

After a train robbery in 1895, the $40,000 taken was put in an iron kettle and buried about a half-mile from Geneva. Presently, it would be east of the Big Oak Golf Course and Pre-Emption Road. In Goshen, there are stories of a chest of gold buried on Crabtree Island, and in Vernon Township, $100,000 is said to be buried. Outside the town of Warsaw, $45,000 of gold coins were buried on Rogers' farm about two miles west of town during the Depression.

In the early 1800s, hermit Moses Follensby buried $400,000 in gold and silver coins close to his cabin. The cabin was at the north end of Follensby Pond, where it enters the lake. The treasure is thought to perhaps be southwest of Tupper Lake on Follensby Road. In Royalton, near the northern part of town, $7,000 in gold nuggets was found near a shanty. It is believed to be part of a miser's fortune found in an old wooden box... perhaps more remains hidden.

Sacketts Harbor, during the War of 1812, was attacked twice by the British. The residents had to flee, perhaps leaving many artifacts behind. In Hicksville, on Long Island, there is a story about a wealthy recluse burying $750,000 in gold and silver coins. In 1960, a bulldozer operator found one container containing $89,000 in old coins. It would seem that perhaps this treasure lore may be true.

A copper Celtic ornament was said to have been found in Westchester County, perhaps on Croton Neck. Treasure hunters are scared away by phantom British troops and Revolutionary ghosts in Pelham, Westchester County. Even Hessian ghost soldiers are found here. Bedford is the battlefield that has been haunted by Dutch and Native American warriors since 1644. Many of the reports describe the ghosts as headless.

Cooper's Beach, Long Island

Cooper's Beach was voted second best beach in the country, after Myrtle Beach, in 2010.

Military Forts

Ticonderoga is an Iroquois word meaning "forks of river" or "between lakes." Mount Defiance and Fort Ticonderoga were used as look-outs for a vital, narrow choke-point that controlled travel along Lake Champlain in the eighteenth century, as it was an important portage between Lake George and Lake Champlain.

There are many Native American relics to be found in Ticonderoga. The seeker should hunt for artifacts between Sandsea or Zandige Creek and Schoharie River. Crown Point Campsite, located off the west end of the Lake Champlain Bridge in Essex County, was where a battle was fought in 1609. Samuel de Champlain killed members of the Mohawk tribe that were raiding other Native American villages there.

FORT NASSOUREEN is found on Castle Island in Lake Champlain and was a Dutch fort in 1615, but was swept away in 1618. The French built FORT FREDERICK in 1731 and then blew it up in 1739, before the British could take it over. The French then built FORT TICONDEROGA, or FORT HUNTER or FORT CARILLON, in 1755. Later, the British built FORT CROWN, but accidently burnt it in 1773. Ruins of both Fort Frederick and Fort Crown are still in the region. Crown Point comes from the French translation of the Native American word Chevelure, meaning "scalp," probably for the battles and massacres that have occurred here. In 1908, the Pell family purchased Fort Ticonderoga. Ironically, there were many old artifacts from other eras still there. One of the Pell's sons tried to fire one of the cannons left and it exploded, killing him instantly.

New York had many forts built by the people who lived there. Every group that has settled in the Empire State would either take over the fort currently standing or build a new one over the old ruins. These military sites are a treasure trove of artifacts. However, they were active forts with battles waged around them. They are also the site of mass burial grounds and, at times, horrifying and painful death, so it's not surprising that many of these places are very haunted with ghosts and have bad, uncomfortable feelings surrounding them. For example, there are claims that a treasure trove is buried near the Jeffery Amherst Fort, located in Essex County. Another example is Cataroqui Lake, an Iroquois word meaning "fort in water." It is thought that they meant Fort Frontenac, which was built by the French in the eighteenth century.

FORT AMSTERDAM was built in Manhattan in 1653, but, amazingly, in spite of the history that surrounds the region, this particular fort never saw battle. Today, the former fort lies under the Custom House in New York City.

New York Harbor forts were the first line of defense at the narrows, the area between Brooklyn and Staten Island. Any enemy entering the Harbor would not be more than 1,000 feet from cannon. As an interesting side note: Britain did not ever try to enter the New York Harbor during the War of 1812, though they did capture Washington D.C.

Manhattan's only lighthouse was built in 1775, off Fort Washington Point. Today, it would be at the foot of 180th Street and the Hudson River. It "had one gun" and was also known as Jeffrey's Hook. It was probably the only lighthouse built *not* to save ships from wrecking, but to *sink* British ships during the Revolution. A British Revolutionary fort, called FORT GEORGE HILL, was built in 1781, east of Broadway and 190th Street. During the Dutch settlement era, it was known as Round Meadow and, in the Revolutionary era, it was known as Laurel Hill. *Author's note: In Saratoga, there is another place called Laurel Hill, which is also known as Snake Hill. Magnetite or Lodestone was discovered there. There is also a geologic oddity found on the hill. Snake Hill is probably the stump of an ancient volcano. Snake Hill is an early name, from around 1810, for the abundant amount of rattlesnakes found halfway up the hill. This is one reason why it is so easy to get confused about treasure sites and place names. Sometimes, the names are exactly the same in the same state.*

FORT WASHINGTON was built at 118th and Ninth Avenue. There is a pond here. While it was being built, workers discovered a deposit of shells and pieces of flint. It is thought that it was probably a summer camp for the tribes. When the British captured Fort Washington, there were eight forts that formed a semi-circle, marking the outer defense of the Americans to the north and east, across Spuyten Duyvil and the Harlem River. British buttons and arrow points were found here in 1890.

CASTLE CLINTON was built in 1808 at West Battery Park to protect the city and guard the Hudson River. Later, it was called Castle Garden. In 1896, it became the New York Aquarium. The wooden door was the actual gateway to Castle Garden when it was a fort. Originally, the fort stood two hundred feet offshore and the workers built a man-made island for it. Battery Park rocks are now under the structures of the park. It was named because in 1693 cannons were placed on these rocks in a line extending from the foot of Greenwich Street to the intersection of Whitehall and Water Streets. In 2006, a rock wall was found, which was part of the fort sea wall in 1766-67. This find proved that the coast was much further inland at that time than it is today due to the landfill. The ruins of two other Revolutionary War forts, Gage and George, are located nearby. Fort George is located in Battery Park.

Earthen forts were found at Ward's Point, which was also known as Billopp's Point during the Revolutionary War era. The Patriots fired on this town on July 25, 1776 from Perth Amboy, New Jersey, and British troops fired back, killing one person here. The Ward Point Battery was part of the Spanish-American War in 1898. It was built to guard the channel leading into Staten Island Sound and make it impossible for a hostile vessel to get past Sandy Hook, and into New York Harbor, by going through Arthur Kill. In 1902, this site became the Sea Breeze Amusement Park. For some reason, it seemed to attract a rowdy crowd and someone was killed here. The place closed and eventually was claimed by the sea. In 2008, pilings of the former dock could still be seen at low tide.

Revolutionary War FORT #8, constructed by the British, is found in the Bronx. FORT #4 and FORT INDEPENDENCE were also built here. On the Bronx East River shoreline, over $3 million in English gold lies buried from ships that sank in the East River throughout the centuries.

In Brooklyn, the Battle of Long Island was fought in Prospect Park in 1776. It was the first battle fought in America as a new country and it was a terrible, bloody battle. The British retreat occurred over Gowanus Creek. There were four battles fought here: Battle Hill, Greenwood Park, at the junction of Fifth, Flatbush, and Atlantic avenues, and at Old Stone House. Other forts found here include FORT STERLING, FORT GREENE, FORT HAMILTON (now known as Fort Lafayette), FORT DEFIANCE near Red Hook on the East River, and FORT PUTNAM. During the battle, the bodies of those who died were buried on a small knoll or island, which is now Third Street, that runs across the area between 7th and 8th Streets. The graves are now well-beneath the ground.

FORT OSWEGO was located near Lake Ontario while FORT ONTARIO, built in 1726 by the British, is found at the mouth of the Oswego River, opposite Oswego. Only ruins remain today.

Not surprising, the Mohawk Valley also has numerous forts. There are FORT HERKIMER, FORT HENDRICK, FORT CANAJOHAIRIE or FORT PLAIN, FORT SCHENECTADY, and FORT JOHNSON; they were all built along the Mohawk River, which was also known as the Canajoharie River by the tribes living here.

FORT HUNTER was located where the Schoharie and Mohawk valleys join along the Mohawk River, also known as Caughnawaga. Most of the stones were used for the building of the Erie Canal, but some ruins remain. FORT DAYTON is found on the edge of Herkimer, near the junction of NY 28 and US 90 in Oswego County, along the Mohawk River. This was a stone fort built in 1722. FORT KLOCK was located in the Mohawk Valley, along the river, on NY 5 in Montgomery County. It was built as a trading post in 1750; much of it still survives today.

For thousands of years, there was an ancient trail that connected the Mohawk River and Wood Creek. This was the only link between the Atlantic Ocean and Lake Ontario. It was called the Oneida Carrying Place because it was located in the Oneida tribe region. Because this trail was so important, there were many battles fought for control of this six-mile trail. Fort Stanwix, in the beginning, was a fortified trading post at the head of the Mohawk River in 1725. It was a perfect post because it was located on the Oneida Carrying Place or Deo-Wain-Sta. Today, nothing remains of this site.

Fort Standwix was built by the British to protect this land in 1758. The Pontiac Rebellion began because the Native Americans in the region were dissatisfied with British rule and wanted them out. The fort, located in Rome, west of Little Falls, was also known as Fort Schuyler. The Battle of Oriskany was fought near here in 1777 and was considered one of the war's bloodiest battles. Paul Revere founded the brass and copper works in Rome in 1801. The town of Utica was settled on the original Fort Standwix site.

Albany was first a Dutch trading post, and they built Fort Nassau on an island in the Hudson River in 1614. It is the second-oldest settlement in the original thirteen colonies. The Dutch also built Fort Albany in 1618, Fort Carilo on the outskirts of Rensselaer in Rensselaer County in 1630, and Fort Aurania or Fort Orange at Albany in 1652. Apparently, they felt threatened and vulnerable to attacks. Fort George was located at the foot of State Street, and Fort Frederick was just a few blocks up the hill, at the other end of the street. The notorious criminal Samuel Green is said to have hidden some of his stolen loot in the area. Albany Post Road was known as Edgar's Lane in 1644. Washington's army camped on the Hudson River somewhere near that road.

Old Stone Fort was built in Schoharie in 1772 as a church, later becoming a Revolutionary War fort in 1777. It was attacked in 1780. A three-pound British cannonball can still be seen in the wall. It is haunted. Footsteps and organ music has been heard and male apparitions are seen. The 1930s organ is still there. A cemetery surrounds the fort and screams are said to be heard there. Captain Christian Brown was in command of the fort when a woman died there during childbirth. The Schoharie Valley, near Middleburgh in Schoharie County, was settled around 1700 by the Palatines. The remains of the old stone fort were located in present-day Gallupville on NY 443. Legend says that settlers hid their valuables before a Native American attack in 1734; all of these settlers were killed during the attack.

Bear Mountain on the Hudson River, at the junction of Interstate Parkway and US 9W in Washington County, contains the ruins of Fort Montgomery and Fort Clinton, which were both captured by the British during the Revolutionary War.

FORT DELAWARE is located north of Narrowsburg on NY 97 in Sullivan County. The site was built in 1750, but the Delaware River has eroded most of it. FORT EDWARD was located on Rogers Island in the Hudson River, connected to the city of Fort Edward by NY 97 in Saratoga County. This area was a Native American carrying place. FORT ST. GEORGE is located off the William Floyd Parkway, near Smith's Point Bridge and Mastic Beach, on Long Island.

At Fort Tryon Park, all that remains today are the earthworks built by the Patriots during the Revolutionary War. FORT KEYSER, near the Palatine Bridge, was located in the area of Stone Arbadia, a 20,000-acre area, in the Mohawk Valley. It was built long before the Revolution and was in ruins at that time. Within two miles of this fort were FORT FREY, FORT WAGNER, and FORT PARIS. FORT LAFAYETTE is hidden somewhere near Verplanck's Point on the Hudson River, opposite Stony Point.

FORT PUTNAM, called "Fortress West Point," was built in 1780 and located within the military academy of West Point. Constructed to protect the Hudson River, it was considered a key defense fort. FORT BREWERTON was located on US 11 near Brewerton on the western edge of Lake Oneida in Oswego County. Only the earthworks remain today. This fort protected the route between Fort Ontario and Albany — and was used during the French and Indian War and Pontiac's Rebellion of 1763-1766. FORT ANNE was also built to protect the Hudson River. FORT ERIE was on Lake Erie, but, before the American troops left, they blew it up. FORT DECKER was in Port Jervis. There is also an unidentified pirate treasure thought to be buried somewhere in town.

Shipwrecks

• The HMS *Hussar* sank in 1780 off Hells Gate with $4 million in gold and silver coins. Some were found by divers in 1965 in the East River.

• The HMS *Lexington* sank in 1781 in the East River with $1.8 million in gold onboard.

• A chest containing $200,000 fell into the New York Harbor at dockside from the ship *Romah* in 1928.

• The steamer *Great Western* was wrecked in 1876 in the East River. There are still artifacts and cash under the water waiting to be discovered.

• The steamer *Black Warrior* wrecked off of Rockaway Beach in 1858. The cargo is still loaded and artifacts can still be found.

Long Island beach

• The steamer *Acaria* wrecked in 1902, near Jones Inlet. Some artifacts have been recovered by divers.

• The ship *City of Norwich* sank in 1866, off Huntington, with $50,000 onboard.

• The cruiser USS *San Diego* sank in 1902, ten miles off Fire Island, and was found by divers in 1960. The cargo was $17,000 in copper.

• The ship *Elizabeth* sank in 1850 on the Fire Island sandbar with rare Italian stones and $16,000 in coins.

• The sidewheeler *Savannah* sank in 1819 and is now buried under Sand Bell Port. This was the first sidewheeler steamer to cross the Atlantic Ocean.

• The liner *Oregon* sank in 1886 in Long Island Sound with over $1 million onboard. Some has been recovered over the years.

• The sidewheeler *Benjamin Franklin* sank in 1854 on the sandbar off Moriches Neck. Much of this wreck has been recovered, but more could be buried beneath the sand.

• A seventeenth century "money ship" is thought to be buried in the sand. Coins from that century have been found. One known wreck off Fire Island was the Dutch ship *Prins Maurtis* in 1657, carrying a great deal of treasure. Many artifacts have been recovered on Fire Island, located just off Long Island. Wrecking was a common vocation here. In 1688, it was called "Five Island," but misread as "Fire Island." Legend of the name says that there were pots of whale oil that glowed on the beach all night, aiding the wreckers. *As an interesting side note: Democrat Point, the western tip of Fire Island, was the first state park on the Atlantic Ocean and a beach where lots of artifacts were found.*

• An unknown schooner was wrecked at Shinnecock in 1816. The Spanish gold coins found on the beach are believed to be from that ship.

• The steamer *Rodo* wrecked off Fire Island in 1908 with $100,000 worth of copper onboard.

• The ship *Ann Hope* sank off Fire Island in 1781 with $500,000 onboard.

• The ship *Pacific* wrecked off Fire Island in 1871 with a cargo of clay pipes. Many have been found on the beach.

• A Spanish frigate, *San Jose*, sank off Fire Island with $500,000 onboard.

• Off the New York shore, in the ocean, the freighter *Oregon* sank in 1941 with more than $3 million of Marino Wool as part of the cargo.

• Off the New York shore, in the ocean, the British liner *Republic* sank in 1909 carrying $2 million in gold.

• The ship *Vineyard* sank in 1836, off Southhampton, with about $54,000 in gold and silver.

Numerous ships were wrecked in the vicinity of Montauk Point, the eastern part of Long Island. One of the richest wrecks here was the American privateer *Marey*, lost in 1763, carrying $100,000 in gold coins and bullion. German gold and silver coins have been found on the beach

Montauk Point in Long Island.

in Montauk, thought to be from the German immigrant ship *Herbert* that wrecked in 1710.

On the State University of New York college campus, located about four miles south of Oswego on Lake Ontario, silver coins have been found. It is believed that they may have come from the sailing vessel *Lady Washington*, which was wrecked here in 1803 carrying a very valuable cargo.

Long Island Lighthouses
Montauk Point Lighthouse

This lighthouse was commissioned by George Washington. You can see Block Island from the top. The tribe called this island Paumanok because of its fish-like shape. The Dutch called this island Seawanhakie, meaning "island of shells." It is the largest island adjoining the continental United States.

Montauk Point
Lighthouse

Devils Belt

Long Island Sound was called the Devils Belt on maps in the eighteenth century and ranges from thirty to three hundred feet deep. The drastic depth change is why there are numerous lighthouses in the body of water. PLUM ISLAND LIGHTHOUSE is located on Plum Island, the largest of the three islands that extend northeastward into the Sound from Long Island. GULL ISLAND LIGHTHOUSE, on Little Gull Island, has been re-built many times due to bad storms and great military battles. Great Gull Island is the site of a former military fort. RACE ROCK LIGHTHOUSE, or Race Point, is located on a land mass that is considered to be one of the most dangerous underwater hazards in the eastern end of Long Island Sound. Not only is Fishers Island considered one of the top-rated golf courses in the nation, but it has also been the scene of numerous shipwrecks, including the *John & Lucy* in 1671, the *Providence* in 1678, and the *Atlantic* in 1846. The NEW LONDON LIGHTHOUSE is considered one of the most haunted places in the northeast. It is seen just before entering the Thames River, near New London, Connecticut. The NEW LONDON HARBOR LIGHTHOUSE, also known as the Pequot Lighthouse, is found at the mouth of the New London Harbor.

New London Lighthouse — Long Island Sound
— considered most haunted lighthouse in Sound.

It was completed in 1761 and is one of the first lighthouses erected in the American colonies. EXECUTION ROCKS LIGHTHOUSE is on a deserted island in Long Island Sound and is extremely haunted. Prisoners of War would be tied to the rocks to await the tide. As it rose, they would eventually drown.

Race Rock Lighthouse

Plum Island Light

Little Gull Island
Lighthouse

The Author's Adventure

The trip across Long Island Sound by ferry was very exciting for me in the summer of 2011. Even the eighteen-wheeler trucks go into the belly of the ferry to cross. The compact cars actually go above the rest of the cars; there is two-tiered parking on the ferry. I get disoriented when I go out to sea. Even in a harbor, with land and islands all around me, I just cannot figure out how to orient myself. Sailors of any era constantly amaze me. I can see why some sort of compass or Lodestone magnetic needle was needed to navigate out here. It was overcast when I headed toward New York from Connecticut, but the sun did backlight the sky at the horizon. It looked eerie, but absolutely beautiful.

Long Island Sound Lighthouse

Orient Point Lighthouse

On the return trip, there was an incredible, violent thunderstorm occurring as we crossed. It was scary, but once the ferry got through it — beautiful sunshine and rainbows emerged. The thunderstorm clouds behind the most haunted lighthouse in Long Island Sound, the New London Lighthouse, makes for an amazing photo.

Fisher's Island — considered one of the best places in the world to golf.

Great Gull and Little Gull Islands in Long Island Sound

Pirates & Pirate Treasure

The area that welcomed the most pirates was East Hampton. The most treasure is thought to be buried on Gardiner's Island, Oyster Bay, and Sayville. This place was the most isolated on Long Island in the 1600s, the pirates' golden era.

It is said that the Devil's Footprint can be found just off Orient Point in Long Island. The boulder is known as Devil's Rock and on top exists a huge footprint that is said to have been created by the Devil. This story starts in Montville, Connecticut. As the Devil was on his way to Long Island, he left his first footprint at the old Mohegan church there. The second step, with his right foot, was left on Shelter Island in Long Island Sound. The impression of the heel is deep, but the toes are lost. Tradition states that the third step was on Orient Point and the last was on Montauk, where he fell into the sea. It is said that if anyone makes a wish when they place their foot into the footprint in the rock, the wish will be granted. It is also reported that no horse could pass this place without rearing in terror. The legend continues by stating that Captain Kidd murdered a woman on this island. Perhaps she was killed to guard a treasure buried?

Sea Skeleton

It is a fact that Captain Kidd stopped and buried treasure on Long Island. Kidd buried the treasure toward the eastern end of Long Island, on Gardiner's Island, in 1699; part or most of it has been discovered. The gold doubloons and pieces of eight were hidden under a marked granite stone in Kidd's Hollow. The Native American name of this island is Manchonet, meaning "the place where many have died." Ironically, the island remained untouched and no one died here during the bloody Pequot War that raged in New England. According to legend, John Gardiner, also known as Lion Gardiner, the owner of the island during that time, rescued Wyanedanoch's daughter from an outlaw; Wyanedanoch was the Sachem or chief of the region and he gave Gardiner the island as a reward. There may be a grain of truth that something happened here because King Philip would not have spared the island during the Pequot War for no reason. Whatever circumstance saved Gardiner from the brutal Pequot War did not last long. In September 1728, the French and Spanish attacked the island and stole all the family's belongings while John Gardiner was tied to a mulberry tree and had to watch. The reason the French and Spanish gave for attacking him was that he was harboring pirates. Perhaps that was true, but there were no pirates found during the attack. Apparently, if they were there, they fled before being apprehended.

Money Pond Trail

It is also said that the attack was actually from a band of about eighty pirates. This band had French, Spanish, and mulatto that terrorized the family on Gardiner's Island and tied John up while they looked for anything valuable. It had nothing to do with Kidd's treasure once being found there.

On Montauk Point, there are two small ponds located at the foot of the hill where Montauk Lighthouse stands. They have been called Money Ponds ever since Kidd's era, supposedly hiding his treasure. One is even said to be bottomless. There is a spot called Kidd Valley on his private island; numerous symbols on the rocks are believed to be clues to where his treasure is hidden. Pirates were also seen at Fisher's Island, north of Gardiner's Island. Coins found on the shore, however, could be from the numerous wrecks off-shore.

There is also a place called Money Hill, south at Croton-on-the-Hudson, where a great treasure is said to exist. Smuggling abounded in earlier times here. After Kidd died, privateering was still popular. The ships that were recorded as being privateers were the *Saratoga* in 1812 and the *General Armstrong*, the *Scourge*, and the *Prince de Neufchatel* in 1813. During the War of 1812, over one hundred ships had permission from New York to be a privateer crew.

In the early 1800s, a pirate named Charles Gibbs is reported to have buried a large treasure in the vicinity of Southampton Beach on Long Island. River pirates in the eighteenth century are said to be based in the vicinity of West Point Military Academy, where they supposedly buried many caches.

The pirate Joseph Bradish is said to have stopped at the east end of the island and his ship sank between Long Island and Block Island. Now, this is where pirate legends can be confusing and probably were to the people of that era. Kidd was known to be in the region. He had a ship named the *Adventure Galley*. The lore of the area says that Joseph Bradish's pirate ship, named *Adventure*, sank in 1699 with $2 million onboard. Are the reports confusing two different pirates? No one is sure. What is known is that Bradish was captured and hanged as a pirate. He was also reported as being a much worse pirate than Kidd. Whatever happened, Bradish is thought to have buried several chests of treasure at Orient Point, on the northeastern tip of Long Island, in the late eighteenth century.

Peekskill

One of Captain Kidd's treasures was sunk in the Hudson River off Jones Point opposite Peekskill. The treasure was scuttled during a storm. In the nineteenth century, this treasure was searched for, but the only person who made any money on the deal was the promoter who ran off with most of the investors' cash.

From the Hudson River, opposite of Peekskill on Royal Island, there is a story of Kidd's treasure. Supposedly, he salvaged the treasure of a ship that sank off the point of the island in thirteen-foot deep water and twenty-seven-foot deep mud. He buried this recovered treasure, said to be $100,000 in gold and $200,000 in silver, before he buried the treasure at Gardiner's Island.

Pirate treasure is also thought to be buried in a cave overlooking a bluff on the Hudson River, called Stony Point, just south of Peekskill. The gold and silver in Kidd's treasure is buried in Bear Mountain State Park. After Kidd's death, his crew supposedly arrived at Dunderberg Mountain at Stony Point to split more treasure. A storm was raging, so the ship was scuttled and the pirates took as much treasure as they could carry and hid the remainder. Though many have tried, no one has been able to find this treasure. Kidd's Plug is part of a steep cliff on the Hudson River, called Cro' Nest, and is said to conceal a cave in which Kidd hid some of his treasure.

In 1696, Albany settlers reported that pirates were at the mouth of the Hudson, including Kidd. On the Hudson River, the narrowest place is called Kidd's Point. There is lore that buried treasure is hidden in that area. It was known as Nassau Island during the pirate heyday.

An interesting side note: Peekskill is one of the only places in the world that has an emery mine. Emery is one mineral that is found next to Magnetite or Lodestone.

Mountain Treasures

There is a legend of a Captain Kidd treasure in the Catskills. A tragedy is said to have taken place with a Spanish girl who was believed to have been Captain Kidd's bride: she murdered by a person named Ballridge, who kidnapped her to ransom for Kidd's treasure, believed to be buried in Kaaterskill Clove on a slope of South Mountain. However, this story may be another telling of a true story. In 1762, well after Kidd was hanged, about eight miles north of the Clove, a member of a rich family is said to have murdered a servant girl by having her dragged behind a horse. He was proven innocent, but it was an interesting tale to tell by a roaring fire in a very strange place. Pirates were always great people to tell stories about, so the legend of Captain Kidd, his buried treasure, and a true murder tale was born. *As an interesting side note: the famous Sleepy Hollow is located at the foot of Kaaterskill Falls.*

In Newburgh, it is said that boys buried a stolen church bell in the swamp here, now one of the Downing Park's lakes. It is said that one can still hear it ringing on summer evenings. Fort Anne or Ann is found midway between Fort Edward and Whitehall on US 4 in Washington County. At Fishkill Landing, on the east bank of the Hudson River, opposite Newburgh, earthworks called Fort Hill were built by Patriots during the Revolutionary War. It is said that Washington himself camped here. It is interesting to note that stories of Washington sleeping everywhere is almost like Kidd burying treasure everywhere. Take both stories with a grain of salt or really research the region to see if the claim is even possible at least.

The story of the sunken treasure chest of Robert Gordon starts in 1775. He left New York heading for Canada where he thought it would be safer for his family during the Revolutionary War. He packed silver in a chest and sank them in a lake somewhere in a marsh. He was killed before he could retrieve the chest. Based on what is known, the location of this chest was sunk in the marsh is along the narrow navigable canal portion of Lake Champlain that is to the northeast of Whitehall and along the western shore of West Haven. However, with dredging and water movement, the chest may have moved further north, but the marsh in the drowned lands is very weedy and dense. There is a main road across for the canal from Adirondack Park.

Niagara Region

Fort Niagara is located at the mouth of the Niagara River on Lake Ontario near Youngstown in Niagara County. This fort controlled the Great Lakes during the colonial era. The French built a fort here in 1726, and it is also known as a "French Castle." The surrounding area could yield many artifacts and the fort is considered a haunted site. Hundreds lost their lives here. In an earlier era, a man was beheaded and it is said he rises from the well. As recently as 2010, footsteps and doors slamming have been heard here, and visitors have reported being touched.

The Devil's Hole Massacre occurred in 1763. Basically it took place between a British troop, formed from Roger's Rangers, and about three hundred Seneca warriors. The tribe believed that the British were trying to take over their territory, and ambushed a wagon train and its armed escort en route from Fort Schlosser to Fort Niagara. Devil's Hole is a heavily wooded area with a deep ravine on either side of the trail at this time. It was a very difficult terrain to navigate and it was the perfect place to attack. About eighty British were scalped and thrown into the ravine. Though the British retreated from this attack, the massacre was supposed to force the settlers to leave, but it only reinforced the British's desire to stay here. Eventually, the British successfully cut off the Seneca tribe from the river and, in doing so, cut off their traditional and only transportation route and source of food and water.

The wealthy French merchant, Clairieux, is said to have buried several kegs of eighteenth century coins near the ruins of his home and store on Grand Island in the middle of the Niagara River between Buffalo and Niagara Falls. In 1888, a cache of sixteenth century silver and gold coins were found near the ruins of a round stone building. During the French & Indian War, some French raiders are said to have buried fifteen chests of treasure somewhere on the island.

In 1893, the steamer *Dean Richard* sank close off-shore at Jerusalem Cors on Lake Erie about ten miles south of Buffalo. The ship contained $191,000 in gold and silver coins. On the Lake Erie shore, about half-a-mile east of Port Colborne, on County 58 in Ontario County, numerous gold coins have been found. Perhaps they are from the steamer *Anthony Wayne*, which wrecked here in 1850 carrying over $100,000 in gold and silver coins. It is about ten miles west of Buffalo.

Silver Creek is located about eight miles northeast of Dunkirk on County 59 on Lake Erie. It is named due to the large number of silver coins found on the beach after a storm. These probably come from the steamer *Atlantic*, which wrecked here in 1852 carrying over $60,000 in coins. The wreckage can be seen on the beach of Lake Erie about four miles northeast of Barcelona, County Road 60 in Chataqua County. Gold and silver coins have been found in the area. In 1873, the steamer *City of Detroit* sank here carrying over $200,000 in gold and silver coins and a large cargo of copper ingots.

Old coins can be found all along the Erie Canal route. The workers of that time also left many artifacts of the era. The canal is 363 miles long, traveling between Buffalo and Albany and was completed in 1825.

INTERESTING SIDENOTE: In 2004, Bigfoot became a protective species in Whitehall. There have been Bigfoot sightings in the Adirondacks for hundreds of years. Even Champlain wrote in his logs the legends of this creature told to him by the Native Americans. The Iroquois and Algonquin tribes called the monster the Stone Giants or Giants of the Mountains. It seems that this town is in the middle of a migratory path of Bigfoot. Think that sightings only happened in the past. The most recent sighting in Whitehall was in 2007. Other towns that have reported sightings of this creature are: Ira, Port Jervis, Newfield, and Amityville. Perhaps there is something unknown and mysterious about this region after all.

Bloody Battlefields

Lake George

Lake George is also known as Bloody Pond, due to so much blood spilling into the lake and discoloring the water during the 1745 Saratoga massacre. Fort Esopus was built by the Dutch near Kingston in 1615. This town was totally destroyed by the British in 1777; the new town was built over the old. There is another body of water, called Bloody Pond, near the present town, located on the east side of Route 9, two miles south of Lake George Village. Over two hundred people were thrown into this body of water after a battle. The water was said to have been stained for weeks and since that time this stagnant pool has been called Bloody Pond. It was the site of a battle, actually the third battle of Lake George in 1755. After the British surrounded the French stationed here, they opened fire and killed everyone. Old Military Road, Route 9 today, was the major road for all military operations during the Battles of Lake George. Numerous artifacts from a battlefield can be usually found along the travel route.

Bloody Pond Road

Bloody Pond in Lake George

Fort William Henry

This fort was built on the south end of Lake George by the British. It is the site of a horrible battle in 1755 that resulted in a massacre when General Marquis de Montclam, with French and Canadian troops and over 1,500 Native Americans from various tribes, burned the fort to the ground, killing all those inside. There is lodestone to be found here, which has been connected to amplifying the effect of very haunted places. Marching sounds and footsteps are heard throughout the fort, and visitors have claimed to be touched during tours.

Fort William Henry

Lake George

Thirty-two miles long and 196 feet deep, there are 176 islands on Lake George; eventually the lake drops into Lake Champlain through the LaChute River, also called the Ticonderoga River. The islands in Lake George have a strange legend about their creation. The story goes that these are sand islands and a new one rises every four years, during a Leap Year. Some of the islands are Three Sisters Island, where Major Rogers camped on March 14, 1758 after the defeat near Ticonderoga; Dome Island, the highest island, is where soldiers used to watch for enemy movements on the lake; Phantom Island, where a hermit lived alone for six years and went insane; Fourteen Mile Island was a battle site between the Patriots and British and Mohawks; and Diamond Island, located in the middle of Lake George, was a military depot for Burgoyne's army during the Revolutionary War in 1777, the same year it was attacked. Diamond-like Quartz found in limestone exists here. They were sold as

Lake George

Lake George Diamonds. The island was also the home of Sampson Paul, a Native American who killed an eight-foot panther with a fishing spear as it swam in the lake. The Algonquin and Iroquois would meet here to smoke a peace pipe, perhaps because it was in the middle of the lake, making ambushes difficult.

Other islands include Recluse Island, the site of the earthquake hoax of 1868 — newspapers in New York claimed the island had sunk eighty feet below the surface of the lake during the earthquake — and Tea Island, the southernmost island and nearest to Diamond. There was a teahouse once here, hence the name, and it was a Revolutionary War lookout. It was also the place where colonial troop pay and supplies were kept while the attack was happening at Fort William Henry. There is a dark story that a person was hanged on this island for stealing the troop's pay and now it is supposedly haunted by his ghost. The pay, as well as gold, is said to be buried on the island. The story continues that the man's descendants may know where the gold was buried. It is also said that General Ambercombie may have buried treasure here, but the details are vague.

In the Ticonderoga region, there are three different treasure stories: Gold and silver coins are thought to be buried near Old Fort Amherst at Crown Point; another story tells of a cache being buried near the banks of Long Pond by retreating British troops during the Revolution; and the last Native Americans are believed to have buried a great deal of loot in the Mount Pharaoh Range a few miles north of Ticonderoga.

Warship Wreck

Warship wreckage from the French & Indian War, 1755-1760, lies underneath the water in Lake George. With its north-south axis, the Hudson River was considered a connecting river between New France and New England in colonial times. Thus, the numerous battles that took place in the Lake George region were for control of the river. Once the war was over, many ships lost in combat were located in the back waters of the lake and ended up at the bottom, awaiting future discovery.

Military Dock

Lake George...where warships may still lie beneath the surface.

Hundreds of easy-to-build bateaux carried troops and supplies during the war; the British would sink these at the southern end of Lake George during the winter — to store them where they would be safe beneath the water and ice — until spring came and the war would resume. British reports state that some of the ships were never recovered. In the 1960s, divers found some of these bateaux and the archeological work continues to this day to find and recover these war relics.

In 1990, divers discovered a wooden wreck in 108 feet of water near an old sunken bateaux in Lake George. It is the oldest known warship wreck in America and the only known example of a radeau, or a floating, self-propelled gun platform.

Lake George Bateau Wreck

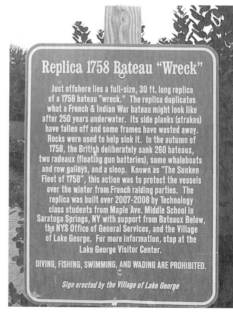

Shipwright Samuel Cobb of Maine built two radeau's on Lake George in 1758 to assist a planned British assault on Fort Ticonderoga. This vessel was named the *Land Tortoise* and was never mentioned in British reports again after it was not recovered.

Saratoga

Two of the bloodiest battles of the Revolution were fought in what is now Saratoga National Historical Park, located on the Hudson River near Bemis Heights, in 1777. Many lives and artifacts were lost during the ferocious fighting. It was actually fought in Schuylerville, also known as Old Saratoga. The German or Hessian soldiers fought with the British here. The battle lines are drawn with posts. The blue posts are the lines of the American defense and the red posts are the British lines. The American troops were basically from New York and Massachusetts. Author's note: The cannons here today are replicas. At an earlier time, the original cannons were on the field, but people stole them. Please leave the parks as you find them. Leave footprints only and take only photos. Always ask permission, if you want to search for artifacts.

Blue means the American defense line.

Saratoga Battlefield National Park

Red means the British attack line.

The cannons are actually facing the direction where they were located during the battle. As you drive through the park, there is an eerie feeling and a sense of history. The American and British lines were half-a-mile apart. The dead were buried where they fell on the field, though burying is a loose term — they were left where they fell. It is strange to know that you are walking on the graves of unknown soldiers. The rangers told me that there were many artifacts still underground here. As an interesting side note: the American cannons are facing away from the British Line. This is not a mistake. It is because the Americans were positive that the British were coming from the south up the Hudson River. They just could not believe that the British would go over the Hudson River Bluffs and over the Bemis Heights hills. The Americans were wrong! The American forces protected the road to and from Albany and the Hudson, thus forcing the British to have to go through thick woods and swamps. The British had a hard time using the artillery they had brought. This battle was considered the turning point of the Revolutionary War.

Cannon at Saratoga — British or Hessian?

It is said that the British buried several treasure caches on the northern shores of Lake Saratoga. Fort Saratoga, now Schuylerville, was a Revolutionary War Fort, located about eight miles from Saratoga at Bemis Heights. It was built in 1691 on the west bank of the Hudson River about a mile south of the current village of Schuylerville. The Saratoga Monument today is the place where the British camped after the Battle of Saratoga on October 17, 1777. They were starved into surrendering after being surrounded by the American forces. A graveyard was also established at this monument, and though digging here is not allowed, the guides state that numerous Revolutionary War artifacts remain in the ground. Many soldiers died in the battle — their ghosts still visit this enticing region.

Cannon at Saratoga — Patriot — notice the strange looking flag of that era.

Saratoga battlefield

Saratoga Monuments at Victory Woods.

This whole region is very familiar with violent battles. In 1673, a battle was fought in Saratoga between the French and the English. The French won and ruled the region. During Queen Anne's War in 1709, a fort was built on the mouth of Batten Kill to protect residents from attacks. In 1745, the massacre of Saratoga occurred — all of the residents were killed. It was a prelude to the French and Indian War.

The British landed here from the Hudson River to come behind the American forces at Saratoga.

Precious Gems, Mines, and Ghost Towns!

Wine Red Garnet is the New York state gem. This means that this gem has been and can be found all through the state. One famous mine is the Barton Garnet Mines. This is the major supplier of garnet to the world. Guided tours are available here. Another site, Hooper Mine, is an abandoned, open-pit garnet mine. One needs permission to enter the site. Both mines are located in the Siamese Ponds Wilderness, off Route 28.

On Long Island, Montauk Point is made of Ronkonkoma terraine. The glacier picked up rocks full of magnetite and garnet from Connecticut and brought it to the beaches here.

Some New York minerals include gold; millerite, which is the richest ore for nickel; halite, which is rock salt; Ilmenite, large crystals; hydromagnesite; tremolite; peridotite; beryl; brown tourmaline; rose quartz; fresh-water pearl; chondrodite; emery; garnet; silver; Titanium; Zinc; Zircon; Mercury; and marble.

The Adirondack Mountains was the first place where raw materials were mined in the United States. Some minerals found in the Adirondacks are magnetic iron ore or Lodestone, graphite, garnet, wollastonite, pyrite, zinc, marble, zircon, various gemstones, and titanium, to name just a few.

Sand dunes on Long Island — what pirates and settlers first saw when they arrived here.

Gold, Silver, and Copper

A lost gold mine near Mount Colden, called the Adolphus Lavigne Lost Mine, is in the middle of Hamilton County while the Lost Truman Hurd Gold Mine is said to be located near the Ashokan Reservoir.

In Jasper, there are stories of a lost silver mine, as well as a treasure cave to be found in Cohocton Valley. The story has existed since the French & Indian War era. Two Quaker brothers named Dickinson came to the area to trade with the tribes in the region. The tribe told of a silver mine, somewhere along Bennett Creek. The cave is said to have a copper kettle filled with the silver, and two ghosts guarding the silver. The Lost Nippletwon Silver Mine is somewhere in the southwest corner of Warren County. A miner, Rufe Evans, buried a cache of silver ore around the village of Accord. The last lost silver mine in New York is said to be in North Elba. William Scott found a silver mine on Nye Mountain, but could never find it again.

Henry Hudson claimed that the Lenni-Lenape tribe discovered a yellow copper mine near New York City. His journals state that there was a "white green cliff" on the banks of the Hudson River that held either a "copper or silver myne." This area was thought to be the Palisades of the west bank of the Hudson River.

Fossils

The first mastodon remains found by Europeans in North America were in Claverack in 1705. Another remain was discovered just a year later, in 1706, in Coxsackie. Many skeletons of mastodons and mammoths have been found in the mud of once-existing glacial lakes. During the glacial period, the weight of the ice depressed New York several hundred feet. The sea came up the Saint Lawrence River at this time and flooded Lake Champlain. Pleistocene-era marine clam shells have been found in the freshwater lake. Mastodon remains have also been found in peat deposits in the Harlem River and Upper Manhattan. These are amazing finds. The lower jaw, foot bone, and head with tusks of a mastodon were found in September 1866. This animal was here 10,000 years ago, pre-glacier. The skeleton was on view in 1867 in the "State Cabinet of Natural History" in the State Capitol Building in Albany. West of Albany, mammoth bones were discovered mixed with gravel in a glacial pothole.

The New York fossil is the sea scorpion, *Eurypterus remipes*. At the fossil site at Eighteen Mile Creek in Erie County, numerous Middle Devonian brachiopods were excavated, including:

- Spinocyrtia granulose
- Mucrospirifer mucronatus
- Meristella barrisi
- Athyris spiriferoides
- Tropidoleptus carinatus
- Pustulina pustulosa
- Productella truncate
- Atrypa reticularis
- Camarotoechia Sappho
- Rhipidomella Penelope
- Stropehodonta demissa

Along the Hudson River, many bones of Phytosaurs from the Late Triassic and Early Jurassic eras have been found. The name means "plant lizards"; however, these dinosaurs were carnivorous and resembled a modern crocodile, but with a bulging forehead and slender jaws with nostrils close to the eyes. They lived in swamps and slow-moving streams. Their prey was probably fish.

Rensselaer Plains was created by beach sand inter-mixed with purple and white quartz and bluish-colored rocks filled with marine fossils. The olive shales start near Lake Ida, found east of Troy, pass northeast through Schaghticoke, and then reappear near the Cambridge Hills in the Owl Kill Valley.

Oysters

The entire New York Harbor was filled with oysters at one time; so many, in fact, that Liberty and Ellis islands were called Great and Small Oyster Islands. Pearl Street is New York City's oldest thoroughfare and named because of the number of pearly shells found near it on the beach. This street was once the shoreline of the East River. The Dutch found shell heaps here, and originally it was called Mother of Pearl Street. As an interesting side note: the logs of the *Mayflower* show that the group almost decided to sail up the Hudson River instead of stopping at Plymouth, following the oysters for food.

In Tottenville, oysters grew here in the brackish waters of Arthur Kill, Raritan Bay, and Prince's Bay. Oyster beds were closed due to pollution in the Hudson River early in the twentieth century. By 1927, the last beds were closed in Raritan Bay. Outbreaks of Typhoid Fever were traced to the oysters of the lower bay and the Kill Van Kull. Arthur Kill became one of the most polluted waterways in the country.

Abandoned Places

Cobble Hill, also known as the Atlantic Avenue Tunnel of Long Island Railroad, is an abandoned railroad tunnel beneath Atlantic Avenue in downtown Brooklyn. Gowanus Canal is the site of abandoned wharves.

Ferry and Cliff streets were once known as the "old swamp." It was the northern boundary of the city and numerous tanneries were located here. In 1905, when buildings were being erected, old tannery vats were found containing tan bark over one hundred years old.

Eleventh Avenue is also known as Death Avenue, where trucks of New York Central Railroad once were. The tracks have been buried, but numerous children were killed here while climbing between the cars.

In Troy, there is an abandoned road called the Cherry Valley Turnpike. Built in 1798, the road was from Albany to Cherry Valley, Utica, and Rome. This path was used for many years before the road was actually built. There were lots of taverns along the road and hundreds of wagons and stages used this road.

The Tottenville Copper Company was erected on both sides of Mill Creek, extending to Arthur Kill, in 1900. It is the site of the old Dissosway Mill. The smokestack could be seen for miles, and it was a copper refining mill. Copper is called the "red metal." The mill produced bands for navy shells during World War II.

The Ballston River is a pre-glacial river running north from Schenectady. Always follow ancient and old river channels. Often, minerals and gems are found in these old riverbeds. For example, there used to be many brooks and rivers in Long Island. Though most are extinct today, one can see the dry brook beds, brinks of waterfalls, and potholes. This is one place where a treasure seeker could find rare minerals and gems.

There are more old water channels to explore. The Rutten Kill used to run through Pearl Street in Albany. Perhaps it was a source of pearls in early times? The ravine of the Rutten Kill is 350 feet wide and fifty feet deep; today, it is used as part of a sewer. It is a neglected, filthy place, yet somehow fitting because this was the last place where gallows were used for public hangings in 1827. Rutten Kill is a traditional name referring to one of the three major streams that flowed through colonial Albany and emptied into the Hudson River. Today, the stream is entirely below surface, still running under modern buildings. Prior to European settlement, a total of five streams flowed through Albany: Rutten Kill; Vosen Kill, meaning Foxes; Beaver Kill, all underground today; Patroon Creek; and Normans Kill, still aboveground. Sheridan Hollow was carved by Foxen Kill and Tivoli Hollow was carved by Patroon's Creek. Empire State Plaza is over the ravine created by Rutten Kill. Lincoln Park is located in the hollow created by Beaver Kill. Washington Lake Park is the end result of damming the remaining part of Rutten Kill aboveground.

Starbuck Island, across the Hudson River from Troy, New York.

The abandoned village of Adirondac and the Tahawus Mines is not open to the public. The mines are located by Henderson Lake and Calamity Brook; iron and titanium were mined here. There is a deserted village to explore near Cold River called Adirondack Iron Works. At one time, magnetic iron ore was mined here. Rock Pond Mine are the ruins of a mine that existed in Pharaoh Lake Wilderness.

In Griffin, old foundations remain of the logging operations that once thrived in this village on NY-8 on the East Branch of the Sacandaga River, near the Wells area. Augur Falls can be found north of Wells, off Routes 8 and 30, about four miles west of Griffin on an old wagon trail. Pickleville is a former community north of Wells. Whitehouse was located in the northwest corner of Wells on West River Road on the north bank of the West Branch of Sacandaga River. All are ghost towns today.

Gem Types Found

MOONSTONE is a sodium potassium aluminum silicate. The name comes from the visual effect caused by light reflecting internally in the moonstone from different feldspars. It has been used as jewelry for centuries, including ancient civilizations. The ancients believed it was the solidified rays of the moon, and it was said to give the possessor good fortune. Also, if you put the gem in your mouth, it would stimulate your memory.

SUNSTONE is a plagioclase feldspar. When viewed from certain directions, it can exhibit a brilliant spangled appearance. The optical effect is due to reflections of red copper, also known as the aventurine-feldspar. The middle of the crystal sparks a lot and is usually a darker color.

BLOODSTONE is green jasper dotted with bright red spots of iron oxide. It was treasured in ancient eras. It is also called the martyr's gem because medieval Christians used the stone to carve scenes of the crucifixion and martyrs. The legend is that this stone was created when drops of Christ's blood fell and stained jasper at the foot of the cross. It is hard to find good specimens of this gem. It is mined in the United States. It was called heliotrope by the Greeks and it was thought to bring change and has been used as an amulet to protect against the evil eye. It is the symbol of justice. If the inclusions in the stone are yellow, the mineral is then called plasma.

BLACK ZEBRA MARBLE is a type of limestone that often looks like the black and white stripes of a Zebra, but can have red or gray hues. It is believed to have a calming or uplifting effect.

AMAZONITE, also known as Amazon Stone, is a green microcline feldspar, The name comes from the Amazon River, but it is doubtful whether these types of stones actually occur in the Amazon River. Some green stones were found there, so all green stones were called this name. The mineral is limited in occurrence. The color may come from small quantities of lead and water found in the feldspar.

ZIRCON is the most ancient mineral or stone found on Earth. The natural color varies between colorless, called jargoon; yellow-golden, called hyacinth or yellow Zircon; red or orange, called jacinth; brown or blue, called azuite; black; and green. The colorless are a popular substitute for diamond and are called the Matura Diamond. Large crystals are rare. It can be found all over the world. The colors are created by heat and occur over hundreds of millions of years. For example, this heating will cause brown Zircon to change to blue and golden. This mineral is the common constituent of most sands. The average age of this mineral is about 4.04 billion years. In the Middle Ages, Zircon was said to aid sleep, bring prosperity, and promote honor and wisdom in its owner. It was even thought to ward off witchcraft. The name is thought to have come from the Persian word Jargoon, meaning "gold-color." Zircon was also found in a meteorite in Chile, estimated to be 4.6 billion years old. Lyncurium, an ancient stone used for signets, is considered to have been either zircon or amber at one time. Zircon is commonly found with sapphire, granite, and limestone.

In Amity , the largest spinel crystal in the world was found, weighing thirty pounds. It was discovered in a lost mine in Sussex County. There is a belt of FRANKLIN MARBLE that stretches across Sussex County, New Jersey, to Orange County, New York. SPINEL is a hard crystalline combination of magnesium oxide and aluminum; it looks like a ruby and is actually the stone that is in some of the most expensive jewelry found around the world, including various crown jewels. In Sparta, spinel has been mined from the Sparta Copper Mine, located south of Sing Sing Prison in Ossining. The mine opened in the early 1800s with several tons of copper ore shipped. The mine is abandoned; today, it is a very dangerous mine shaft.

The Herkimer Diamond is a generic name for double-terminated quartz crystals, which were first discovered in outcrops in Middleville and Little Falls in Herkimer County and the Mohawk River Valley late in the eighteenth century. Sometimes they are called the Middleville Diamonds and Little Falls Diamonds. This quartz can also be found in Fulton and Montgomery Counties.

Limestone from the breccias ledge, east of Lansingburgh Station, contain quartz crystal known as Manitou aseniah, meaning "spirit stone." The Dutch and French called the stone Arbia; the English called it Diamond Rock.

Mineral Sites

- ESSEX COUNTY (in general): Anorthosite, Zircon
- Monroe County in general: Magnetite or Lodestone
- ORANGE COUNTY (in general): Spinel, large crystals, Zircon, magnetite in Ramapo Mountains as well as in Rockland County in the dumps of nineteenth century iron mines
- ST. LAWRENCE COUNTY (in general): Phlgopite, marble, from the Edwards Mine, Diposide, and opaque green Zircon
- BALMAT, ST. LAWRENCE COUNTY: Apatite at the Gouverneur Talc Mine and magnetite
- BEDFORD, WESTCHESTER COUNTY: Asteriated Rose Quartz, Biotite, and Bertrandite
- BLOOMING GROVE, ORANGE COUNTY: Bloodstone
- BREWSTER, PUTNAM COUNTY: Phrrohotite, magnetite, choridroite, titanite, Clinohlore, and Chrysotile

- CLINTONVILLE, CLINTON COUNTY: Jasper at the Arnold Mine
- DEKALB, ST. LAWRENCE COUNTY: Moonstone, Diopside, Brown Tourmaline in old Marble quarries, and Uvite
- FONDA, MONTGOMERY COUNTY: Quartz, Herkimer Diamonds
- GENESCO, LIVINGSTON COUNTY: Coral
- GORE MOUNTAIN, WARREN COUNTY: Garnet
- GOUVERNEUR, ST. LAWRENCE COUNTY: Brown Tourmaline, Tremolite, and uvite
- HARRIMAN STATE PARK, HUDSON VALLEY: Magnetite or Lodestone Mine
- JOHNSBURG, WARREN COUNTY: Serpentine from the Asbestos Mine near Garnet Lake
- KEESVILLE, CLINTON COUNTY: Serpentine near Buttermilk Falls
- KINGFIELD ON THE HUDSON RIVER: Copper was discovered by the Dutch in 1640 in the Puhaquarry Mine
- MALONE, FRANKLIN COUNTY: Sunstone
- MANHATTAN: Marble on Seaman Avenue and Isham Street
- MIDDLEVILLE, HERKIMER COUNTY: Quartz or Herkimer Diamonds
- MINEVILLE, ESSEX COUNTY: Sunstone at the Fisher Hill Mine and Black Magnetite
- NATURAL BRIDGE: Blue Zircon
- NEWCOMB, ESSEX COUNTY: Moonstone, Brown Tourmaline
- NORTH CREEK, WARREN COUNTY: Almandine Garnet
- OLMSTEDVILLE, ESSEX COUNTY: Moonstone
- PIERREPONT, ST. LAWRENCE COUNTY: Apatite, Black Tourmaline, marble, uvite, brown tourmaline
- PLATTSBURGH, CLINTON COUNTY: Zebra Marble
- PORT HENRY, ESSEX COUNTY: Rose Quartz
- ROCHESTER, MONROE COUNTY: Agate
- ROSSIE: Apatite, marble, calcite
- ST. JOHNSVILLE, MONTGOMERY COUNTY: Quartz or Herkimer Diamonds
- SARANAC LAKE, FRANKLIN COUNTY: Moonstone, Labradorite
- SARATOGA SPRINGS, SARATOGA COUNTY: Chrysoberyl, Quartz Crystals from the Gailor Quarry, Zircon
- SHAWANGUNK MOUNTAINS, ULSTER COUNTY: Gold was prospected here in the 1900s; these mountains are also known as the Crystal Mountains
- SPRING GLEN, ULSTER COUNTY: The Horseshoe Mine is located at the base of a mountain waterfall; the water falls over mouth of the mine
- STATEN ISLAND: Marble discovered at the Slossan Avenue exit
- THURMAN, WARREN COUNTY: Serpentine in marble
- Ticonderoga: Graphite
- WADING RIVER, LONG ISLAND, SUFFOLK COUNTY: Agate and Jasper in beach pebbles at Wildwood State Park
- WEST CHAZY, CLINTON COUNTY: Fossil Limestone
- WOLCOTT, WAYNE COUNTY: Larvikite or Fossil Limestone and Epidote

On Jones Beach on the south shore in Nassau County on Long Island, I was told a story from a person who was stationed here through the Coast Guard. He told me that a friend was walking along the beach and found a sand cavern with numerous clay-covered marbles inside. He picked them all up, put them in his pocket, and, as he was walking along the beach, he would throw one into the ocean every once in a while. When he got home, and his pants went through the washing machine, he found a small clay marble still in the pocket. When he touched the marble, the clay dissolved and a small gem was left in his hand. He had thrown large marbles into the ocean and, though he tried to find another cavern filled with clay marbles, he never did. Jones Beach is a barrier island and a state park. The south beach faces the open Atlantic Ocean, so it is possible that something was buried or washed up from the numerous shipwrecks that occurred here throughout the years.

The Bluestone found in New York was quarried in the Moss Hill Quarry in the town of Alcove. The rock found in New York and Pennsylvania, known as Pennsylvania Bluestone, is defined as *feldspathic greywacke*. This stone was deposited in the Catskill Delta during the Middle to Upper Devonian Period of the Paleozoic Era, approximately 370-345 million years ago. The term "bluestone" is derived from deep blue-colored sandstone first found in Ulster County. The Catskill Delta was created by runoff from the Acadian Mountains, which are the Ancestral Appalachians that covered the area where New York City now exists. This Delta ran in a narrow band from southwest to northeast and today provides the base material for the high-quality bluestone that was quarried from the Catskill Mountains and Northeast Pennsylvania.

Coeymans is a town in the southeast corner of Albany County. Baeren or Barren Island, called Kaxhaxki by Native Americans, and Shad Island are part of the town. There is a thread of marble that extends across the town from the north to south, about three or four miles from Coeymans Creek called Onisquethau by Native Americans. This creek eventually empties into the Hudson River.

Hudson River

Twenty-three miles north of Lake George is Natural Stone Bridge and Cave Park. This is the largest marble cave found in the east. A massive stone bridge arch, originally named Ponte de Dios, meaning Bridge of God, by early explorers marks the entrance to the cave. The marble here is unusual, because it formed quickly just during the last ice age by an east-west trending fault that exposed a layer of ancient marble to raging acidic floodwaters from melting glaciers.

Catskill Mountain Lost Treasure Words

Henry Hudson's mate, Robert Juet, commented on the Catskills Mountains that he saw, as he sailed on what he called the "Great River of the Mountaynes." He noted that he saw indications of metals in the highland just below Newburgh Bay: "The Mountaynes looked as if some metal of mineral were in them. The trees that grow on them were all blasted and some of them barren with few or no leaves." Near the site of Hoboken today, he wrote, "The cliffs seemed to glow with silver or copper." It was hoped by the Dutch that this mountain range had a great deal of mineral wealth. Is it no wonder then that Europe believed that North America was filled with precious metal just waiting to be taken?

Legends abound about treasure that was buried either naturally or artificially. Travelers to the region were often encouraged to search for this treasure. In 1874, there was a legend told by the Native Americans about a gold mine in the Catskills. The treasure seekers during that time had a medium — an enchanted stone — but no gold was ever found.

There is a lost silver mine mystery here as well. When the Europeans first arrived to the town of Blenheim in Schoharie County just north of Utsayantha Mountain, around thirty-five miles southwest of Albany, they found the Iroquois tribe wearing a variety of silver jewelry. They refused to say where they got the silver. After the Revolutionary War, settlers were very interested in the silver. After some searching, they felt that perhaps it was located a little east of the Schoharie Creek, but nothing was found. Finally, in 1804, a treasure hunter thought he found the source of the silver on a farm owned by the Becker family, close to the junction of Mine Kin and Schoharie Creek. Before he could tell anyone the exact location, however, he died. The Lost Blenheim Silver Mine remains hidden somewhere on the northern side of Blenheim Mountain. There is also a story that it was sealed off during the Revolution and a landslide covered it completely after that.

The Schlechtenhorst Lost Silver Mine is thought to be located within a five-mile radius of Woodstock in Ulster County. During the Revolution, some Tory raiders are said to have buried a great treasure in the woods on the northern side of the town. The Lost Shawangunk Silver Mine is located in the Catskill Mountains between Lakes Mongaup and Hodge Pond in the northern part of Sullivan County.

In Mahopac, gold mines existed on Kennicut Hill at the Crow Hill Mine in 1902. At the German Flats Mine, a fault was encountered and the ore was lost. It is located about one and three-quarters mile north of Mahopac Falls. The mine was abandoned in 1895. Quartz and Feldspar were also found. In the iron mines here, there were many cave-ins with tools and machines still underground. This town and waterfall site played central roles in the history of Putnam County. Originally, it was occupied by the Wappinger sub-tribe of the Algonquin's. Revolutionary War camps were built all through this region. It was a crossroads between key colonial forts.

So ends this journey for supernatural treasure hidden in the vastly different regions of New York State. On to the next...

Smile greeting from Pennsylvania!

Section Three:

Pennsylvania

Overview of the Keystone State

Welcome to the Keystone and Quaker state! A keystone is the top interlocking stone of an arch. It is the "key" stone that holds the rest of the arch in place. If one places the thirteen original colonies in an arch, Pennsylvania would sit in the middle, with six colonies located to the northeast and six to the southeast, hence the name. This state ties the north and south together, ties the Great Lakes to the Atlantic Ocean, and was a key state, or gateway, at the start of America's journey into the western territory. Just as the Europeans followed the sun west to search for precious treasure, so did Americans.

Native American Settlements and Geology

More than twenty-two percent of Pennsylvanian soil is glacial in nature and coal is what was taken most from the land here. A glacial line is found from Olean through Ralston, Berwick, Eckley, and Belvidere, New Jersey, to Amboy, New Jersey, along the Delaware River. In some places on this line, the ice was 3,000 feet thick.

This whole region was created in an old Silurian sea. Cryptozoon *proliferum* is a spectacular form of ancient cauliflower, called Eozoon, found in the mountainous regions. During the time the sea was surrounding the mountains, a barrier reef was created and when the glaciers scraped by, they exposed on the mountain sides "petrified sea gardens," which can be seen near State College. This species generally grew in crumbling layers that formed biscuits or domes that spread out over the mountainside.

Water damage shown in the rocks in the region.

The mountains here are probably the tops of islands with Late Devonian forests on top. Remember that the pre-Atlantic Ocean surrounded the region during the Late Devonian era. These mountains were a moist environment with lots of streams flowing toward the sea. Where the streams and saltwater met, deltas were formed. These deltas spread until they formed a lowland area covered by the early first forests. The first trees grew in swampy woods. These trees were different than the swampy woods found in New York. The trees here are called Lepidodendron, and they had drooping foliage, more like the present-day Araucaria, which is a fern-type of foliage.

Summit view from Pennsylvanian Mountains

The coal age began when the seas continuously retreated, leaving debris. They also left lots of fossils to be discovered. There are Late Carboniferous formations in the western part of the state containing thirteen important coal beds, which are six to fourteen feet thick. The amount of plant fossils found here stagger the mind; these marine, swamp, and river fossils are called cyclothems. Since there is a huge abundance of coal found, there are also numerous mines. Not all mines lead to precious gems or metals, but all are very dangerous. Extreme caution should be used when venturing into these places—and permission is always needed before proceeding into a mine shaft.

Pennsylvania has fossils just waiting to be found. The official State fossil is Tirlobite, *phacops rana*, a marine animal that lived 540-245 million years ago. On Red Hill, in Clinton County, just northwest of Lock Haven, there is a large bedrock exposure of Late Devonian-age rocks. However, the fossils in these rocks are vertebrate fossils of a quality not seen anywhere else in the Appalachian Mountains. Fossils here are the oldest amphibian remains found in North America. This fossil is called *Hynerpeton bassetti* and it was a four-footed creature that swam in rivers and walked on land about 350 million years ago. Recently, the lower jaw bones of another tetrapod, the *Densignathus rowei*, were recovered here. The other fossils found here include armored fish (*placoderms*), ray-finned fish (*actinopterygians*), and lob-finned fish (*sarcopterygians*).

Mount Davis is the highest point in the state. Dinosaur footprints have been found throughout the state from the species named Atreipus.

Buffaloes used to roam the upper Allegheny. The salt spring where herds of the bison would travel to was thought to be located on Onondargo Lake, near Conewango. Early settlers state that there would be no less than 10,000 bison coming through. The French called French Creek, La Bouffe Riviere, or the buffalo river, due to the amazing amount of bison that roamed. Buffalo Valley is where the last buffalo in Pennsylvania was killed in 1799. The last Elk to have ever been seen in this region was on a rock in Clarion County—it was shot on Elk Rock, in a blinding snowstorm, by a Native American named Jim Jacobs, in part of the Cattaraugus Reservation in 1867. Copperheads and rattlesnakes still frequent this area. The area between Oil City and Warren is noted as one of the most prolific snake territories in the world. Knowing where animals would go may lead a treasure seeker to find Native American artifacts, as the tribes would follow the game.

The very first settlers here were the Eastern Woodland American Lenni-Lenape Tribe, followed by the Algonquin and Shawnee Natives. The territory of the Attiwandaronk and Kahkawh, also known as the netural nation, was originally in the central part of the state. However, even though they were an Iroquoian tribe, they were annihilated by the Five Nations. Many artifacts have been found in the region, including pottery, spear points, knives, Hammerstones, net sinkers, hoes, axes, polishing stones, beads, vessels, and pipes. Sometimes, artifacts can be discovered by interpreting a place name. For example, Shohola Creek is an Algonquin word meaning "glue" — it was where the water was collected to make the glue for arrow feathers. It would make sense that some Native American artifacts may be found along this waterway. Another place where Native American village sites were located is on the Susquehanna River. The Monsey or Muncy tribe had a village near the west branch, and Catawissa was a site on this river too. Asylum is the home of a standing stone, or a large rock, in the stream. It was a landmark to the tribes who hunted here and is found on the east side of the river. There was once a fort here too. Frankstown was the Native American village called Assunepachla, and the town of Cornplanter was named for the Native American chief who lived here. In Juanita County, in the Tuscarora Valley on Licking Creek, are numerous Delaware tribe villages. There were many battles between the tribal villages here for control of the area.

In Avella, the first item was discovered that gave the earliest evidence of people living in North America. The relic was a tool called atlatl or spear thrower. This item is over 15,000 years old. In 1973 through 1977, James Anovasio excavated the Meadowcroft Rock Shelter in the southwestern part of the state. He found baskets and stone blades dating over 20,000 years old. The theory is that people who lived in this area came across the Bering Land Bridge around 12,000 years ago, so the question remains: who left the tools over 20,000 years ago? That answer remains a mystery.

Pennsylvania tribes from west to east are the Erie; the Shawnee, who are scattered throughout the state; and the Ohio Valley tribes or Ohio Mound builders, called the Monongahela People. Their artifacts are found all along the Ohio and Allegheny rivers. Next are the Seneca; the Wyandotte; the Nanticoke; the Iroquois Honniasont, meaning "wearing something around the neck." This refers to the Black Minqua who wore a black badge around their neck—they were destroyed by the Susquehanna Tribe. Then came the Susquehannock who lived along the Susquehanna River and were called the White Minqua. Next in line were the Lenape or Delaware, Unalachtigo clan, who resided along the Schuylkill River; the Munesee or Muncy and the Lenape or Delaware, Unami clan, both of which lived along the Lehigh River.

These Native American trails were the first roads into northeastern Pennsylvania. Pioneers from Connecticut and Rhode Island followed three trails into the state. The Native American paths were narrow and deeply sunken because of new usage; some were not even two feet wide and seldom ran through the mountain gaps.

The first trail was called different names, probably because it led to various Native American villages called Cochecton, Shohola, Salem, and Capouse. This was the Minisink Path Trail that connected the Shrewbury Inlet with Minisink Island in the Delaware River. Minisink was a Native American tribe related to the Munsee. The word is said to mean "rocky land." This trail was found about four miles south of Milford, opposite the island where the main Minsi village location was. It led out of Wyoming, heading east to Coshutunk, or Cochecto, the name of the Native American village, and followed the upper Delaware River to the village of Capouse. The second trail was the Bethany-Montrose Trail. The third path was called Easton, Wilkes-Barre path, also known as the Warriors Trail. This path was from Tioga to Sunbury, following the west bank of the Susquehanna River. It is named because it was the path followed by the military to various battlefields in the state. Warrior Run, in this case, the word run means a "moving body of water." The name comes from a stream in the area called Warrior Stream. The trail next to the stream is called Warrior's Path, where one hundred survivors of the Wyoming Massacre were said to use this Native American trail to escape being scalped. The spot is located between Nanticoke and Sugar Notch.

The Connecticut Trail was a Native American path between the Delaware River and the Susquehanna and Lackawanna valleys from the east coast to Pennsylvania. It is called the Connecticut Trail because Connecticut, at one time, claimed this part of Pennsylvania; the claim started in 1662 and was contested for numerous years after. Cochecton was the first Connecticut settlement in Pennsylvania. It was located around the same area as the Native American village once known by the same name.

Susquehanna Avenue

Connecticut still seems to want to have a place in Pennsylvania. This casino is operated by the Mohegan Tribe located in Connecticut.

Wyalusing is an ancient village of a tribe called Gahontoto, whose inhabitants were exterminated by the Cayugas. The entire Susquehanna Valley was known as Wyalusing in the pre-Revolutionary War era. At the place where Sheshequin Path and Minisink Path meet is called Diahoga, or Tioga, Point. This place was guarded by an Iroquois Sachem who refused entrance to all who failed the examination. This point leads to the southern part of the Iroquois territory. Native American trails were usually twelve to eighteen feet wide and sometimes a foot deep. Today, many Pennsylvania Native American trails follow the railroad tracks. The name Tioga was taken from the Native American language, meaning "our gateway" or "at the fords." It is thought that the gateway was the meeting of the Chemung River, which was called the Tioga River, and the Susquehanna River, leading from the Delaware Tribe land to the south and the Iroquois Tribe land to the north.

As an interesting side note: Runners could go one hundred miles per day on these trails to give information about or warn of enemies coming.

Old railroad tracks in Scranton, Pennsylvania.
These tracks often followed Native American trails.

"Old Sullivan Road," in Carbon County, is where General Sullivan marched his troops. It was part of a Native American trail. Many of the stories about this road come from soldiers' diaries. These men crossed over the Poconos through Monroe County, to the top of what the soldiers called "Hungry Hill," and then south to Locust Ridge, to the Headwaters of the Lehigh River. Looking down from here, the soldiers called the spot "Hell's Kitchen" or "The Kitchen." Nesquehoning was the Native American name for Hell's Kitchen, meaning "narrow valley." At a point just above the falls of the Lehigh River crossing is what's called "Shades of Death," thought to perhaps have something to do with a Native American battle. As an interesting side note: Hickory Run, a state park today, is another place that early colonials called "shades of death," for the dense forests, swamps, and poor soil. Little remains of the now ghost town of Hickory Run. Why the name? No one is really sure because not many hickory trees were found here. As the road steeply descends into Wilkes-Barre, it was sometimes called the "Giants' Despair" because it was difficult to navigate from below.

The Appalachian Trail passes 221 miles through Pennsylvania and is considered the rockiest part of the route. The plant Indian Pipes are found here. The white flower on this plant is part of the Native American legend that those who touch the "corpse plant" would have bad luck. Another tale of this plant is that if one picks the flower and it turns black…you would die.

A Native American path also led from Cayusa Lake, New York, to the Susquehanna River. Eventually, it became a turnpike.

In 1753, there was only one road going through Pennsylvania; this was called the French Road. It was the only road for over forty years. To the Native Americans, this trail was called the Venango Trail. For the treasure seeker, this would be a good place to start the search for "Charlie No-Face," a deformed ghost who has haunted the Pennsylvania country roads for decades. The legend is said to have really started from a man named Raymond Robinson, who was horribly disfigured as a child. He would stay indoors most of the time, but would walk in the evening. People would gather to see him and they called him Charlie No-Face or the Green Man. Even though he died in 1985, there are claims that his ghost walks to this day.

Near the Native American village of Capouse, named for Chief Capoose, along the trail on the Lackawanna River to the Roaring Bridge, one can find Nay Aug Falls. This Native American village extended from Providence on the north of Roaring Brook, also known as Gully Creek, and along both sides of the Lackawanna River. A graveyard and old apple tree was all that was left of the village in the seventeenth century. The apple tree was used as a sign post for the town of Providence. In the late 1800s, the apple tree was destroyed by a storm, and since then the site of the graveyard has been lost. Scranton, was also known as Capouse. He was the father of Winola, who became the Sachem or Chief of the Munsee tribe, for which Muncy is named. Scranton has also been called Slocum Hollow, Deep Hollow, Unionville, Harrison, Lackawanna Iron Works, Scrantonia, and Armstrong.

It is not surprising to find Dutch artifacts in Pennsylvania since, across the Delaware River in Delaware, the first Dutch settlement was founded in 1631 on Lewis Creek in Delaware Bay, called Swanendael, meaning "valley of the swans." When the Dutch returned in 1632, the settlement was burnt to the ground, with no survivors ever found. The Native Americans said that there was a massacre at the settlement, but it was not the tribes who attacked. This ended the Dutch settling here for awhile.

Scranton garage graffiti. It was great!

Scranton garage graffiti. An absolutely beautiful surprise!

The state was named by King Charles II for William Penn, the founder of Pennsylvania. William Penn's ship was called *The Welcome*. The suffix "sylvania" is the Latin word for woods, so it was Penn's Woods. Dundanion Castle, also known as Tammany Hall, is located in Cork Harbor, Ireland, the place from where William Penn originally sailed to the New World. The word "Tammany" comes from Tamanend, which perhaps may be another name for Thomas Osborne, the Delaware Native American who supposedly welcomed Penn to Pennsylvania and signed the lost treaty of Shakamaxon in 1682 with him.

This is a fascinating story. Thomas Osborne is said to have signed the treaty of peace for the land purchase under an elm tree at the village of Shakamaxon. This treaty has never been found. However, who this man was is the real question. According to the *Maryland Genealogical Society Bulletin Winter 1992* (vol. 33, No. 1), Russell Slagle, a member of the Susquehannock Tribe, made this statement about the lost treaty question:

In 1663, the settlers supposedly murdered a tribe member along the Bush River. The tribe retaliated by kidnapping the eldest son of the Osborne family. He was never seen by his family again, but this tribe member stated that he became a chief of the tribe later in life. It is said that it was Thomas Osborne, who then made a verbal treaty with Penn, giving Pennsylvania to the settlers. Shakamaxon was the Native American village near present-day Philadelphia. Later, Penn said that he signed a treaty with the Delaware tribe, but now you know the missing treaty story.

Waterways

During colonial times, many streams and rivers were not bridged and needed to be forded. This was very difficult and dangerous. Many artifacts were lost in the water because of this. Also, many roads would cross the waterways, but one would still actually have to go through the water. In 1677, the old road The King's Path crossed Pennypack Creek. Many towns have a roadway named "Water Street" located in them. The name comes from the fact that early wagon, when faced with a lack of good roads, would choose to travel along the bed of a shallow stream, turning the road for a time into a virtual street made of water.

The great Earthquake of 1811 damaged and changed numerous river channels here. It is also said to have destroyed islands in rivers. Those changed riverbed courses are a great place to start a treasure quest.

Waterways

The Pymatuning Reservoir is north of Jamestown. This area was once a swamp. When the dam was built in 1934, it completely filled with water. It is used to regulate the Beaver and Shenango rivers. It is an Iroquois word meaning "the crooked mouthed man's dwelling place" and refers to someone's deceit. It makes sense though; after all, the region was the hunting grounds for bear and wild cats for the tribe, so maybe it was thought to be a good name when the area became a man-made lake instead.

River Street and Water Street are so named because in many places they used to be waterways.

The great Delaware River was called Poutaxat, Makiriskitton, Makarish Kisken, and Whitituck by the Native Americans. The Dutch called it Zueydt, meaning the "South River," in relation to the Hudson River to the north, or the Prince Hendrick's or Prince Charles River. The Swedes called it New Sweden Stream or Godyn's Bay. The Delaware River takes the name for Lord de la Warre, governor of the English colony of Virginia. No one is really sure where the Delaware rises. The upper Delaware River is really just a lot of mountain streams and brooks that race toward the ocean. The river itself begins when the East Branch and West Branch meet at Hancock, near the Pennsylvania border. At the end of the river's course, it opens into a thirty-mile across bay, ending as mysteriously as it begins. Petty Island, located in the Delaware River, is a spot where many colonial relics have been found. However, there is also a dark side to the river: South of Milford on the Delaware River is where one finds the Death Eddy, where settlers were once killed by Native Americans.

In 1700, there was a mineral springs in Bristol called the Nasty Water. Why nasty? That answer is not clear because in 1720 the area became a health spa region. Today, the actual site of the springs has disappeared. Yellow Springs is named for the color of the water, but they are considered healing waters.

The Lehigh River goes through a gap called Die Lecha Wasser-Kraft. The Native Americans called it Buch-Ka-Buck-Ka, which means "the mountains butting opposite each other," or lechauwekink, meaning "where there are forks." One of the main Native American trails crossed the river. The water drop here is about 1,210 feet. It would take a lot of talent and skill to canoe here. On a personal note, I did whitewater raft on this river and it was a major ride. We did not go through this gap, but I did hear the stories as I traveled on the river. This is an amazing place. Onoks Falls here is a ninety-foot drop and Fort Allen was built here in 1755. Devil's Pulpit is a rock formation located in Washington Township in the northern Lehigh Valley on the west side of the Lehigh River. The sandstone rocks are said to resemble a pulpit.

Amber color of water in region.

The Fishkill River was called two different names, the Wawaset or Wawassan, meaning the lower river, and Wawasiungh or Suspecough, meaning the upper river, by the Native Americans. There is an error in the records though: Sespecough means "marsh creek," probably named by the Wawaset tribe who fished here. It was a spawning river with edible fish. There were lots of floods and natural disasters that occurred here. When that happens, one can often find artifacts from that era. There was also copper mining and smuggling along the river in earlier times.

Warren was the site of a small Native American village called Chauougon. The Europeans arrived here in July 1749. There are legends that these settlers buried six lead plates all along the river, basically claiming this river as their property, and that the Ohio River belonged to the King of France. The Native Americans dug up at least one of these plates, the one in Warren. Another is said to have been buried at the mouth of the Muskingum River and was found by boys swimming there in 1798. The third was buried near the mouth of the Great Kanawha River in 1846. No others have been found. One is said to be buried near the big Indian Rock about nine miles below Franklin, another lies somewhere down the Ohio River between Wheeling and Parkersburg, and the last one was placed at the mouth of the Big Miami River.

Before the Ice Age there was no Allegheny River. Actually two rivers converged here: one from the Warren area that actually flowed backward through the valley and the other, is the current headwater of the present river. Grinding ice changed the landscape, hence creating the current river course. Rose Quartz was discovered here, yet the reason why remains a mystery. The nearest source of quartz is 1,200 miles away. The original headwater of the river was once in Clarion. The present Clarion Valley was the upper Allegheny River. There is a legend about a tribe living along this river an ancient tribe called the Allegewi who were defeated by the Lenni-Lenape. However, it was not this tribe that built the mounds here; legend states that an earlier tribe did. The name Allegheny is derived from the Allegawi Tribe. The Allegheny River is a Native American word, meaning "most beautiful, fine, or best stream." It is actually the upper part of the Ohio River. The Allegheny and Monongahela rivers join to form the Ohio River. It was the easiest way through the western part of Pennsylvania in earlier times.

Today, the headwaters of the river begin in Olean, New York. It is the head of navigation of the Allegheny, Ohio, and Mississippi rivers. It is over 250 miles long with about 130 islands in it. The river may have been traveled as early as 1669. There are stories that a French geographer, Rene Robert Cavalier Sieur de La Salle, left Canada to "see the west." It is possible that he traveled this river, though it's not absolutely known. The man did not keep great notes, and in April 1682, his crew murdered him for getting them lost while looking for the mouth of the Mississippi River. There are other reports that people have actually jumped into this river and ended up in New Orleans, but this may be more folklore than fact. However, there are reports that in March 1879 and in the late 1930s people did complete this stunt.

Native American villages once existed all along its shores. The lore of the Allegheny River Tribe is that one day several hunters found a dead rat along the shore. They had never seen an animal like this before and brought it to their chief. He stated that this animal came from the Delaware River Valley, where the tribe once lived. It was found just before the Europeans came and was considered a very bad omen. This story about the rat that was supposedly found was just a few years before 1749 and the arrival of the first European. As an interesting side note: If it is said that the Europeans brought rats to the country, it should also be said that they brought honeybees to the New World too!

The town south of Pittsburgh called Ohiopyle is a Seneca word, meaning "beautiful river" or "large creek." Originally, both the Ohio and Allegheny rivers went by these names and the Iroquois of upstate New York considered the rivers to be one and the same. The name Ohiopyle or ohiopehhla is also said to be the entire word for Ohio, which is said to mean "white frothy water."

The Pennsylvania rivers, Allegheny and Monongahela, eventually flow into the Gulf of Mexico. The site of Nemacolin Castle, a Native American village, was located on Front Street in Brownsville and was a trading post on site of the old Fort Burd. This fort guarded the Ohio to Maryland trade route on this river.

Brandywine River or Creek is sixty miles long and enters the Delaware River. The word creek is from the Teutonic language, signifying a winding estuary, cove, or a watery shelter where a ship could sail. Today, it means a small river or branch of a river.

The Lenni-Lenape Tribe lived just north of the Brandywine River in Christianham. This was a trading post and meeting place of the tribe. The name Lenni-Lenape means "true or old men." This tribe was part of the larger Delaware Nation. They were enemies of the Iroquoian Susquehannas, also known as Minquas. This enemy was called the black Minquas because they wore black ceremonial paint. They may have been part of the Erie tribe, but no one is absolutely sure. In 1674, the Iroquois Seneca Tribe destroyed the Susquehanna Nation. The Erie and Seneca tribes fought, with the Erie tribe ultimately being exterminated, over a lost game. The Erie tribe suggested that the Seneca tribe had not really won, thus a war started.

The Susquehanna River name comes from the Native American word sisquehanne or Sisku, meaning "mud" and hanne, meaning "river," so it literally means "muddy river." It has also been said to mean "long reach river," "crooked river," or "great bay river." The river goes into the Allegheny Mountains. The town Cherry Tree is found on the west branch of the Susquehanna River, which was navigable in colonial times into the western third of the state. At the place where canoes could no longer travel, they were carried to the next place that they could be put back into the water called carries or portages. For this reason, this spot was known for many years as Canoe Place. At or near this spot was a huge cherry tree that was the official boundary, called the "purchase line," between the Iroquois land and the territory acquired by William Penn. The tree was also used to help set the boundaries between three local counties: Great Bend, also known as Lodersville, is found in Susquehanna County, just south of New York. It was named because the Susquehanna River heads toward Great Bend from Binghamton and then takes a turn, *or makes a great bend*, and heads back to New York State. Alongside the river, was a stagecoach road, following the old Native American trails over Mount Pocono and the Abingtons. It was also known as the Old Connecticut Road (talked about earlier in this section of the book) and it took two days over a tough road to get from Philadelphia to Providence, Pennsylvania.

Susquehanna River

Chickies Rock, located on the Susquehanna River, has a Native American legend attached to it: A warrior who fought a battle with another for a maiden it seems that many of these legends start this way won the battle. The maiden, however, wanted the other warrior to win. They both jumped or one jumped and one was forced to jump in after, but the end result was that both died in the river by this rock. The Susquehannock Tribe had a village and fort on the opposite shore of mouth of the Chickies Creek.

Wissahickon Creek in Penn's era it was called Whitpaine's Creek is also known as Wysihicken or Wissinoming Creek or Sissimocksink or Little Wahank on various maps. The Native American name is derived from Wissachgamen, meaning "a place where grapes are." This is a stream found in the southeastern part of the state. It runs about twenty-three miles, passing through and dividing Northwest Pennsylvania, before entering into the Schuylkill River at Philadelphia. The last few miles flow through a deep gorge that is part of the Fairmount Park system. The entire valley is known as one of six hundred National Natural Landmarks in the United States. The name comes from the Lenape tribe language and means "catfish creek" or "stream of yellowish color." There is a main trail alongside the stream called Forbidden or Wissahickon Drive. It is a gravel road, originally called Upper Wissahickon Drive, and is called Forbidden Drive because cars are not allowed to travel on it. The Devil's Pool is found downstream of the Wissahickon Creek at the mouth of Cresheim Creek. The lore of the region is that the Lenape tribe used this pool as a spiritual area. Today, it is very polluted and should not be used for swimming.

Lake Winola also has a tragic legend attached to it: Winola, the Native American name meaning "water lily," was a daughter of a Native American chief. Her involvement with a captive European settler brought dishonor and once, while looking at her reflection in the lake, she saw an image of her father in war paint. Fresh scalps hung from his waist and she recognized the scalp of her lover. Winola threw herself into the lake and was never seen again.

Nuangola Lake, south of Nanticoke, the word may mean "people of the north," is said to be named after the Native American maiden who drowned there. The story reminds one of the Lake Winola story. Both stories are a lot like the lore behind Winona Falls, south of Matamoras. It is said that the Native American Princess jumped to her death from a cliff overlooking the falls once she learned her tribe had declared war on the tribe of her lover. The lake is shaped like a heart, but was originally called Triangular Lake and Three Cornered Pond.

Sinking Spring, in the Reading area, got its name from the large number of underground streams here—the water carving the limestone and forming sinkholes. To early residents, one spring seemed to rise and sink quickly, thus inspiring the name.

Lake Erie

This name comes from the Erie tribe and means "raccoon," "at the place of the panther," or "long tail." The warriors wore the pelts of wildcats. The tribe was also known as the "cat nation," and the raccoon, being considered a wildcat, appears on the tribe's totem pole. Early French maps describe Lake Erie as Lac du Chat, meaning "the lake of the cat." The Iroquois name for Lake Erie was Erie Tejocharontiong, shortened to Lake Erige, also meaning "Lake of the cat." The tribe was not part of the Iroquois Nation, and was wiped out in 1656 by the Seneca tribe. They were known as the Neutral Nation, resisting all attempts at peace with the settlers. All efforts were abandoned until the Seneca tribe took control of the valley, and the war culminated in the extinction of the Erie tribe.

Lake Erie's geography is not like any other in Pennsylvania. It has three different geological features: lake bluffs, lake plains, and ravines and gorges formed by streams emptying into the Great Lake. During the last ice age, as water levels lowered, many beaches grew where old lakes once were. Across from Erie, on the Presque Isle Peninsula, there is a seven-mile-long, one-mile-wide sandy formation. As sand accumulated here, it moved the peninsula east about one mile every two hundred years. The region is not rich in minerals, but two Paleozoic formations are unusual: the Vergent Flags and Vergent Shales. *Flag* is fine-grained sandstone and *Shale* refers to a mass of gray, blue, and olive shale.

Erie is the second cloudiest city in the United States. The entire region is referred to in the French journals as the Niagara Valley. In 1679, Robert Cavelier founded the first French colony, near an outlet of Lake Erie that flowed into the Niagara River. He built the *Griffin*, which was the first sailing vessel launched into Lake Erie. He was searching for the Northwest Passage to China. Ironically, he managed to cross Lake Erie, Lake Huron, and Lake Michigan. On its return, the vessel vanished in the lake. The remains may have been found recently, but there are legal issues with the discoverers, the State of Michigan, the federal government, and the government of France and so the ruins of his ship lay where they sank in 1679.

Mountains

There are seven dominant hills in the Pennsylvania highlands: the STONE HILLS; SOUTH MOUNTAIN; SCHUYLKILL HILLS; BLUE MOUNTAIN; the RED HILLS, called this because they are made with Triassic red sandstone; GINGER HILL, named because of the ginger-colored brown soil; and BARREN HILL, made of white sandstone and named because this is not a good crop soil.

Shickshinny is found on Route 11, midway between Nanticoke and Berwick. It is named for the nearby Shickshinny Creek. The Native American word means "five mountains" because five mountains converge near here. They are Newport, Knob, Lee's, River, and Rocky Mountains. However, the name could also be a Munsee word, schigi-hanna, meaning "fine stream," or even an Algonquin word, meaning "turkeys aplenty."

The Allegheny Mountains has huge boulders and sculptures, including Griffis Sculpture Park in Ashford Hollow, off Route 219, and Rock City Park in Olean, New York. Why? About 500 million years ago, this area was at the bottom of a prehistoric sea. The quartz found here is called "pudding stone," same as what is found in New York. As the mountains were created, the stones lifted with the land. This is where signal rock is found and where the Native Americans created signal fires to warn of danger. Mountains are named after streams. Seven Mountains region in Bear Meadows State Forest Monument contain two rare plants: the pitcher plant and the sun-dew.

The Pocono Mountains are really not mountains at all, though the ghosts of a bloody past are still said to roam here. The Lenape tribe lived in the region and had hard feelings against the land grab that the European settlers made for their territory. Many Native American massacres occurred in this region in the eighteenth century. An old Native American trail crossed the ridge of Mount Pocono. The mountains were first discovered or viewed in 1725 by French Huguenot, Nicholas DePuis. It was over-logged during the timber heyday. Though it may be hard to believe, the Poconos were once under a shallow sea. A Mastodon skeleton was found in a peat bog near Marshalls Creek in the 1980s.

Big Pocono Mountain

Points of the Supernatural

The Pennsylvania Dutch have a rich, dark history here. Some Native American lore is that Pequea is the site of a Shawnee tribe village and Hempfield was named because hemp was once the main crop. The Native American village here was called Shawano.

In the Black Forest region, one can find the legend of the Thunderbird. This huge bird lore started with the Quillayute, a tribe living near the Quillayute River. It is said that the Sachem of the tribe asked the Great Spirit to save his people. This large bird gave his tribe a whale that it carried from the sea. The "Thunderbird" name comes from the beating of its wings, which created thunder. This legend is not restricted to just this location, though. The Comanche and Potawatomi tribes also had legends of this great bird that could carry victims away to be eaten. It is said to have a two-canoe-length wingspan and was fifteen to eighteen feet long. It is thought that perhaps the extinct condor from the Pleistocene era could be the origin of this legend. However, settlers in the 1840s also claim to have seen this bird in the sky. Still not completely convinced that there may be something to this story? In 2002, a report in the *Anchorage Daily News* stated that "a bird the size of a small airplane was recently said to be seen flying over southwest Alaska, puzzling scientists." There are two types of Thunderbirds: very helpful and very dangerous. Petroglyphs have been found of the Thunderbirds. They are said to be black, feathers five feet long with a hooked beak, and a wing span of fifteen to twenty-five feet.

In New Castle, there is an old nursing home, which was built in 1926 and has since been abandoned, that is considered very haunted. There have been Unidentified Flying Object, or UFO, sightings reported throughout Bucks County and there is supposedly a UFO crash site located in Kecksburg. Pennsylvania is also a hotspot for Bigfoot sightings.

The town of Archbald in the Lackawanna Valley region is known as White Run. A run refers to a body of water with a current or running water. The lore of the region states that Native Americans, paid by the British to torment and attack the residents, hid their payment of British gold in an Archbald cave.

Wind Gap exists in the Kittatinny Mountains. This is a non-water made gap, but there was a Native American trail and, later, a road about one hundred feet higher than the river or where Water Gap is to the northeast. The Native Americans have an oral tradition that says water once passed through here, but there is no real evidence of that fact. There have been gold occurrences reported here since 1828.

Centralia in Columbia County is the least populous borough in the state. It was known as Centreville before 1865. The underground mine fire that forced the town's evacuation is predicted to burn for another two hundred years if left unattended.

Buckhorn lore is that the name comes from the place where antlers of a deer were gouged into an oak tree along a Native American trail near this Columbia County town. It is said that the antlers remained there for years and became an encouraging landmark for travelers, signifying that a town was now within walking distance. Hornbrook Creek is supposedly named for the large horn or tusk of a mastodon, nine feet long, taken from the riverbed in 1844 or perhaps it was from deer horns found embedded in a tree near the creek at an earlier date.

Mountain summit view

Sheshequin Township, found in the north central part of the state, is a Native American word meaning "place of rattle," not for snakes, but where the medicine men would use their rattles. This was a ceremonial site for the tribes.

Canton, Bradford County, is the site of the Minnequa Springs Hotel. The resort opened in 1869 and drew many people to seek a cure of rheumatism or other ailments. The legend is that Minnequa was a Native American maiden who was near death until she drank from these healing waters at this spring. A darker legend is that she met a tragic death here and was buried near the spring. Ingham's Spring was called Aquetong by the Native Americans and is the largest spring between Maine and Florida. Hundreds of thousands of gallons of water flows here each day.

The Clarion River is named because the first surveyors thought that its distant sound had the silvery mellow sound of a clarion. On the darker side, Gallows Hill is located southeast of Bethlehem. In the 1700s, a local Native American was charged with murder and hanged at a spot called Pegg's Run. A crowd gathered on this hill to witness the event.

Half Moon, located near State College, was settled in 1784. It is named for the half moon marks found carved on trees along a Native American trail through this region. Picture Rocks, located in Muncy, were created by petroglyphs carved by the Munsee tribe who lived in the Muncy Creek Valley. Unfortunately, the pictures on the cliffs above Muncy Creek have long disappeared.

Plains Township was originally occupied by the Wanami, a sub-tribe of the Delaware Tribe. Wanamie, found southwest of Nanticoke, was another village of the Wanami Tribe. Laceyville, also known as Braintrim and Skinner's Eddy, was the camping grounds for the Tuscarora tribe. Nanticoke was the early village of the Nanticoke tribe. The Nay Aug Park, the Native American name comes from naw-yaug, meaning "roaring brook" or "noisy water," which passes through the park. In the 1600s, the Nay Aug tribe may have lived around here.

Macungie, near Allentown, is a Delaware tribe word meaning "feeding place for bears." Quakeake is a Schuylkill County town and stream; the Native American word means "pine woods." Paxtang is where several Native American trails met. It was located near Harrisburg; the name is a Susquehannock Native American word meaning "still waters." Meshoppen is the Native American word for "glass beads." Perhaps it was an early trading post where glass beads were accepted as a medium of exchange.

Providence merged with Scranton in 1866. The township was founded in 1770 by settlers from Providence, Rhode Island. It was also known as Centerville, not to be confused with Centreville, Pennsylvania, or The Corners, or Razorville. During the tornado in 1834, called the "great blow," almost every home was destroyed here in seconds.

The town of Queen Esther was the rendezvous place for the Six Nations. The Native American castle, or village, of Queen Esther was located at Tioga Point; it was destroyed after the July 1778 Battle of Wyoming, with the other villages of Standing Stone, Sheshequin, and Wyalusing. Mount Achsinging is an Algonquin term meaning "standing stones."

The Standing Stone was found in Bradford County. It is sometimes referred to as "Oneida." It was about six feet square and stood fourteen feet high. The rock formation was at the meeting of the Juniata River and the Standing Stone Creek in Huntingdon. It is believed to have marked the cross waters point of the two streams. Though was it left there by the glacier in that spot or was it placed there by people living here is the unanswered question. It was the site where Native Americans and Europeans met to trade. The settlers reported that when they first arrived here they found a Native American camp, where the lodges were arranged in a circle around the stone, which was covered with petroglyphs. The legend was that if the stone was ever moved, the tribe would no longer exist. When the tribe left, they took the stone with them. There was another standing stone monument above the Susquehanna River. It stood about forty-four feet tall, located opposite Wysox. It was part solid rock beneath and has stood through many storms for centuries.

Snowshoe is not far from the geographic center of Pennsylvania. In 1773, local surveyors found a snowshoe hanging from a tree, not far from the site of an abandoned Native American camp, hence the name. Towanda is a corruption of the Nanticoke name for area, which was tawundeunk, meaning "where we bury the dead" or "from here our great dead are resting." In essence, this was a Native American burial ground. Shavertown is also known as Bloody Run, not because of the battles or human death that happened here, but because of the number of butchers who worked on the main street.

An airplane crash in 1948, carrying $250,000 in paper currency, occurred at Mount Carmel near the town of Ashland. It was said by the survivors that the money was thrown out of the plane before the crash. The mountain name comes from the Bible. In 1812, a settler opened a stop called the Mount Carmel Inn on the toll road that passed here.

The name Slippery Rock Creek comes from the type of moss that is found here. When water combines with the clay and silt washing over the stone, it causes the rocks to become slippery. There are other stories though that may be the reason for the name. It is said that George Washington was retreating from Native Americans in the area and chose to dash across Slippery Rock to safety. The pursuing tribe member lost his footing on the rocks and misfired his gun, barely missing the future President of the United States. This story has been told many times in battlefields of the Revolutionary War. It has been said that angels themselves helped stop the bullets during the war. Another story is that the creek was named during the French & Indian War. As a British commander and army marched down the Native American trail and across the creek, his horse fell on a large smooth rock, severely injuring the man. His soldiers called the creek slippery rock. Still, another reason for the name of the stream reflects the fact that the water at the spot had a peculiar texture and contained many small stones and riffles. The combination allowed the rock to collect slime easily.

In Harrisburg, ironically the town that recently filed for bankruptcy, $15,000 was once found at an old farmhouse. In Mill Grove, located on Roaring Creek, in the northwestern part of town, a farmer buried gold coins near the old covered bridge. In Hillsboro, about four miles northeast of town in Allegheny County, gold coins valued at $350,000 are said to have been hidden on a miser's property in 1890.

Spanish Hill is found on the Susquehanna River, about a mile south of Sayre close to the New York State line. Legends state that a large cache of Spanish treasure was buried in the hill before the first settlers arrived. The treasure is said to be buried under the plateau between the Chemung and Susquehanna rivers that were said to be traveled on by the Spanish. Native Americans oral tradition says that the Spanish came here with chests filled with coins and concealed them in a cave in the Carantouan Mountain. Spanish Hill, in Carantouran, is mentioned as early as 1614 by the Dutch. In 1795, the French visited the junction of Chemung and Susquehanna rivers and found some remains of entrenchments. The local tribe called them the Spanish Ramparts. In the 1840s, a medal was found that is documented to have been made in 1550. Later, a Spanish sword, crucifix, and a black, water-logged boat were found. Local tradition also says that the hill was used by the mysterious Iroquois Mound Builders, or the early French, and by three soldiers from a Swedish boat that was thrown off course and buried treasure here, as well as the Spanish. Much of the stories are just theories. The Spanish story is that the Spanish built the hill about 1550. The tribe says that men in iron hats came to the mountain to escape other men who were after them. The tribe called the mountain Espana or Mispan and said that none of their ancestors would visit the place because it was cursed. The men were supposed to have brought chests filled with coins and buried the chests in caves. The Spanish were attacked and killed by the tribe soon after they arrived. In 1810, a surveyor who was in the area reported that the tribe still would not go near this area and said that the ghosts of the Spanish still guard their treasure. In the 1820s, Joseph Smith, founder of the Mormon Church, is known to have searched Carantouan for the money chests with a divining rod, but without success.

Wampum, found northwest of Pittsburgh, is the Native American word for string of shell beads, which were used as money between the tribes. Wapwallopen is a Native American word meaning "where the wild hemp grows" or "the place where the messengers were murdered." Who was killed or what happened is not known.

Philadelphia

William Penn was searching this completely unknown territory in 1682 when he landed at the city. It was called wicacoa by Native Americans, meaning "pleasant place." Philadelphia is called the "City of Brotherly

Love." Lumbee villages and enclaves were found here. When the Lumbees first had contact with the colonists, they spoke English. Legend say that they were the descendants of Sir Walter Raleigh's lost colony and were a mixed race of European and southeast Native American.

The Betsy Ross home was built with Delaware River bricks filled with gold dust. It is also haunted. There are strange sounds and whispers heard, especially in the basement. The ghost is said to be an angry or sad ghost.

The geology of the Atlantic Coastal Plain is largely made up of sands and brick clay that can be found on the sandy shores of the Delaware River. Colonial homes were made by bricks created with material from the Delaware River. In 1880, it was determined that these bricks hold a significant amount of disseminated gold, enough to pay off the national debt at that time, but it would cost $10 to get $1 worth of gold out of the bricks. It really is not worth looking for gold in the Delaware River.

Betsy Ross home in Philadelphia.

Close-up of Delaware River "gold" bricks on Betsy Ross home

Treasure, as well as beauty, truly lies with the finder or beholder. Sometimes the best items or artifacts ever found and considered the most precious by archaeologists were once waste items; an example of this would be the discovery of waste products from the Bonnin and Morris porcelain kiln in Philadelphia. These items gave information about the shapes, fabrics, and decoration of one of the first American ceramic factories.

The Schuylkill River is a Dutch word meaning "hidden stream or creek." The Native American name was Gan-sho-han-ne, meaning "mother of waters" or "rushing and roaring waters." When the Dutch explorers first passed the mouth of the river, they completely missed it, hence the name. This seems to refer to the river's meeting the Delaware River, which was nearly hidden by dense vegetation. The river is also known as "hideout creek." Perhaps it was used to hide valuable items from prying eyes throughout the years or it may refer to the place where a Swedish ship hid to attack Dutch ships.

In 1609, Henry Hudson explored the lower Delaware Valley. By 1634, voyagers from Virginia established a small fort at the mouth of the Schuylkill River, near Philadelphia. It is not documented, but one wonders if this group was from the lost Roanoke Island colony? If not, they probably did help the tribe living here learn English. The Swedish settlers, led by John Printz, came to the island in 1638, building a fort from the ships *Vogel Grip* and *Kolmar Nyckel*. Numerous artifacts from all eras are found. If you travel Route 13 from Philadelphia to the south, cross a bridge between Brandywine Village and Wilmington, you will be in the exact spot where the streams fell into a great pool and where ships once sailed from the Delaware River to the Atlantic Ocean. It was called Great Falls by the pioneers. In 1643, the first Europeans had settled in Pennsylvania, at Essington, which was called Tinicum Island. On the darker side of the city, this was also a site of witchcraft trials.

Gettysburg

This region is called the Triassic Lowlands. Gettysburg resides in magma rock that hardened. This magma was once 1,000 feet deep. It is an unusual rock formation. There is no doubt that there are Civil War era artifacts throughout this whole region. It is illegal to dig in most of the Gettysburg sites, so though I would recommend visiting the area, you will need permission to go search for treasure here. This being said, Gettysburg is considered one of the most haunted Civil War sites in America and the battle was the bloodiest fought in the United States. Over 51,000 people died in this small Pennsylvanian town. This is a prime spot for the combination of ghosts and treasure stories and they do run rampant in the area. It is even said that Lincoln had a dream about this horrible war, preceding the firing on Fort Sumter that he told General Grant about. In this same dream, he saw the horrible deaths that would occur in Gettysburg, Bull Run, Vicksburg, and other places.

Allegheny Region

General Braddock was buried in Unionville after a defeat at north Turtle Creek on the Monongahela, below Pittsburgh on Chestnut Ridge. His men carried him south for three days until he died. The legend is that he lost the battle because he would not let his men fight the way Native Americans fought, hiding between trees, waiting to attack. While any battlefield may still contain military artifacts, they are usually in a local, state or federal park.

Fort Roberdau or Fort Roberdeaux was founded in Altoona. It was built in the spring of 1778 to guard the mining and smelting of lead in a lead mine. The American army needed the supply of lead found near here. Also, settlers found safety in the Sinking Valley fort during raids. The town of Altoona is named from the Latin word altus, meaning "high" because it is located in the Allegheny Mountains. It is also said that the name comes from the Cherokee word allatoona, meaning "high lands of great worth."

There are shipwrecks still to be found in Allegheny County, including:

• The *Warren*, which sank near Pittsburgh just off the Lake Erie shore in the Spring 1864.
• The *Florence Bell*, which was caught and sank by ice at Creighton in January 1910 at the mouth of the Allegheny and Monongahela rivers.
• The *Forest* and *Pulaski*, which both collided and sank about twenty miles above Pittsburgh in 1843.
• The *Liberty 2*, which struck a pier of the St. Clair Bridge in Pittsburgh in 1855 and sank at the spot.
• The *Alice*, which exploded and sank near Glenfield on the Allegheny River.

Pittsburgh

Pittsburgh was first seen by George Washington in 1753 because he thought this was the best place for a fort. Washington suggested that a fort be built at the "Fork of the Ohio"; in other words, here. This was where the Monongahela and the Allegheny rivers meet to form the Ohio River. Others, however, settled here before Washington arrived. There was a Native American fort here, in a high area about two miles below this place. The native tribes who lived here on the Ohio headwaters were the Mohicans and Iroquois.

Pittsburgh already was the site of Fort Duquesne. In 1754, this region was a barren, forsaken, marshy, mosquito-infested area. The French fort was named after Marquis Duquesne, the Governor of Canada. In 1755, twelve Englishmen were tortured just outside the fort by the Native American tribe living here, yet the French did not or could not stop this event. It is said that for a long while no grass would grow on the banks of the Allegheny River at the spot where these men were brutally murdered. In 1758, three years after this event, the English army arrived after hearing Washington's report, and the French left with no battle. The fort became Fort Pitt; hence, the town became Pittsburg, later Pittsburgh. Roads were cut through here to the Great Meadows, and Washington camped here, ultimately meeting the French in battle. The camp at the Great Meadows was called Fort Necessity, located about eleven miles east of Uniontown. The fort was built by Washington in 1754; however, the exact site of the stockade is still unknown. There was also a fort found at the Forks of the Ohio Point State Park, otherwise known as Pittsburgh's golden triangle. There are no traces of Fort Pitt found, but archeologists have discovered parts of Fort Duquesne.

Lake Erie

This Great Lake is also known as the Dead Sea of North America, perhaps because it was very polluted at one time. Gold coins have been discovered on the shore of Lake Erie in the vicinity of Lawrence Park in Erie County. They are believed to have come from the steamer *Erie*, which was wrecked during a storm carrying over $200,000 in gold coins. Twelve miles northeast of Orchard Beach, an old wreck can be seen off-shore. Large amounts of American silver dollars from the late nineteenth century have been found.

In 1890, $60,000 in gold coins and paper currency were robbed from the Emporium Bank and buried on one side of the Kinzua Railroad Bridge, which crossed the Kinzua Creek about five miles northeast of Mount Jewitt. It is thought that the stolen money has never been recovered.

Many of the cannon balls used in the War of 1812 by Commondore Perry on Lake Erie were made in Pittsburgh. Wagon loads were hauled overland to the lake, but not all got there. Many pioneer and settler diaries talk about finding these cannon balls on the road to the lake. Some may still be buried by years of sediment build up.

Wilkes-Barre

In August 2011, I visited Wilkes-Barre. It was about two weeks after Hurricane Irene ravaged the northeast. The Susquehanna River overflowed and I saw lots of damage all along the road coming toward the river. Flooding was a major issue with the Delaware and Susquehanna rivers here. Tens of thousands of residents completely lost their homes in the flooding. It was unbelievable!

From 2011, Hurricane Irene's destruction along the Susquehanna River in Wilkes-Barre

Debris left by flooding of Susquehanna River

Destructive power of rushing water

Crane reaching under the bridge over the Susquehanna River to dig out debris

Wilkes-Barre is also the site of the Knox Mine Disaster. This mine went under the Susquehanna River. In 1959, the ice-laden river broke into the mine and twelve miners did not have time to get out as 10 billion gallons of water flooded the mine. It was a coal mine, but this disaster effectively ended deep-mining under the rivers in Wyoming County.

Knox Mine Disaster

In the Wyoming Valley, just below Wilkes-Barre on the upper Susquehanna River, the Battle of Wyoming occurred July 3, 1778. It was considered a massacre. The Delaware Tribe lived here, and it is said that this tribe was more inclined to peace than the Shawnee or Muncy tribes that also were living around the area. This region was considered a very bloody place, with numerous skirmishes occurring between the Native Americans and settlers. Many graves have been found in the region, with the skeletons having the marks of the tomahawk. Many scalping knives and bullet holes in the skeletons have also been discovered. As an interesting side note: This battle was reported to be a Native American massacre against the settlers, but actually, it was a combined British, Tory, and Native American band of about 1,100 that massacred the settlers in the town of Wyoming.

Fort Wyoming was located at the site of the Old Court House in Wyoming. Fort Wilkes-Barre was found on the Susquehanna River. It was built in the spring of 1778 because of the news that the Mohawk, Onondago, Cayuga, and Seneca tribes were amassing for an attack of this region from Niagara.

Battle of Wyoming

Cannon from Forty Fort.

Susquehanna River island — brown trees were destroyed by Hurricane Irene.

1

Pirates, Military, and Shipwrecks!

Pirate Lore

In 1696, Pennsylvania made charges against the pirate, John Avery, stating that he was attacking ships along their rivers.

In Gardeau, on present-day County Route 155 in McKean County, there lies a treasure thought to be worth about $1.5 million dollars in silver bars buried by Captain Blackbeard. This is not the Blackbeard of pirate lore, though it is claimed to be a pirate story. This Blackbeard was a British admiral in the War of 1812. He was trying to get to Canada quickly, and silver is very heavy. He buried it in this region, and it is thought that a landslide covered the treasure spot. He was seen in Renovo, burying the treasure in the mountains outside Emporium.

The town of New Hope, however, does have a pirate-connected treasure story. In Washington Crossing State Park, on Bowmans Hill on the Delaware River, the spot where Washington and 2,400 soldiers crossed the Delaware River on Christmas 1776, buried gold is said to lie beneath the park. Around 1700, before General Washington used Bowmans Hill as a lookout prior to the Battle of Trenton, a mysterious man lived here. Doctor John Bowman was reported to be an associate of the pirate Captain Kidd. He is thought to have buried treasure on his property, located on Bowman's Hill in Bucks County. This was his cut of the pirate loot. He buried the treasure because he did not want to be connected to Kidd and hanged.

Privateers during the Jenkins Ear War in 1742 captured the Spanish merchant ship, *San Ignacio El Grande*, heading for the home port of Philadelphia. They did not want to give the English King his entire share of the plunder, so they buried twenty-two ceramic flasks of mercury and 38,000 pieces of eight on the west bank of the Delaware River about three miles southwest of Chester. Later, they were unable to relocate the spot. The Jenkins Ear War, caused by Robert Jenkins, was between England and Spain. Jenkins was the captain of a British merchant ship who exhibited his severed ear to Parliament, reporting that this horrible disfigurement occurred due to the boarding of his vessel by Spain in 1731.

The famous pirates Blackbeard and Captain Kidd are said to have roamed the Delaware and Schuykill Rivers and to have buried treasure in Philadelphia. It is said that Spanish currency used by pirates and merchants in Philadelphia, such as silver Double Reals and pieces of eight and pistoles, are all buried under the Society Hill section of the city. Society Hill is named because of the mercantile establishment "The Free Society of Traders," which had an office here in 1682. They had an office and warehouse on the west side of Front Street near the south side of Dock Creek. The pirate treasure was hidden somewhere called the "Cherry Garden," which was a locale on Society Hill.

Military

Forts

FORT ZELLER can be found half-a-mile north of Newmanstown in Lebanon County. It is the state's oldest surviving fort, built in 1723 by the pioneers. Any place where there were military battles or encampments built, there may be artifacts left from the people of that era. It was sometimes easier to leave the items behind than continue to carry them, especially if the people were retreating from an enemy or an advancing army.

FORT CHRISTINA existed on Minquas Kill, called Christina's Creek by the Swedish settlers, near Wilmington. FORT WALTOUR was built in the vicinity of Strawpump and Penglyn. Pioneers here were of German descent. FORT NASSAU was located on the Delaware River in Wilmington. This fort was under Swedish rule in the early years. FORT ELFSBORG OR ELSINBOROUGH was built by the Swedish, who called it Myggenborg, and then abandoned it. Perhaps the reason for them abandoning it is obvious by the meaning of the name, "Fort Mosquito." FORT CASIMIR was built at Sand Huken, today New Castle, on the Delaware River about five miles below Fort Christina. FORT WILSON was built at the southwest corner of Third and Walnut streets in Philadelphia. FORT DURKEE was at the park, just below Fort Wilkes-Barre. FORT PITTSTON was on the corner of North Main Street and Parsonage Street in Pittston. It was first called Lackwanna Fort. FORT WINTERMOUNT is found between Forty Fort and Fort Jenkins. The site of Fort Jenkins is at the upper crossing bridge from Pittston to West Pittston, on the right side. FORT LIGONIER is in Legonier in Westmoreland County. The town was founded on the site of this wooden fort. FORT PRESQUE ISLE was built in 1753 on Mill Creek near Lake Erie. It fell in 1763 because the Native Americans came to the gate, saying that they had furs to sell, and, when the gates opened, they attacked.

FORT HAMILTON was the companion to Fort Penn, being established by Ben Franklin in 1756. It was one of the chain of forts located along the Kittatinny Mountains, stretching all the way from the Delaware River to the Maryland River. This is the way mountain gaps were fortified. Forts were placed between them so that no settler would be far from a place of refuge from Native American attacks. This fort is located in East Stroudsburg and abandoned in 1757.

Site of Fort Hamilton

Bust of Ben Franklin

FORT PENN was located in Stroudsburg, just below Mount Pocono. It was the first fort reached in 1778 by the fugitives from the Wyoming Massacre. FORTY FORT is also a town, named for the forty settlers from Connecticut who arrived here and built a fort in 1769. The area became a flash-point for the armies trying to dominate the region, finally ending in the Wyoming Massacre of 1778. Below the fort is the Wyoming Monument. Three hundred Patriots were massacred nearby by 1,100 British troops, Tories, and Indians. The survivors fled here after the massacre. The Monument is found near the Susquehanna River.

BARREN HILL, also known as Fort Hill or Militia Hill, is found just northwest of Philadelphia. In 1778, a battle was fought between the French and the British. The French were victorious. Fort Le Bocuf is found in Waterford near Lake Erie. It was built by the French in 1760 and destroyed during the Pontiac War in 1763. This was a war between the British and the Iroquois Tribe early in the century. Only the foundations remain.

FORT BEDFORD is located in Beford in the southern part of the state. Bedford Springs were healing waters said to be found by a man in 1786 who was searching for gold and thought he found it when he saw markings on the stone left by the mineral water. Still, others say that a fisherman found the spring in 1804 and it cured his rheumatism. There were covered bridges over this spring at one time. FORT RAYSTOWN was located in the Fort Bedford State Park in Bedford. Today, it is completely gone. Raystown Ray is a lake monster who also lives here. The Native Americans called lake monsters, "pond devils." They have been reported in numerous lakes throughout the world for a long time. Raystown Lake is found in Huntington County.

FORT MIFFLIN is located on the Delaware River on the eastern edge of Philadelphia International Airport. It is called the "Alamo of the Delaware" and is considered very haunted. A number of relics from the Revolutionary War era have been found here. There is a faceless soldier that is seen and a screaming lady heard. She lost her child here and her screams have been heard so often that the police have been called numerous times. Near the blacksmith's shop, noises of someone working here have been reported. However, the casemates are the most haunted spot here. This was the prison cells during the Civil War, when the fort was a Confederate Prison Camp. A lamplighter is seen near dark and both Revolutionary War and Civil War ghosts have been seen. There was a British payship wrecked here in 1812. The cargo lies under the river today.

FORT DELAWARE was built in 1754 to protect Philadelphia. It was completed in 1859, just before the Civil War era. It is built on Pea Patch Island, named due to a legend dating to colonial times. There was a ship filled with peas grounded here on the sandbar. The roots of the pea plants grew, until the island of 178 acres appeared on the surface of the water. There are parts of the island actually three feet below sea level. In 1861, a thousand prisoners were interned on this island. By 1863, over 12,000 prisoners were here, most taken at Gettysburg. This island was only supposed to hold 4,000 men. It was a horrible place, ripe with dirt, misery, lice, rats, and disease. The only water source was the rainwater that washed off the flat roof of the fort. When the dead exceeded the capacity of the cemetery on the island, the northern government decided to bury them on the Jersey Shore at Finn's Point on what is the Fort Mott reservation. A government tug, called the Osceola, went back and forth carrying the dead, almost 2,400, and they were dumped in a mass grave. Cannon balls, some weighing as much as 107 pounds, still remain on the island.

During the Revolution, a paymaster was attacked by Native Americans, but he managed to bury $150,000 in gold and silver coins. He was killed, but was in the area of Laurel Hill near the Farmington, close to Fort Necessity. The log structure Fort Necessity was a battlefield site found on Route 40. This place was the opening battle of the French & Indian War. The fort was built by Washington near Uniontown.

Sunbury is the site of a Native American village called Shamokin, which was located in the junction of the north and west branch of the Susquehanna River. FORT AUGUSTA was a wooden fort built here in 1756. It was located on Pennsylvania Route 14, near Sudbury in Northcumberland County. It was never taken over due to the large size and heaviness of the garrison. During the Revolution, the Patriots fought the Iroquois from this fort. Bloody Spring was named because a man was tending cattle outside the fort in 1756; he was shot and scalped as he drank from the spring about a half-a-mile from the fort. There are many horror tales about the Native Americans and settlers fighting in this area. It is now under a railroad structure.

FORT HORN was in Clinton County in Pine Creek. In 1776, the Declaration of Independence from the Crown of England, stating that the citizens of this settlement were free and independent, was buried in a tin box. It was probably written within hours of the Declaration that was accepted by the Continental Congress in Philadelphia. In 1778, the Six Nations wiped out the settlement of Pine Creek. Fort Horn was burned and no trace of the town could be found. This valuable piece of paper is still missing to this day.

Battlefields!

The Conojacular War was fought in the 1730s between Maryland and Pennsylvania. It was basically a war between the sons of William Penn and Charles Calvert over the northern boundary of Maryland and Pennsylvania. The story is that a man, Thomas Cresap, purchased land on the Conojohela

Flats and called it Pleasant Acres, which was about the same latitude as Philadelphia, and was in Pennsylvania. However, he stated that he lived in Maryland, not Pennsylvania. A series of violent incidents between Cresap and the Pennsylvania authorities occurred and this became known as the Conojacular (or Conojocular) War. Eventually, Cresap was taken into custody and, in 1738, the temporary line was agreed upon nineteen miles south of the 40th Parallel. During the battle at Cresap's home, one person was killed and the house was set on fire, burning to the ground. Today, the place where this "war" occurred is drowned land under the Susquehanna River by the dam.

The Revolutionary War Battle of Germantown was fought not far from the Wissahickon Creek. This was an all-wilderness area during that era, with rough terrain and no way through. The travel was so hard that the American John Armstrong had to abandon cannons in the valley. Other legends tell that this terrain helped American spies by allowing them to sit on a rock overlooking the valley and drop balls of yarn to the Americans with notes inside that detailed the movement of British troops during the occupation of Philadelphia. The Battle of Germantown was fought on October 4, 1777. The Americans lost this battle due to fog enveloping the area on this day. The American army was shot at by members of their own troops, as they thought they were shooting at the enemy.

The Battle of the Clouds was a major conflict between the British and Patriots, which took place near Malvern, Chester County, in 1777. Just before this battle, a record-breaking rainstorm caused the Patriots to lose much of their equipment. Covering 30,000 acres, the Brandywine Battlefield Park is another famous battlefield. The conflict occurred there on September 11, 1777. As an interesting side note: The date, September 11, 1777, seems to herald major events in other states as well, such as New York. The Patriots lost this battle. The Bushy Run Battlefield is located north of Jeannette and east of Harrison City. British troops were headed for Fort Pitt and were attacked by Native Americans. Both sides suffered great losses. Thompson Island, found on the Allegheny River, is the only Revolutionary War battle fought in this part of the state.

Wilkes-Barre in the Wyoming Valley was the site of terrible battles during the Revolutionary War. This was the area that Connecticut even claimed at one time. The Delaware Tribe called the valley "m'chwewormink," meaning "extensive meadows." The town of Wyoming was once called New Troy and the county of Wyoming was called Putnam. The remains of Fort Wyoming are in the center of Wilkes-Barre. It was built in 1771 and was destroyed when the town of Wyoming was destroyed in 1778 — that town was located about six miles northeast of Wilkes-Barre on the Susquehanna River.

Wyoming Avenue

Military Loot?

Palmyra, Burlington County was a hiding spot of British plunder during the Revolutionary War, when Philadelphia was sacked. In the Potato River, near Crosby, it is told, about $5 million in gold and silver bullion treasure was buried by Colonel Noah Parker in 1812. Welch Mountain, near Warwick, was a known outlaw hiding place. General Washington's army also camped here. The Warwick iron furnace was reported as making many imperfect cannons during the Revolutionary War. These cannons are said to be buried on the banks of French Creek.

Revolutionary War Tories are thought to have buried several chests on the McMillan Farm, located about two miles east of Bloosbery, in Tioga County, near the Tioga River. Also, Tory raiders buried plunder in a cave overlooking the Delaware River about two miles north of Easton. During the Revolution in 1775, a band of Tories buried $100,000 in gold, silver pate, silver coins, and jewelry in an abandoned well about a mile south of Wernersville in Berks County.

A British spy admitted to burying a number of gold coins near the tavern on Pond Street, directly opposite Burnington Island on the Delaware River in Bristol, during the American Revolutionary War. Hessian soldiers are also said to have tossed a cannon filled with gold coins into the Delaware River near Chester during the Revolution.

Confederate raiders robbed several banks in central Pennsylvania and then buried the loot in barrels around the Mountain House, near the summit of the Snowshoe Mountains in the Allegheny Range, about a mile west of Wingate. Also during the Civil War, Confederate soldiers are said to have buried fifteen tons of silver bullion in a cave about two miles north of Uniontown in Fayette County.

During the Civil War era, around 1863, a Union payroll army wagon carrying twenty-six bars of gold, weighing fifty pounds each, was attacked and only one person survived, escaping to tell the tale. Searchers found dead mules in this area and, in the 1870s, human skeletons were found at Dent's Run. It is thought they were the soldiers from this wagon. The survivor said that they buried the gold before being attacked. Dents Run is located where Elk and Cameron counties meet. The wagon left Driftwood and was never seen again.

Lackawaxen is a Native American word, meaning "where the way forks" or "where the roads part." This area is near Minisink Ford, New York. It is the site of the only major Revolutionary War battle, called the Battle of Minisink, fought in the upper Delaware River region. A few dozen American soldiers were killed in the battle that took place in 1779. It took the widows over forty-three years to get the bones of their husbands' home. Even sixty-five years after the battle, the bones of one of the men were found here.

Other Plunder and Treasures

Outlaw Plunder

Outlaw Joe Fracker buried gold and silver coins in Jack's River, north of Lewistown. In 1888, Michale Rizzalo robbed a bank of $12,000. He buried the loot near Laurel Run Creek in the Laurel Run Mountains, located about four miles east of Wilkes-Barre. Hand's Pass in Coatesville was a favorite spot for robbers to stop the stage. This part of the stage route was uphill and the stage would have to slow down. The robbers took advantage of this, particularly the Sandy Flash gang. It is possible that loot may have been quickly hidden and never recovered in this area.

The Belsano Train Robbery occurred on October 11, 1924. The train was carrying a payroll of $33,000 and was robbed outside Cambria County. Legends say that though the robbers were captured, not much money was recovered. It is thought to have been buried somewhere around where the train was stopped.

Counterfeit coins, created by Cyrus Cole, are thought to be buried in Eldred, McKean County in the 1900s. They are said to be counterfeit silver half dollars and gold coins. It is thought that he knew he was being watched, and, before he was caught, buried the coins near here. Warrior Gap is the spot where the $70,000 payroll of a lumber company is thought to be buried. It is possibly about three miles south of Wilkes-Barre, just north of Highway I-81, along Warriors Run. In Buckingham, the Doane outlaw gang buried a cache of gold and silver coins on the Preston Rich Farm that was located on Mechanicsville Road in the late 1700s. During the 1800s, the Kirk gang had a hideout in a place called Dulaneys Cave, now called Laurel Caverns, in Uniontown and buried a large amount of treasure there.

The criminal David Lewis is said to have buried a saddleback full of $10,000 in gold in a small cave along the Juanita River at Juanita Terrace, south of Lewiston, in Cumberland County. However, he did return for it, but the river flooded and washed away his trail. His lost loot was left in a Conodoguinett Creek cave that he used as a hideout, about one and a half miles from Carlisle. The cavern was described as having an antechamber ninety yards long and a man could stand in it. Three passages branched from it. One of these led to the "Devil's Dining Room." It was said to have been a Native American storehouse before Lewis took control of it. It was also said that parts of it was used as a tomb, though those stories are vague. Lewis met a tragic end. He was captured by the authorities and died in prison.

Silver and Gold!

Lost silver bars buried in McKean County in northern Pennsylvania in the town of Gardeau are valued at over 1.5 million dollars. In 1811, the British Admiralty tried to raise the wreckage of a Spanish galleon that had gone down during a hurricane in 1680. After retrieving the silver bars, the Commodore of the expedition started to worry about how to get it back to England. Tensions were high right before the War of 1812 broke out between Great Britain and the United States. A plan was made to go over land to Canada and ship the silver out of America to England. The Commodore decided to follow the Susquehanna River due north to present-day Williamsport and from there took the Sinnemahoning River north-westward until he reached the present-day town of Emporium. Here, there would be a twenty-three-mile portage, or carry, over the Keating Summit to the headwaters of the Allegheny River, near Port Allegheny, to continue the trip. The journey would go on up the Allegheny River to the mouth of Conewango Creek, near present-day Warren, and then up to Chautauqua Lake or Jamestown. From there, the silver would be put on a ship heading toward Canada. Sailing through Lake Erie, the British felt they would be home free, since Britain controlled Erie in that era, and so the wagons were loaded with silver and headed to Canada. It was a very difficult journey, to say the least. During the trip, Britain and America declared war, and the Commodore decided that perhaps he should bury this silver after he got over the portage, so, in the southeast corner of McKean County, near the village of Keating Summit, this treasure was buried near an old saltlick. The treasure was never found again.

Here is a gold story from Potter County that takes place in 1690 before the Europeans came. A party of French voyageurs left New Orleans by raft to return to Montreal. They started at the Mississippi River to the Ohio River, which Native Americans called "The Beautiful River," to the twenty-three-mile portage/carry over the Keating Summit to the headwaters of the Allegheny River near Port Allegheny. This was known as Canoe Place and had been used as a way to travel here for three hundred years. They would travel up the Allegheny River, at the present Golden Triangle, to the mouth of the Conewango Creek, near present-day Warren and then up to Chautauqua Lake or Jamestown. From there, they would travel to Lake Erie. As they approached Warren, the leaders feared the Seneca Tribe and were terrified of an attack. It is thought that they did reach North Coudersport, where they decided that perhaps they should bury the kegs of gold, mark the site, and continue as quickly as possible, so they turned south to the valley known as Borie. Near a rock, on the Allegheny River, which they marked with a cross chiseled into it, they buried the $300,000 in gold. They never returned to retrieve the gold. For many years, the Seneca talked about a huge rock with a strange marking on it, but said that they never dug there. If this story sounds a lot like the story above, the real truth is that this was the only path through the state to Canada. With so many people passing along the exact same route, it is not a coincidence that there would be many ghostly treasure tales along the route.

There is a lost silver lode awaiting discovery in Sweden Township in Potter County, about five miles from the town of Coudersport in northern Pennsylvania, also known as God's Country. This silver mine was supposedly known to the Iroquois Nation for two hundred years before the Europeans arrived. Though the Native Americans would never tell the settlers where they were getting the pure silver ore from, in 1894, the townspeople secretly followed a Seneca warrior. He headed in the direction of Sweden Valley, entering the valley about a half-a-mile from present-day Route 6. Within hours, he reemerged near the base of Ice Mountain. The townspeople decided that perhaps using a divining rod might find the silver. Halfway up the mountain, the forked stick lurched forward and they started digging. They reported that they found a sheet of ice, a shaft, pottery, and human bones, but no silver. However, they did discover the strange Ice Mine, a place that is covered in ice in the summer, but ironically has no ice in the winter.

Captain's Braddock's gold may be found in the North Huntingdon area. Braddock was at a camp called Three Springs Encampment with his troop near Circleville and the Youghiogheny River, and was planning to attack Fort Duquesne, which was occupied by the French. It was decided to pay the men after the battle with the King's gold that they were carrying, because some would be killed. At that time, it was also decided to hide the gold rather than carry it into battle, so three men and Braddock followed Crawford Run to the River, buried the gold under a Walnut Tree, and returned to camp.

The Revolutionary War army moved south in the direction of the river, but for some reason they believed it was the Monongahela, not the Youghiogheny. They followed the river to the forks of another river located at present-day McKeesport. This second river was the Monongahela, but Braddock thought it was the Allegheny River. The French were waiting in ambush and it was almost a total massacre; Braddock and the men who knew where the gold was buried were killed. Braddock's body was buried near Fort Necessity and the gold was never recovered.

2.
Precious Gems, Mines, and Ghost Towns!

Coal-Oil Johnny is a generic name for anyone who squanders an oil fortune. The name is said to have come from John Washington Steele, who inherited a fortune in 1864. He acquired a farm in Oil Creek. At the age of twenty-one, he is said to have spent $1 million in six months. He died in poverty and the story is told to show the consequences of foolish spending. Perhaps this is one reason why people would hide their treasures to be safe for another day.

Redington is where the mineral Cat's Eye Quartz can be found on South Mountain. Dead Woman Hollow, found on South Mountain, is where the Native Americans have a legend about a settler woman who was bitten by a snake here and died. It is thought that the Confederate Army marched through this region during the Civil War. Often, there are military artifacts to be found where armies camped or marched through. The Appalachian Trail does pass near here and it would make sense for armies to use well-defined trails rather than have to make roads.

The Appalachian Trail was a pre-historic trail and it must be remembered that it was at one time the only way to traverse through the thick woods that once existed here. There are legends of numerous graves and ambush spots found all along the trail. For example, there is a place around the South Mountain region called Indian Breast Works. There are two stories about the creation of this place. The first concerns the Native Americans. When the settlers used this trail to travel south in Pennsylvania, the Native Americans would shoot arrows at them from a stone barricade on Big Rocky Ridge. It is also said that the large boulders on the side of the mountain were put there to be pushed at settlers along the path. The second story starts in the Civil War era. It is possible that Confederate soldiers used this valley to get from the south to Chambersburg. It also makes sense that this stone fence area was actually put together by the soldiers, not the Native Americans, and was used to shoot at enemies that passed through. There is not much left here today, only about twenty-five feet.

At Fuller Lake, near South Mountain, there is a water-filled ore pit created by the iron ore mined for the Pine Grove Furnace. It is ninety feet deep. The mining of ore had to be stopped because the water came into the quarry so quickly that it could not be pumped out. Some of the mining machinery is said to be at the bottom of the lake. Because it is a mining hole, the sides are very steep.

Cornwall Furnace was near Cornwall in Lebanon County. This rich iron source was discovered in 1742. The Durham Village site, located near Riegelsville in Bucks County, is a ruined furnace site that functioned between 1727 and 1789. They built heavy cargo boats; some were used by Washington in his famous crossing of the Delaware River in 1776. Hopewell Village is about five miles southeast of Birdsboro in Berks County. It was founded in 1770 as an iron-making center, and the area represents the beginning of the iron industry in America. Ruins can still be seen there. The story continues that there was once a cave close to the furnace called Devil's Hole that was destroyed by the operations of the furnace. This cave once was filled with stalactites and passages that tourists would travel through. Though the entrance may have been destroyed, perhaps the cave passages still exist.

Gold, Silver, and Copper

There are gold regions in Pennsylvania. Sites are found in northern York County in Dillsburg, Grantham, Wellsville, and Rossville. There are also rivers that have gold in them, including Stony Run, Fisher's Run, Beaver Creek, North Branch, Wolf Run, and Yellow Breeches Creek. Gold can be found in the mountain areas too, especially in Tunkhannock on Messhoppen Creek and Stony Brook Creek in Wyoming County, as well as in the Susquehanna River. Gold was found in Reading at the New Albany gold mine on Route 220, in Sweden Valley at the Kress Gold Mine on Route 6, and in Noxon, where gold was reported being found on a farm. In Wyalusing, a gold nugget was found behind a hotel. There is said to be a lost gold mine in Mapleton at the base of Jack's Mountain.

There are lost Native American mines, as well as both gold and silver mines, in the vicinity of McConnellsburg, in the nearby Cove and Dickeys Mountains. The Lost Bear Jasper Mine is located in the area of Raubville along the Delaware River in Northcumberland County. The Pequea Silver Mine, located near Conestoga in Lancaster County, was worked from before the Revolutionary War to 1875.

On the Delaware River, in the New Hope region, is the site of Solebury Copper Mine. The real question is, did the Native Americans also mine here? Oral tradition states that only the Europeans mined here well before the Revolutionary War, but who were they? Perhaps it was the Swedish settlers who did live on the Delaware River in 1637. In

1854, the mine entrance was found. It was proven that it was being used almost two hundred years earlier and there was a heap of debris at the entrance. Trees growing on the waste pile were destroyed, but thought to be over one hundred years old. Who were the miners? Maybe they were the ancient Mound Builders, but that was not what the Native American legend stated. Perhaps they were the workers for the West India Company who traded with the Native Americans at the Falls of the Delaware. The mystery remains today.

The lost cave of silver is said to be in the Allegheny National Forest, west of the town of Tionesta, and contains a lot of silver veins. During the 1700s, a settler got lost and sought shelter in a cave where he saw the silver. He managed to find his way out, but could not find it again. It is said that it was a Native American silver cave, and it was thought to be about fifteen miles upstream from the town.

Deep Run is also the site of a Native American silver mine. It is really a lost cache of silver ingots that was hidden here. Almost on the state line of Pennsylvania and Maryland, it is believed that it is located in Adams County. The legend is that a German silversmith was allowed to work a mine owned by the local tribe. Somehow, his daughter stole silver from the mine — the father and daughter vanished, along with any knowledge of the location of the mine. There is mention of a stream and a large flat rock, and steps that lead underground, which may mean that it's not a natural cave. Supposedly it is located 1.5 miles outside of Union Mills, at the base of the hill. *As an interesting side note: Geologists say that the mineral conditions are right for silver to exist in this region.*

In 1825, in Keating, on the west branch of the Susquehanna River, residents claimed to see a band of Native Americans go upstream, carrying knapsacks and small axes. When they returned, they had bags filled with silver. The trail leads upstream to Birch Island Run, where the tracks of the tribe disappeared. The Natives never told anyone where they got the silver.

In McConnelsburg, on State Route 16 in Fulton County, a Native American silver mine is located in James Buchanan State Forest. In the pioneer era, settlers told of tribe members obtaining silver in this area that they traded with them, but would never say where they got the silver to begin with.

Thunder Run drains into Johnson Brook in Pike Township, near Caleton in Potter County. The name comes from the continuous roar, like distant thunder, as it travels out of the hill near the Brook. The noise comes from the tumbling of the water in the hill. There is a story of a diamond mine in Johnson Brook. During the Civil War, a gang of horse thieves hid in Sandstone Hollow, which drains into Pine Creek and at Thunder Run. There is supposedly a natural cave or tunnel connecting the two streams, which are about half-a-mile apart, that may hide something.

Susquehanna River

Ghost Towns

OLD FORGE was also known as Mudtown, which was an abandoned forge in 1800. When the settlers returned over a quarter of a century later, they referred to the area as "old forge." The forge was near the confluence of the Lackawanna River and Ascension Brook.

STEENE is the name of a hamlet that no longer exists in Wayne County, but it was rail stop number 16.

OLD ECONOMY is a ghost town located several miles outside of Ambridge in Beaver County. It was an industrial community between 1825 and 1905. Only seventeen buildings remain in this town today.

SIZERVILLE was founded in 1838 and is located about three miles from present-day Sizerville. The ghost town was burned in 1897 and abandoned.

EPHRATA is a ghost town near the junction of US 222 and 322, near the present-day town of Ephrata. It was founded in 1728 by German Baptists and abandoned in 1880. Located in the Lancaster area, it took its name from the Biblical city of Ephrath, which is the ancient name for Bethlehem. It was also known as Dunkertown, which is a reference to the practice of water immersion during baptism.

The site of NEW SWEDEN was on the Delaware River in the Prinshof National Historic Park about five miles northeast of Chester in Delaware County. This was the first permanent European settlement in Pennsylvania, founded by the Swedish in 1638. In 1643, they also settled on Tinicum Island in the river and built a fort there. Both settlements were completely destroyed by the Dutch in 1655.

AUSTIN is in Potter County. This was once one of the most prosperous towns in northern Pennslyvania. On September 30, 1911, the Bayless Dam, just two miles north of the town, burst and destroyed Austin, as well as the town of Costello about three miles further south.

Pennsylvania Dutch

The superstitions are easy to find here. One way to find water was to suspend a gold coin in a drinking glass. The number of times the coin swings against the side of the glass denotes the number of feet beneath the earth the stream is located.

Rural tradition of the Pennsylvania Dutch people in Hamburg, located a few miles north of Reading, near Windsor Castle, state that there is a vacant field where witches, ghosts, and others would dance. There is a deep circle in the field said to be created by the people dancing or walking in the field.

On the banks of the Sacony River in Berks County, a main tributary of Maiden Creek, is where the Crystal Cave is found. In Kutztown, a farmer was blasting limestone in 1871 when he discovered a dark, narrow hole only eighty feet from the farmhouse. After pulling away the dirt, he was able to reveal an opening large enough to crawl through. After exploring, he climbed out and said he found diamond-like crystals on the walls of the cave. Hence, the name was born. These minerals, however, were not diamonds, just quartz. It is considered one of the greatest natural wonders in the United States.

Minerals and Gems

The world's first discovery of the mineral Celestine was in 1791 or 1797, the dates differ, in Bellwood, Blair County. The color of the mineral is pale blue. Oolite, also known as egg stone, is sedimentary rock formed from ooids, or spherical grains, composed of concentric layers — the name comes from the Hellenic word *ooion* or egg. In Pennsylvania, it is found in the Conococheague limestone of the Cambrian age. Lots of marble and gold bricks are found in Philadelphia. There is a marble tomb for Ben Franklin, where people throw money for good luck. Palaeozoic marble quarries can be found here. Green Serpentine and red sandstone, as well as quartzite, and blue gabbro are all found in the state. Many rare minerals are also found here, including corundum in sapphire and diaspore, garnet, beryl, and tourmaline. There are many abandoned quarries. As an interesting side note: the Dupont Company became famous due to the powder found in Pennsylvania.

Ben Franklin's tomb in Philadelphia.

Eastern Pennsylvania is made up of marine deposits. The Highlands are formed by crystalline and volcanic rocks that culminate in the Allegheny Plateau. The mineral belts run across the state from the northeast to the southwest. The Hematite found is why the Triassic rocks are red in color.

Minerals found in the state include anthracite or pure carbon, chromite, sepiolite, copper, pisolitic limestone, and magnetite or lodestone. Quartz is very abundant here, including chalcedony; jasper; smoky quartz; rose quartz; black tourmaline, which is basically found in the southeastern part of state; almandite garnet, of which red is the most common; brown Zircon; amethyst; beryl; sunstone; moonstone; amazonite; and rutile.

Mineral Sites

Limestone is found on Wissahickon Creek as well as a very unique rock called Wissahickson Schist. This is Precambian to Cambrian Stone, and has flecks of mica and garnet. Quartzite is also found in the valley. Almandine Garnet and Magneitite were found near Bells Mill Road, located close to Devil's Pool. One can also find the mineral talc, so soft that it can be scratched off with a fingernail. Other minerals can be found at the following sites:

- CHESTER COUNTY (in general): Microline, Stalactitic, pyrite, emery deposits, margarite, clinochlore, blue moonstone (in West Nottingham Township), and sunstone
- SOUTHERN YORK COUNTY (in general): In the Susquehanna River, Platinum flakes were found west of Quarryville. In the Delta area found in the southeastern corner of York County, there is a small community known as the Delta Slate resources. In 1850, Peach Bottom Slate mined here was considered the best in the world. Gold flakes have also been found here. Three and a half miles west of Delta, along the Mason-Dixon line at Constitution, Rutile was found. Rutile is nicknamed the "money stone." Gold is also found in Peter's Creek (Platinum flakes too), Fishing Creek, and Bald Eagle Creek. There are numerous volcanic rocks found here as well.
- ADAMS COUNTY (in general): Gold can be found at Devil's Den in Gettysburg. However, there is no panning allowed here.
- LANCASTER COUNTY (in general): Gold was discovered in Muddy Run Park, south of the Holtwood Dam and Normanwood Bridge
- LEBANON AND BERKS COUNTIES (in general): Magnetite
- ARCHBALD, LACKAWANNA COUNTY: The largest and most impressive glacial pothole in the world exists. The original size was forty-five feet deep and twenty-five feet in diameter, and the walls showed a whirl of stones in its formation. Apparently, it was created by a stream of considerable volume

falling from an elevation, but where did the stream go? It is thought that the ice here was 1,800 feet thick, perhaps 2,000 feet thick.

• ASHTON TOWNSHIP, DELAWARE COUNTY: Sunstone and moonstone that shows double reflections are found

• AVONDALE, CHESTER COUNTY: Aquamarine; golden beryl; garnet in the old Leiper, now Faccenda quarry; quartz crystals; and amethyst

• BART, LANCASTER COUNTY: Smoky quartz is found at the Gap Nickel Mines

• BLACK HORSE, DELAWARE COUNTY: Amazonite; garnet on Mineral Hill along the road from Media; Sunstone from an old corundum pit; and green quartz

• BOOTHWYN, DELAWARE COUNTY: Amethyst, rutilated quartz, and quartz crystals from the East Branch of Naaman's Creek

• BRIDGEPORT, MONTGOMERY COUNTY: Jasper and Quartz are found in the Dolomite Quarry of the Bethlehem Steel Company

• CHESTER, DELAWARE COUNTY: Amethyst, Beryl, Smoky Quartz at the Shaw & Esrey's Quarry, and Almandine Garnet in the soil above Peter's Mill Dam in Green Creek

• COATESVILLE, CHESTER COUNTY: Beryl, amethyst, and smoky quartz

• CORNOG, CHESTER COUNTY: Blue Quartz and smoky quartz with epidote is found at the Keystone Trap Rock Quarry

• DARBY, DELAWARE COUNTY: Beryl

• DARLINGTON CORNERS, CHESTER COUNTY: Serpentine and beryl are found at the Brinton Quarry

• EASTON, NORTHAMPTON COUNTY: Topaz, Serpentine, and marble

• EUREKA, BUCKS COUNTY: Smoky Quartz was discovered in the Eureka Quarry

• FAIRFIELD, PENNSBURY TOWNSHIP: Sunstone

• FRENCH CREEK IRON MINES IN PENNSYLVANIA DUTCH COUNTRY: Chalcopyrite, Pyrite, and Magnetite are mined

• GLADHILL, ADAMS COUNTY: Copper in Rhyolite was found at the Bingham Mine

• GLENDALE, DELAWARE COUNTY: Beryl

• HARRISBURG, DAUPHIN COUNTY: Agate and garnet are found in Swarata Creek. It is also reported that gold deposits have been found here for years.

• JENKINS CORNER, LANCASTER COUNTY: Serpentine and Williamsite were found in the Cedar Hill Quarry

• KENNETT SQUARE, CHESTER COUNTY: Tourmaline, plus Sunstone was found at the Pierce's Paper Mill

• KUNKLETOWN, MONROE COUNTY: Quartz and gold were reported in Paint Ore Mine around the Civil War. This mine was located on the Appalachian Trail.

- LEIPERVILLE, DELAWARE COUNTY: Blue and golden beryl, thulite, quartz crystals, and Andalusite
- LENNI, DELAWARE COUNTY: Sunstone, amazonstone, moonstone, and amethyst were found on Chester Creek
- MIDDLETOWN TOWNSHIP, DELAWARE COUNTY: Moonstone and salmon sunstone
- MINERAL HILL, MEDIA, DELAWARE COUNTY: Amethyst, Amazonstone, Moonstone at the Crumps Quarry, beryl, and red and green sunstone
- MORGAN STATION, DELAWARE COUNTY: Amethyst
- MORGANTOWN, BERKS COUNTY: Garnet, epidote, and quartz found at the Grace Mine of Bethlehem Steel Company.
- MT. HOLLY SPRINGS, CUMBERLAND COUNTY: Agate nodules were found
- NESHAMINY FALLS, BUCKS COUNTY: Moonstone was found at Vanartsdalen's Quarry
- OXFORD, CHESTER COUNTY: Serpentine and Williamsite were found in the Wood's Chrome Mine on Octorara Creek
- POCOPSON, CHESTER COUNTY: Amethyst
- PRICETOWN, BERKS COUNTY: Brown Zircon discovered in magnetite
- QUARRYVILLE, LANCASTER COUNTY: Serpentine and Williamsite were found in the Stillwell Quarry
- STATE COLLEGE, CENTRE COUNTY: Oolite
- STROMVILLE, MONROE COUNTY: Quartz is found on Crystal Hill. It is called Crystal Hill because of the shiny quartz.
- SYCAMORE MILLS, DELAWARE COUNTY: Smoky Quartz, Amethyst near Dismal Run, and Green Quartz
- TRAINER STATION, DELAWARE COUNTY: Smoky Quartz, Quartz crystals, and green beryl were found.
- UNIONVILLE, CHESTER COUNTY: Corundum, serpentine found on Corundum Hill, and clinochlore.
- UPPER DARBY, DELAWARE COUNTY: Smoky quartz
- VALLEY FORGE, CHESTER COUNTY: Amethyst was found in the abandoned Jug Hollow Mine.
- VERA CRUZ, LEHIGH COUNTY: Jasper

So this is the sunset or ending to the discovery of the haunted treasure sites found in New York, New Jersey, and Pennsylvania. We have traveled as far west as we can in this book. Always remember that the best part of any search is the journey itself. Enjoy the quest!

The journey of the Susquehanna River continues

Bibliography

Books

Aron, Paul. *Unsolved Mysteries of American History*. New York, New York: John Wiley & Sons, 1997.

Art, Henry William. *Ecological Studies of the Sunken Forest – Fire Island National Seashore, New York*. Washington, D.C.: Government Printing Office – National Park Department, 1976.

Boyle, Robert H. *The Hudson River*. New York, New York: W.W. Norton & Co., 1969.

Bradley, Hugh. *Such Was Saratoga*. New York, New York: Doubleday, Doran, & Co., 1940.

Braider, Donald. *Rivers of America, The Niagara*. New York, New York: Holt, Rinehart & Winston, 1972.

Bregman-Taney, Janet & Clark, Kenneth R. *The Pocono Mountains*. Guilford, Connecticut: The Globe Pequot Press, 2003.

Brown, Henry Collins. *From Alley Pond to Rockefeller Center*. New York, New York: E.P. Dutton & Company, 1936.

Brown, Kenneth & Mendrick, Michael J. *The Insiders Guide to the Adirondacks*. Plattsburgh, New York: Press Republican, 1997.

Burns, Cherie. *The Great Hurricane: 1938*. New York, New York: Atlantic Monthly Press, 2005.

Cahill, Robert Ellis Curious Customs and Cures. Salem, Massachusetts: Old Saltbox, 1990.

Caldwell, Mark. *New York Night – The Mystique & Its History*. New York, New York: Scribner, 2005.

Canby, Henry Seidel. *The Brandywine*. Atglen, Pennsylvania: Schiffer Publishing, Ltd., 1941.

Carson, Russell M.L. *Peaks and People of the Adirondacks*. Garden City, New York: Doubleday, Doran, and Co., 1928.

Cawley, James & Margaret. *Exploring the Little Rivers of New Jersey*. Princeton, New Jersey: Princeton University Press, 1942.

Coenraads, Robert R. *Rocks & Fossils – A Visual Guide*. Buffalo, New York: Firefly Books, 2005.

Committee on Science, History, & Art of the Hudson-Fulton Celebration Commission. *Hudson-Fulton Celebration*. New York, New York: Committee on Science, History, & Art of the Hudson-Fulton Celebration Commission, 1909.

Cramer, Carl. *Dark Trees to the Wind*. New York, New York: William Sloane Associates, 1949.

Crofton, Ian. *The Totally Useless History of Science*. London, England: Quercus Publishing, 2010.

Cromie, Alice. *Restored Towns & Historic Districts of America*. New York, New York: E.P. Dutton, 1979.

Cunningham, John T. *Colonial Histories – New Jersey*. Camden, New Jersey: Thomas Nelson & Sons, 1971.

Daughters of the American Revolution of Allegheny County, Pennsylvania. *Pittsburgh Founded, November 25, 1758*. Pittsburgh, Pennsylvania: Reed & Witting Press, 1914.

Delgado, James P. *Lost Warships*. New York, New York: Checkmark Books, 2001.

Donaldson, Alfred L. *A History of the Adirondacks, Volume 1*. New York, New York: The Century Company, 1921.

Evers, Alf. *The Catskills, from Wilderness to Woodstock*. Garden City, New Jersey: Doubleday & Co., 1972.

Faris, John T. *Old Trails & Roads in Penn's Land*. Philadelphia, Pennsylvania: J.B. Lippincott Company, 1927.

Federal Writers' Project of the Works Progress Administration for the Erie County Unit. *Erie: A Guide to the City and County*. Philadelphia, Pennsylvania: The William Penn Association, 1938.

Federal Writers' Project of the Works Progress Administration for the State of New Jersey. *Stories of New Jersey.* Newark, New Jersey: M. Barrows & Co., 1938.

Fenton, Carroll Lane and Mildred Adams. *The Fossil Book.* New York, New York: Doubleday Dell Publishing Group, 1958.

Funk, Wilfred, Litt.D. *Word Origins.* Avenel, New Jersey: Outlet Book Company, 1950.

Greylock, Grace. *The Hoosac Valley: Its Legends & Its History.* New York, New York: G.P. Putnam's Sons, 1912.

Haring, H. A. *Our Catskills Mountains.* New York, New York: G. P. Putnam's & Sons, 1931.

Harshberger, John W. *The Vegetation of the New Jersey Pine Barrens.* New York, New York: Dover Publications, 1970.

Hislop, Codman, *Rivers of America – The Mohawk.* New York, New York: Rinehart & Co., 1948.

Hoppe, E. O. *Pirates, Buccaneers & Gentlemen Adventures.* Cranbury, New Jersey: A.S. Barnes & Co., 1972.

Hume, Ivor Noel. *A Guide to Artifacts of Colonial America.* New York, New York: Alfred A. Knopf, 1970.

Ivory, Karen. *Off the Beaten Path: Philadelphia.* Guilford, Connecticut: The Globe Pequot Press, 2003.

Jameson, W. C. *Buried Treasures of the Atlantic Coast.* New York, New York: August House, 1998.

Jamieson, Paul F. *The Adirondack Reader.* New York, New York: The MacMillan Co., 1964.

Johnston, Captain Henry S. *The Thousand Islands of the St. Lawrence River.* Boston, Massachusetts: The Christopher Publishing House, 1937.

Kane, Joseph Nathan, Steven Anzovin, and Janet Podell. *Facts About the States.* New York, New York: The H. W. Wilson Company, 1989.

Famous First Facts, Sixth Edition. Bronx, New York: The H. W. Wilson, Co., 2006.

Kime, Patricia. *Hidden Philadelphia & the Amish Country.* Berkeley, California: Ulysses Press, Berkeley, 2006.

King, Philip B. *The Evolution of North America.* Princeton, New Jersey: Princeton University Press, 1959.

Klein, Philip S. & Ari Hoogenboom. *A History of Pennsylvania.* New York, New York: McGraw-Hill Book Co., 1973.

Kunz, George Frederick. *The Curious Lore of Precious Stones.* Philadelphia, Pennsylvania: J.B. Lippincott, Co., 1913.

Landman, Neil H., Paula M. Mikkelsen, Rudiger Bieler, & Bennett Bronson. *Pearls: A Natural History.* New York, New York: Harry N. Abrams, Inc., 2001.

Leonard, Jonathan Norton and the editors of Time-Life Books. *Atlantic Beaches*. Chicago, Illinois: Time-Life Books, Inc., 1972.

Lessem, Don & Donald F. Glut. *Dinosaur Encyclopedia*. New York, New York: Random House, 1983.

Lopate, Phillip. *Waterfront*. New York, New York: Crown Publishers, 2004.

MacFall, Russell P. *Gem Hunter's Guide*. New York, New York: Thomas Y. Crowell, 1975.

Rock Hunter's Guide. New York, New York: Thomas Y. Crowell, 1980.

Malinowski, Sharon and Anna Sheets. *The Gale Encyclopedia of Native American Tribes*. Detroit, Michigan: Gale Research, Inc., 1998.

Maney, J. Arthur. *The Mohawk Valley: Its Legends and Its History*. New York, New York: G. P. Putnam & Sons, 1901.

Manley, Sean. *Long Island Discovery*. Garden City, New York: Doubleday & Co., 1966.

Maple, Eric. *Origins: Superstitions and their Meanings*. Pleasantville, New York: Reader's Digest, 1978.

Marx, Robert F. *Buried Treasures You Can Find*. Dallas, Texas: Ram Publishing, 1993.

Matthews, John. *Pirates – Most Wanted*. New York, New York: Atheneum Books for Young Readers, 2007.

McKay, Richard C. *South Street – A Maritime History of New York*. New York, New York: G. P. Putnam's Sons, 1934.

McPhee, John. *The Pine Barrens.* New York, New York: Farrar, Straus & Giroux, 1967.

Basin & Range. New York, New York: Farrar, Straus & Giroux, 1981.

Morris, James. *The Great Port, A Helen & Kurt Wolff Book – Harcourt.* New York, New York: Brace & World, Inc., 1969.

Mottana, Annbale, Rodolfo Crespi, and Giuseppe Liborio. *Simon & Schuster's Guide to Rocks & Minerals.* New York, New York: Simon & Schuster, 1977.

Murphy, Robert Cushman. *Fish-Shape Paumanok.* Philadelphia, Pennsylvania: The American Philosophical Society, 1964.

Nevius, Michelle & James Nevius. *Inside the Apple.* New York, New York: Free Press, Simon & Schuster, Inc., 2009.

Newbury, Lida, Editor. *New Jersey: A Guide to Its Present and Past, 2nd Printing.* New York, New York: Originally complied by the Federal Writers Project of the Works Progress Administration in the State of New Jersey, Hastings House, 1977.

Niles, Grace Greylock. *The Hoosac Valley, Its Legends and Its History.* New York, New York: G.P. Putnam's Sons, 1912.

O'Kane, Walter Collins. *Trails and Summits of the Adirondacks.* New York, New York: Houghton Mifflin Co., 1928.

Overton, Jacqueline. *Long Island's Story*. Garden City, New York: Doubleday, Doran, & Co., 1929.

Parker, Amasa J. *Landmarks of Albany County*. Syracuse, New York: D. Mason & Co., 1897.

Pound, Arthur. *The Golden Earth*. Norwood, Massachusetts: Norwood Press, 1935.

Powell, Lyman P. *Historic Towns of the Middle States*. New York, New York: G.P. Putnam's Sons, 1899.

Rattroy, Jeannette Edwards. *East Hampton History*. Garden City, New York: Country Life Press, 1953.

Reader's Digest Editors. *American Folklore & Legend*. Pleasantville, New York: Reader's Digest Association, 1983.

Off The Beaten Path. Pleasantville, New York: Reader's Digest, 2003.

Reid, W. Max. *The Mohawk Valley: Its Legends & Its History*. New York, New York: G.P. Putnam's Sons, 1901.

Rovin, Jeff. *Did you ever wonder...* Boca Raton, Florida: Globe Communications Corp, 1997.

Santelli, Robert. *Guide to the Jersey Shore*. Guilford, Connecticut: The Globe Pequot Press, 1986.

Sceurman, Mark & Mark Moran. *Weird N.J.* New York, New York: Sterling Publishing, 2005.

Schumann, Walter. *Gemstones of the World*. New York, New York: Sterling

Publishing, Co., 1963.

Minerals of the World. New York, New York: Sterling Publishing Co.,

1992.

Shaw, Charles G. *Oddly Enough*. New York, New York: Farrar & Rinehart,

1938.

Shepherd, Barnett. *Tottenville, The Town The Oyster Built*. Staten Island,

New York: Preservation League of Staten Island & the Tottenville

Historical Society, 2008.

Sherman, Steve & Julia Older. *Appalachian Odyssey*. Brattleboro, Vermont:

The Stephen Green Press, 1977.

Simpson, Jeffrey. *The Hudson River, 1850–1918*. Tarrytown, New York:

Sleepy Hollow Press, 1981.

Sinnott, Trip. *Tea Island – A Perfect Little Gem, The Story of a Lake George

Island*. Clinton Corners, New York: The Attic Studio Press, 1983.

Snow, Dean R. *The Archaeology of New England*. New York, New York:

Academic Press, 1980.

Snow, Edward Rowe. *Ghosts, Gales & Gold*. New York, New York: Dodd,

Mead, & Co., 1972.

Stewart, George R. *American Place Names*. New York, New York: Oxford

University Press, 1970.

Stockton, Frank R. *Buccaneers and Pirates*. Mineola, New York: Dover Publications, Inc., 2007.

Stoltie, Annie & Elizabeth Folwell. *The Adirondack Book*. Madison, Wisconsin: The Countryman Press, 1992.

Stone, William L. *Reminiscences of Saratoga and Ballston*. New York, New York: Worthington Company, 1890.

Storm, Rory. *Monster Hunt, The Guide to Cryptozoology*. New York, New York: Metro Books, 2008.

Sugar, Bert Randolph with C.N. Richardson. *The Ultimate Book of New York Lists*. New York, New York: Skyhorse Publishing, 2009.

Thorndike, Joseph J. *The Coast*. New York, New York: St. Martins Press, 1993.

Todd, Charles Burr. *In Olde New York*. New York, New York: The Grafton Press, 1907.

Turner, G. *Descriptions of the Chalybeate Springs near Saratoga*. Syracuse, New York: Gaylord Brothers, 1908.

Ulmann, Albert. *A Landmark History of New York*. New York, New York: D. Appleton-Century Company, 1939.

Van de Water, Frederic F. *Lake Champlain and Lake George*. New York, New York: Bobs-Merrill Co., 1946.

Vandeis, Iris & Paul F. Kerr. *Mineral Recognition.* New York, New York: John Wiley & Sons, 1967.

Ventura, Varla. *Beyond Bizarre.* San Francisco, California: Weiser Books, 2010.

Wall, Diana diZerega & Anne-Marie Cantwell. *Touring Gotham's Archaeological Past.* New Haven, Connecticut: Yale University Press, 2004.

Wallower, Lucille. *Colonial Pennsylvania.* Nashville, Tennessee: Thomas Nelson & Co., 1972.

Way, Jr., Frederick. *The Allegheny.* New York, New York: Farrar & Rinehart, Inc., 1942.

Weyburn, S. Fletcher. *Following the Connecticut Trail.* Scranton, Pennsylvania: The Anthractie Press, 1932.

Weygandt, Cornelius. *The Blue Hill – Rounds & Discoveries in the Country Places of Pennsylvania.* New York, New York: Henry Holt & Co., 1936.

Whitlock, Herbert P. *The Story of the Gems.* New York, New York: Lee Furman, Inc., 1936.

Wildes, Harry Emerson. *The Delaware.* New York, New York: Farrar & Rinehart, 1940.

Williams, Deborah. *Country Roads of New York.* Lincolnwood, Illinois: Country Roads Press, 1994.

Winn, Christopher. *I Never Knew That About Ireland.* New York, New York: Thomas Dunne Books, 2006.

Workers of the Writer's Program of the Work Projects Administration in the State of New York. *New York – American Guide Series.* New York, New York: Oxford University Press, 1940.

Websites

http://abandonedmines.net

http://frontierhistory.blogspot.com

http://www.nativer-languages.org

www.accessgenealogy.com

www.adandonedmines.net

www.brigantinebeachnj.com

www.dcnr.state.pa.us

www.galleries.com

www.PAgold.com

www.thepiratesrealm.com

www.treasure-adventure.com

Index